Practical CSS3

DEVELOP AND DESIGN

Chris Mills

Peachpit
Press

Practical CSS3: Develop and Design

Chris Mills

Peachpit Press

1249 Eighth Street
Berkeley, CA 94710
510/524-2178
510/524-2221 (fax)

Find us on the Web at: www.peachpit.com
To report errors, please send a note to: errata@peachpit.com
Peachpit Press is a division of Pearson Education.
Copyright © 2013 by Chris Mills

Acquisitions Editor: Rebecca Gulick
Development and Copy Editor: Anne Marie Walker
Technical Reviewers: Peter Gasston, Bruce Lawson
Production Coordinator: Myrna Vladic
Compositor: David Van Ness
Proofreader: Patricia Pane
Indexer: Valerie Haynes-Perry
Cover Design: Aren Howell Straiger
Interior Design: Mimi Heft

ISBN-13:   978-0-321-82372-4
ISBN-10:   0-321-82372-9

9 8 7 6 5 4 3 2 1

Printed and bound in the United States of America

ACKNOWLEDGMENTS

I'd like to give a shout out to all the spiffing chaps and chapesses of awesomeness and beauty that have helped and inspired me during this time, and driven me to get this book written!

My colleagues and friends at Opera for being almost like a second family, for teaching me so much, for helping me fix my code, and for making web standards fun. ODevRel2012: Andreas, Bruce, Daniel-san, Karl, Luz, Mike, Patrick, Shwetank, Tiffany, Vadim, and Zi Bin. And thanks to all the other talented people who make Opera a great place to work.

My allies in the wider web dev community for giving me much inspiration and smiles, mainly on Twitter: Jake74, Dan Donald, Phil Sherry, Shaun/Leslie Jensen-Inman, Doug Schepers, Jon Hicks, Chris Murphy, and the rest of the Irish posse, Remy Sharp, Anna Debenham, Mark and Emma Boulton, and the rest of the FSS crew, Henny Swan, and the W3C Web Education Community Group—phew. If I forgot your name on this list, please abuse me on Twitter: @chrisdavidmills.

Peter Gasston for an awesome tech review job on this book. I owe you mate.

Anne Marie Walker, Rebecca Gulick, and the rest of the Peachpit crew for kicking my ass into delivering this thing and helping to shape it.

Conquest of Steel (Vic/DD/Dan/Claymore) for being almost like a third family, or maybe more like having four whinging girlfriends. Cheers guys for the 15 years and counting of heavy metal. \m/

My friends in other far-flung places for always giving me love and support, even if they didn't understand this interweb thing.

My parents for "bringing me up proper." I love you both very dearly.

And most of all I'd like to give thanks and love to Kirsty, Gabriel, Elva, and Freida for putting up with me for four months while ignoring them to write this book, and for being the main reason I get out of bed in the morning.

CONTENTS

ONLINE RESOURCES

Throughout this book I use several third-party, online resources that include scripts and stylesheets, and I present and reference many examples that I wrote to illustrate the concepts in this book. The third-party resources are referenced where appropriate, so you'll be able to find them when needed. To find my examples is even easier: You can download them all at http://peachpit.com/practicalcss3.

But that's not all! Also available at http://peachpit.com/practicalcss3 are the following:

- **A bonus chapter.** In Chapter 9, "Styling HTML5 Media and Forms," I discuss building custom-styled controls for your HTML5 ‹video› and ‹audio› elements, and styling form elements using the form-related pseudo-classes in CSS3.

- **A cheat sheet.** This reference document details the syntax of all the new CSS3 features I use in this book and how they are supported in browsers. Print it out and hang it on your wall as an at-a-glance guide! I'll update this reference as the data changes.

Both are courtesy of your very generous author.

WELCOME TO CSS3

CSS3 provides you with exciting new tools for your web development toolbox, allowing you to accomplish many styling tasks in a much easier, more flexible, and less hackish manner than you've been used to when working with CSS2. The following chapters will introduce you to the most useful, new CSS3 features and show you how to use them in real

HTML AND CSS BASIC KNOWLEDGE	THE LATEST, GREATEST BROWSERS	OLDER, LESS-CAPABLE BROWSERS
This book assumes you are well versed in basic HTML(4) and CSS(2) features and techniques. But just in case you need to look up any of the basics, keep some decent reference material to hand. A wealth of excellent tutorials is available on the W3C Web Education Community Wiki at www.w3.org/community/webed/wiki/Main_Page.	Be sure to install the latest versions of desktop Opera, Firefox, Chrome, Safari, and Internet Explorer (IE). Ideally, you should have a testing environment available for all modern browsers; have as many to hand as you can.	Have older, less-capable browsers available for testing fallbacks, polyfills, and graceful degradation. Run older versions of IE on multiple virtual machines (VirtualBox is an acceptable, free option at www.virtualbox.org). Camino is a good option for a test Mac-based browser that doesn't support most of the new CSS3/HTML5 features.

projects today, as well as provide alternatives and fallbacks for less-capable browsers. Before you start this book, make sure you have the following prerequisites. Now that you have all of the tools you need laid out in front of you, you're ready to go and make beautiful CSS3 music. Let's get going.

ALTERNATIVE BROWSING DEVICES

To test sites on different screen sizes, resolutions, and control mechanisms, have at least one or two alternative browsing devices. Mobile phones and tablets are essential fodder. A web-enabled TV would also be fun!

DEBUGGING ENVIRONMENTS

When it comes to choosing debugging environments, you have so many choices! Dragonfly on Opera, Firebug on Firefox; hell, every browser tends to come with a respectable debugging environment these days. Be sure to become familiar with as many as possible so you'll have the best chance at tracking down irksome bugs.

A DECENT TEXT EDITOR

A good text editor is all you need to write CSS and HTML. Coda on the Mac is awesome (http://panic.com/coda), but it's not free. Good free alternatives are Notepad++ for Windows, Text Wrangler for Mac, and Bluefish for Linux. WYSIWYG environments are not recommended, especially for learning. I'm a big fan of Jared Spool's quip about them being more like "WYSI … WTF"!

1

INTRODUCTION TO CSS3 AND MODERN WEB DESIGN

CSS3, the new, modular version of the CSS3 spec, contains many awesome new features that will make your web design work easier, more flexible, and more interesting. What's not to love? Browser support is not complete yet, but many of the features have enough support to be useful in a production environment, and you can work around nonsupporting browsers.

In this chapter I'll provide the rationale behind why the new version came about and gently preach a manifesto of modern web design to you. Then I'll provide a brief roundup of the CSS3 modules before examining some of the general new features of CSS3 that are useful to explore as background knowledge before you go any further.

WHY **CSS3?**

CSS3 has been around for longer than you might think. In fact, work had started on the earliest parts of CSS3 at about the same time as the CSS2 spec was being finished in the late 1990s. CSS2 has many very powerful features, and you can do a lot with it, but it was clear all those years ago that despite this a number of features were missing from the spec. This was evidenced by the fact that web designers tried to do many tasks using weird and interesting hacks or unusual techniques, often involving lots of nested <div>s or other semantic backstabbery, images, or even proprietary technologies like Flash. Some examples that spring to mind include:

- Font embedding. Downloading custom fonts for use on websites has been available in Internet Explorer (IE) since version 4 but wasn't standardized until years later with CSS3 web fonts. Before web fonts gained popularity and cross-browser support, web developers used to rely on all kinds of weird replacement techniques, such as image replacement and siFR (Scalable Inman Flash Replacement—see http://en.wikipedia.org/wiki/Scalable_Inman_Flash_Replacement) if they wanted custom fonts in headings.

- Bulletproof CSS. Back in the late 1990s and early 2000s a lot of pioneering techniques started to spring up for creating CSS UI features that wouldn't break if the text was resized. The text wouldn't spill messily out of its containers; instead, the design would expand along with it. These techniques were referred to as "Bulletproof CSS," and they worked well if done properly. But often they required a number of nested <div>s, each with a single background image hung off it. Bulletproof rounded corners on a container required four nested <div>s! Such designs were inflexible as well. If you wanted to then change the color of the background, you'd have to go back into your preferred graphics editor and update all the background images each time. This is exactly the kind of problem that properties like border-radius were created to fix.

- Multiple column layouts. It is very common to use CSS floats to create multiple column layouts; this everyone knows. But this is somewhat of a hack. Floats were never originally intended for this purpose. They were intended for simple magazine layout image floats.

- Dynamic UIs. Many "dynamic UI features," such as layouts that automatically adapt to different screen widths and smooth animations and transitions for user feedback, have been traditionally done using JavaScript. There was no way to achieve them using CSS alone until recently; hence, the rise of DHTML in the late 1990s (yuck!) and more recently, the overwhelming popularity of JavaScript libraries, such as jQuery and Dojo.

And the list goes on. CSS3 was created not to give users a completely new set of amazing features to play with and create "spangly web innovations" (a great design agency name if ever there was one), but more to provide users with standardized, more flexible ways of solving existing problems.

There are now more than 40 modules in CSS3 at various stages of completion and browser support. The modular system is beneficial in many ways. It makes CSS3 easier to write by the spec teams and implement by the browser vendors: It is always easier to tackle small chunks than a single giant monolith. It also makes it easier for web designers and developers to get their heads around, and in my opinion, it makes it easier to "sell" to clients who may have issues about using "unfinished" technologies in their sites (yes, CSS 2.1 was technically only finished in 2011, but hey).

MODERN **WEB DESIGN** PHILOSOPHY

FIGURE 1.1
It's highly impressive to be able to create web pages like this, just using open standards (see http://operasoftware.github.com/Emberwind and http://helloracer.com/webgl).

I am a great supporter of CSS and the rest of the open standards landscape. The last couple of years have been very exciting for open standards. You've seen browsers leap forward in terms of rendering speed, feature support, and so on. New web technologies like CSS3 and HTML5/WebGL really do allow you to create some amazing digital experiences (**Figure 1.1**).

SITE BEST VIEWED IN GOOGLE CHROME

FIGURE 1.2 "Best viewed in Google Chrome" sounds like a step back to the days of "Best viewed in IE4." Now, I'm not saying that all content should be accessible to all people: It is not always that simple. But you should make such allowances whenever possible.

But everyone needs to take a step back when considering such innovations and not lose sight of the original qualities and best practices that made the web great, such as accessibility, usability, and graceful degradation.

ACCESSIBILITY COMES FIRST

In terms of my perspective on web design, I am really a "web 1.0" kinda guy. Innovative technologies are exciting, and you can fully appreciate their importance in the evolution of the web. But what is more exciting is the universal nature of the web. It's the fact that you can take the same content, style it in a million different ways, and still have it remain accessible to all web users the world over regardless of how they use the web—be it on a mobile phone, using only keyboard controls, or via a screen reader.

It is something designers and developers shouldn't lose sight of, but often we do. Whenever an exciting new web technology comes to the forefront, too many sites tend to pop up that go wild with the shiny and forget about the basic tenets. Recently, you've seen a sad reemergence of "This site is best viewed in..." messages, which should have been eliminated after the original browser wars ended a decade or so ago. And what about important text content rendered in <canvas>, which is therefore inaccessible? And how about CSS3 features that could work across multiple browsers but don't because the designer has only used the -webkit- prefixed version of the property? That designer might say, "Oooh, but it's an app; therefore, it's important to lock out anyone who isn't using a device of the correct level of shininess" (**Figure 1.2**).

USABILITY NEXT!

Once your users have managed to access your content and services, can they make sense of it and glean the information they wanted from it? This is a simple, perhaps obvious point to make, but I've lost count of the times I've gone to a company website and scratched my head in vain while trying to find contact details, opening times, or an address. Instead, I find nothing useful amidst the sea of marketing BS, cheesy videos, and other propaganda being presented.

Why do people not think more about what information is most useful to people viewing their websites and how to present that information in an easily digestible way? A simple, well-written, and clearly available bit of copy is nearly always more effective than reams of flashy, whizzy, technical stuff.

My mantra for usability (and many other people's, too) is "don't make me think." Don't make your users think about how to get what they want. If you've not already read it, Steve Krug's book *Don't Make Me Think: A Common Sense Approach To Web Usability, 2nd Edition* is essential reading.

GRACEFUL DEGRADATION AND PROGRESSIVE ENHANCEMENT

Graceful degradation and progressive enhancement were two terms that first became popular (or at least noteworthy) about a decade ago. Both were used when talking about what happens to content when the browser viewing it doesn't support all the features used to create it.

Graceful degradation means that the content falls back to something simpler but still perfectly accessible and usable. So, for example, if a content box is built and then styled using lots of CSS3 glitz, older browsers should still be able to display the text in a readable form, even if it doesn't look as nice.

Progressive enhancement means that the base content is accessible by all, but then usability and stylistic enhancements are built on top of that base for those browsers that support those enhancements.

FIGURE 1.3 Dan Cederholm said it best with this cheeky little site.

These are design philosophies that I have always held dear. They have not always been easy to uphold, because you often meet clients who are "obsessed with pixel perfection across all browsers" or some similar weird fetish. But they are certainly becoming cool again, especially with all the CSS3 features to make use of and lots of mobiles and other alternative browsing devices to make your content work across. Oh, and IE6, 7, and 8 still have significant market share and often need to be supported.

The wide variety of new devices you have to support these days (mobile phones, tablets, TVs, etc.) actually makes things easier in terms of clients craving pixel perfection across all devices: It is impossible for sites to look and function the same across all desktop and mobile platforms, and indeed it doesn't make sense (as aped by dowebsitesneedtolookexactlythesameineverybrowser.com, seen in **Figure 1.3**). It is all about context. What makes sense on a standard desktop computer might well provide a bad user experience on a touchscreen mobile device or tablet.

The good news is that CSS3 is fairly easy to progressively enhance and gracefully degrade, and otherwise get to work OK across old browsers. Most of the features, if used in the right way, will degrade gracefully so that the base content will still be accessible in nonsupporting browsers. Also, there are mechanisms that allow you to build in support or provide alternative content if need be.

THOUGHT PROCESS FOR CONTENT

A good thought process to go through when implementing shiny features on a website interface is as follows:

1. Create a base of accessible HTML content. The styling and behavior you build on top of this content should, wherever possible, be usability and stylistic enhancements, and not essential for accessing the content.

2. Consider whether you need to use all the cool, cutting-edge technologies or whether you just want to because you're a cool kid who wants to be in with the in crowd.

3. Check whether your proposed implementation will gracefully degrade while leaving the base content accessible.

4. Test whether the content is accessible and OK looking across varying devices (e.g., different screen sizes, control mechanisms).

5. In cases where the content is not accessible without the CSS3, WebGL, or whatever, or not accessible to certain users, do your best to build in alternative mechanisms that will provide access to that content.

You should constantly look at making content work for as many users as possible by:

1. Keeping graceful degradation/progressive enhancement in mind.

2. Providing alternatives for inaccessible content using built-in features (e.g., alt text, transcripts for video).

3. Building in your own alternatives when no built-in mechanisms exist (e.g., feature detection and provision of alternative styles using Modernizr).

4. Using polyfills to provide support for features where none exists.

The rule I used for deciding what to cover in this book was to include a CSS3 feature only if it has support across at least two major browsers and if you can make designs employing it work in older browsers that don't support it via polyfills, alternative content, graceful degradation, and so on. I've broken this rule a few times, but only when I thought a feature was very significant and likely to have more implementations soon, and when nonsupport didn't completely break sites.

> **TIP:** A great site to consult for quick summaries of which CSS3 and HTML5 features are ready to use on production sites, and whether fallbacks and the like should be provided is http://html5please.us by Divya Manian, Paul Irish, et al.

Let's look at a brief roundup of the major CSS3 modules you'll be utilising and their main features. You can find more details on the latest status of each module at the W3C CSS Current Work page at www.w3.org/Style/CSS/current-work.en.html. As you'll see, many of the modules are not yet finished, but this shouldn't stop you from using some of those features. Many such features are already supported in browsers, albeit with vendor prefixes (see the section "Vendor Prefixes" for more details).

The major CSS3 modules featured in this book include:

- CSS Color (www.w3.org/TR/css3-color). CSS Color defines the many ways to specify color in CSS3, including RGB (red, green, blue), HSL (hue, saturation, lightness), RGBA and HSLA (same as before but includes an alpha channel to specify transparency), and a separate opacity property to apply transparency to a whole selection of elements.

- CSS Fonts Level 3 (www.w3.org/TR/css3-fonts). As well as containing the definitions for downloadable web fonts (previously in a separate module known as, you guessed it, CSS web fonts), this module also contains definitions for other font-affecting properties, such as `font-feature-settings`. I won't talk about many of these beyond web fonts, because many do not have much browser support yet. You'll mostly meet these in Chapter 3.

- CSS Text Level 3 (www.w3.org/TR/css3-text). This goes hand in hand with CSS Fonts Level 3 to give you more power over your words! As well as housing familiar items from CSS2, such as `letter-spacing` and `text-transform`, CSS Text introduces new friends, such as hyphenation and text shadow.

- Selectors Level 3 (www.w3.org/TR/css3-selectors). Selectors Level 3 defines a much more powerful, robust set of mechanisms for selecting the elements you want to apply styles to than was available in CSS2. Pretty much all of these selectors have good support across modern browsers. These are discussed later in the "CSS3 Selectors" section of this chapter.

- Media Queries (www.w3.org/TR/css3-mediaqueries). The primary means by which you can now serve optimized different layouts of the same content to widely differing browsing devices—for example, wide screen and narrow screen. You'll mostly meet these in Chapter 8.

- Backgrounds and Borders Level 3 (www.w3.org/TR/css3-background). Backgrounds and Borders defines anything to do with background and borders, including rounded corners (`border-radius`), drop shadows (`box-shadow`), and fancy border effects (`border-image`).

- CSS Multi-column layout (www.w3.org/TR/css3-multicol). CSS Multi-column layout defines an easy way to break up content into multi-column layouts that reflow nicely rather than having to hack it with imprecise floats. You'll meet these in Chapter 7.

- CSS transforms (www.w3.org/TR/css3-2d-transforms and www.w3.org/TR/css3-3d-transforms). These two specifications define mechanisms for transforming the size, position, and shape of elements in two and three dimensions. I'll mainly talk about these in Chapter 5.

- CSS transitions (www.w3.org/TR/css3-transitions). CSS transitions give you a way to smoothly animate changes in state, such as a change in link color or an increase in banner size on hover. You'll mainly see these in Chapter 5.

- CSS animations (www.w3.org/TR/css3-animations). CSS animations allow you to implement Flash-style declarative animations using keyframes detailing different property values, which the browser then "tweens" between. These are also covered in Chapter 5.

- CSS Flexible box layout (www.w3.org/TR/css3-flexbox). Mainly intended for equally distributing the height or width of rows or columns, this module defines new values for the `display` property to allow more powerful layout techniques. This is supported to varying degrees across modern browsers, but it is definitely worth mentioning.

- CSS Image Values and Replaced Content Level 3 (www.w3.org/TR/css3 -images). This module contains some useful features for controlling background images and replaced content, some of which is starting to be supported across browsers. I'll cover linear and radial gradients among other features.

GENERAL **CSS3** FEATURES

To whet your appetite, let's now look at some general CSS3 features. These features are grouped together because they are general features that you'll meet time and time again throughout different chapters: They are useful in many different circumstances.

VENDOR PREFIXES

Vendor prefixes are not exactly specific CSS3 features, but at the time of this writing (and for some time after), you'll meet them repeatedly when working with CSS3. The reason is that many of the modules you'll be using features from aren't finished.

The idea is that before a CSS feature is completely "finished" (e.g., the spec is not quite stable, and changes may be made before the final version), it can still be implemented inside browsers. At this stage, browser vendors add their own vendor prefix to the start of the feature and use the prefixed version. This allows each vendor to support the feature inside its own "sandbox," as it were, so if the spec changes and future versions work differently, this won't result in a single property that works differently across different browsers. As an example, CSS transitions are currently supported across browsers with vendor prefixes. A sample block of code might look like this:

```
a:link {
    background-color: #666666;
    -webkit-transition: 1s all;
    -moz-transition: 1s all;
    -ms-transition: 1s all;
    -o-transition: 1s all;
    transition: 1s all;
}

a: hover {
    background-color: #ffffff;
}
```

I've put the prefixed properties in my example in the order they are in for two reasons. First, it looks aesthetically pleasing to have the widest prefix first and the narrowest last.

Second, at the time of this writing, a number of non-WebKit browser makers were discussing adding support for -webkit- prefixed versions of some properties, as well as their own prefixed versions. By putting -webkit- first, you can make sure that if this happens, such browsers will end up using their own prefixed version if it is present, not -webkit-, because the others all appear afterwards in the cascade.

Using the correct prefixed property will always be better and more accurate than relying on faked -webkit- support, especially considering that in some cases you might feed the different browsers different property values because of varying support. For example, at the time of this writing Opera does not yet support 3D transforms, so you could provide Opera with this 2D transform that would work:

```
-webkit-transform: rotate3D(1,0,0,10deg) translateX(300px);
-o-transform: translateX(300px);
```

Why are other browsers considering adding -webkit- support? Because so many developers have been harboring an ill-conceived idea that WebKit is the only browser engine worth supporting. So they were using lots of CSS3 features only with the -webkit- prefix, thereby making those features arbitrarily fail in other browsers that support them. As far as users are concerned, it is the browsers that are at fault. The average site visitors don't know any better, and neither should they be expected to. Messy as it is, non-WebKit browsers adding -webkit- support is a somewhat desperate potential measure to try to fix this browser support mess to some degree.

To sum up, it may sound nightmarish having to include five different versions of the same property in such situations. Quite a few people think that you shouldn't use vendor prefixes at all in production projects, and that they are only for testing purposes (this is the W3C's official stance too). But don't let that stop you. As you'll discover throughout this book, it is easy in most cases to retain an acceptable user experience in browsers that don't support those properties, as long as you give it a bit of forethought!

If you want to use prefixed CSS3 features, please do so responsibly and use all the different prefixes for all supporting browsers. And don't make your sites dependent on a particular feature that doesn't have cross-browser support!

This transition shorthand property tells the browser to smoothly transition every property that changes when the link's state changes over a duration of 1 second (see Chapter 5 for more details). In this case it is just the background color that changes. The aspect to focus on in this code is the fact that there are five copies of the transition property. The first four include vendor prefixes. At the time of this writing, you need to include these so the effect will work in Chrome and other WebKit-based browsers (-webkit-), Firefox and other Gecko-based browsers (-moz-), IE (-ms-), and Opera (-o-). I've also included the fifth—prefixless—property so that when browsers start to support the prefixless version instead of their own specific prefixed property, the code will still work for them, and you won't have to update it unless the spec has changed since then.

There is no single correct way to order the vendor prefixes in your code, and different people have different opinions about how it should be done. I'm just presenting my opinion of what I think works best.

CSS3 COLORS

The new CSS3 Color units (www.w3.org/TR/css3-color) are most useful, particularly because they allow you to programmatically define transparency for colors. This allows you to create advanced graphics and features that blend nicely into each other and their backgrounds without having to create loads of transparent PNGs all the time.

Table 1.1 shows what current support looks like.

TABLE 1.1 Browser Support for CSS3 Color Units

BROWSER RGBA, HSL, HSLA, AND OPACITY	
Opera	Since 10
Firefox	Since 3.0
Safari	Since 3.1
Chrome	Since 4.0
Internet Explorer	Since 9
iOS	Since 3.2
Android	Since 2.1
Mobile Chrome	Since beta
Opera Mobile	Since 10
Opera Mini	Since 5

RGB AND RGBA

RGB (actually available since CSS2) works in a similar way to hex values. You define red, green, and blue channels, but you do it using numbers between 0 and 255, not pairs of hexadecimal numbers:

- `rgb(255,0,0)`. ■ Equivalent to #ff0000 or red
- `rgb(255,255,255)`. ☐ Equivalent to #ffffff or white

RGBA takes this a step further, adding a fourth value that specifies the alpha channel, or the opacity of the color. This value is between 0 and 1; 0 is completely transparent, and 1 is completely opaque:

- `rgba(255,0,0,1)`. ■ Full red with full opacity
- `rgba(255,0,0,0.5)`. ■ Full red but 50 percent transparent
- `rgba(255,0,0,0.2)`. ■ Full red but 80 percent transparent

HSL AND HSLA

HSL—hue, saturation, and lightness—is a different way of defining a color, which makes a lot of sense to many people, especially designers who are used to using graphics editors. The syntax looks like this:

- `hsl(0,100%,50%)`. ■ Equivalent to #ff0000 or red
- `hsl(0,0%,100%)`. ☐ Equivalent to #ffffff or white

The first value—hue—takes a value between 0 and 360. It's basically a point around a standard color wheel circle.

The second value—saturation—takes a value of 0–100% and refers to how bright the color is; 100% is full color, and 0% is greyscale.

The third value—lightness—takes a value of 0–100% and refers to how light the color is; 100% is completely light/white, and 0% is completely dark/black.

HSL makes sense in a lot of ways; for example, you could select complementary shades of red to go with the preceding red color, just by varying the lightness, like this:

hsl(0,100%,30%)

hsl(0,100%,40%)

hsl(0,100%,50%)

hsl(0,100%,60%)

HSLA works in the same way as RGBA. You just add the alpha channel value to the existing color like this: hsla(0,100%,50%,0.5), which results in full red but is 50 percent transparent.

OPACITY

A separate opacity property is available in CSS3. You can add it to any element to set a level of transparency for that entire element and everything within it, including all child elements. As you'd expect, it takes a value of 0–1:

opacity: 0;

This property makes elements completely vanish!

The content is still available in the DOM, just invisible to sighted viewers (in contrast to other methods of hiding content, such as display: none;, which renders the content inaccessible to screen-reader users). I mainly find this useful for hiding certain content and then making it appear again when you mouse over/focus on a certain area of the document, as in pop-up information boxes and suchlike.

NOTE: Because old versions of IE do not support transparent CSS colors or opacity, you'll need to make provisions for this by adding in support or alternatives. You'll learn various ways of doing this throughout the book.

SIZING TEXT USING REMS

CSS3 introduces a few new size units (see www.w3.org/TR/css3-values); one in particular that seems stable and is getting good browser support is the rem, or root em. This makes text styling a lot easier because all sizes defined in rems are relative to the text size of the root element—<html>. Rems get rid of the complications caused by ems and percentages: They work relative to the sizing of their parent elements. So, for nested elements, you'll often have to do all kinds of weird calculations to work out what values to use to get the font size you want. Consider the following example (see rem_example.html in the chapter1 code download folder):

```
<h1>Example <em>rem</em> exploration</h1>

<p>This example is written to show why the new CSS3 rem unit
→ is useful. It allows you to much more easily size text and
→ boxes, as rem sizing is always relative to the size of the
→ <code>&lt;html&gt;</code> element.</p>
```

Here you can start off by sizing your text like so:

```
html {
    font-size: 62.5%;
}


h1 {
    font-size: 3em;
}


p {
    font-size: 1.4em;
}
```

This is simple CSS. You start with the tried and tested 62.5% font setting to take the base font size for the whole document down to 10px (62.5% of 16px, the standard default body text font size in all browsers). Then you set the <h1> size to three times that, which results in a computed size of 30px. The <p> is set to 1.4 times the size of the base font, or 14px.

The trouble starts when you try to resize children of those elements. If you wanted to, say, size your <code> element at 11px, how would you do that with ems? Well, 1.1em wouldn't work, because it would be 1.1em of 14px (the size of its parent element). The actual value you need is 11/14 = 0.786em. Extrapolate this to more complicated and precise designs, and you're looking at a whole load of complicated math and hair pulling.

Rems make text sizing a lot easier. If you instead used rems for these text sizes, everything would be relative to the font-size on the <html>. So getting 11px code font would be a matter of using the following:

```
code {
    font-size: 1.1rem;
}
```

Table 1.2 shows the current state of browser support for rem units.

TABLE 1.2 Browser Support Matrix for Rem Units

BROWSER REM UNITS	
Opera	Since 11.6
Firefox	Since 3.6
Safari	Since 5.0
Chrome	Since 6.0
Internet Explorer	Since 9
iOS	Since 4.0
Android	Since 2.1
Mobile Chrome	Since beta
Opera Mobile	12
Opera Mini	No

IE only supports rems since version 9, so support for older versions needs some attention. The best way to handle this is to provide fallbacks in pixel sizes so older IE versions at least get the same sizing, albeit with a lesser degree of flexibility. For example:

```
code {
    font-size: 11px;
    font-size: 1.1rem;
}
```

TIP: IE6 and IE7 don't resize text set in pixels, so for accessibility's sake, if you are planning on using rems for text sizing, you might want to consider bumping up the text size just for these browsers using an IE conditional stylesheet (see Chapter 2.)

CSS3 SELECTORS

CSS3 features an entire toolbox of new selectors that allow you to select more specific elements for styling while nullifying the need for a lot of those arbitrary IDs and classes you tend to often include to select "the last item in the list," or "the first paragraph in the post that always contains the introduction," or even "the twelfth div across on the 17th shelf because I want it to be the prettiest."

I won't discuss every selector exhaustively. If you want a detailed reference for each one, consult a resource such as www.w3.org/community/webed/wiki/Advanced_CSS_selectors. Instead, I'll provide a quick reference in **Table 1.3** for all the selectors, and then showcase some of the most powerful and interesting ones (as well as some seldom-explored selectors first included in CSS2) to give you a good flavor of what selectors are now capable of.

TABLE 1.3 CSS Selectors Reference

SELECTOR	EXAMPLE	DESCRIPTION	BROWSER SUPPORT
Universal	*	Selects everything on the page.	All
Attribute	img[alt]	Selects all of the specified elements that have the specified attribute. Ideal for accessibility testing if you want to highlight images with and without alt attributes.	Not IE6 or earlier.
	img[src="alert.gif"]	Selects all of the specified elements that have the specified attribute with the specified value. Useful for selecting specific images or other elements without needing extra IDs or classes.	Not IE6 or earlier.
	img[src^="alert"]	Selects all of the specified elements that have the specified string at the start of the attribute value.	Not IE6 or earlier.
	img[src$="gif"]	Selects all of the specified elements that have the specified string at the end of the attribute value.	Not IE6 or earlier.
	a[href*="uk"]	Selects all of the specified elements that have the specified string somewhere inside the attribute value. These are useful for adding special styling or icons to specific content—for example, links to resources just about the UK or links to PDFs.	Not IE6 or earlier.
	article[class~="feature"]	Selects all of the specified elements that have the specified string inside the attribute value, but only if it is a single value in a space-delimited list of values.	Not IE6 or earlier.
	article[id|="feature"]	Selects all of the specified elements that have the specified string inside the attribute value, but only if it is a single value in a hyphen-delimited list of values. These last two selectors might be potentially useful if you are trying to select elements based on some kind of horrible tagging system inserted into attributes by a CMS.	Not IE6 or earlier.

TABLE 1.3 CSS Selectors Reference *(continued)*

SELECTOR	EXAMPLE	DESCRIPTION	BROWSER SUPPORT
Descendant	nav a	Selects the element on the right only if it is nested somewhere inside the element(s) to the left. You can chain more than two together—for example, nav li a.	All.
Child	body>header	Selects the element on the right only if it is a direct child of the element(s) to the left. You can chain more than two together—for example, body>header>p.	Not IE6 or earlier.
Adjacent sibling	h1 + p	Selects the element on the right only if it comes immediately after the element on the left in the source order, and they are siblings at the same nesting level. It's perfect if, for example, you set paragraphs to have an indent on the first line but want to remove that indent for the first line after each heading.	Not IE6 or earlier.
General sibling	h1 ~ img	Selects the element on the right only if it is a sibling (at the same nesting level) as the element on the left. It's great for setting that indent mentioned previously on each paragraph after a heading or giving a special styling only to images inside an article at the same level as a heading.	Not IE6 or earlier.
UI element pseudo-classes	a:link	Styles the default state of a link.	All.
	a:visited	Styles links when they've already been visited.	All.
	img:hover	Styles elements when they're hovered over.	All.
	input:focus	Styles elements when they're given focus (e.g., with the keyboard).	All.
	a:active	Styles links while they are being activated (e.g., by being clicked on).	All.

continues on next page

TABLE 1.3 CSS Selectors Reference *(continued)*

SELECTOR	EXAMPLE	DESCRIPTION	BROWSER SUPPORT
UI element pseudo-classes (continued)	`input:valid`	Styles form inputs that contain valid data. These types of selectors are very useful for giving users hints about whether their form data is valid or not.	Not supported in IE.
	`input:invalid`	Styles form inputs that contain invalid data.	Not supported in IE.
	`input:enabled`	Styles enabled form inputs.	All.
	`input:disabled`	Styles disabled form inputs.	All.
	`input:in-range`	Styles form inputs that contain data that is inside the valid range.	Not supported in IE.
	`input:out-of-range`	Styles form inputs that contain data that is outside the valid range.	Not supported in IE.
Negation selector	`input:not([type="submit"])`	Styles the specified element if it isn't selected by the simple selector(s) inside the parentheses. This is useful in cases where you have several similar elements and want to select them all except for one of two. For example, when laying out a form you'll want to give most of the inputs an equal width but not the `submit` or `file` inputs. You can include multiple selectors to negate inside the parentheses in a comma-delimited list—for example, `input:not([type="submit"], [type="file"])`.	Not IE8 or earlier.
Language selector	`p:lang(en-US)`	Styles the specified element only if it has the language inside the parentheses set on it via the `lang` attribute.	Not IE6 or earlier.
Target selector	`article:target`	Styles the element only if it is the target of a link. It's incredibly cool for making content appear at the click of a button, such as overlays, information boxes, or different tabs in a tabbed interface, without needing JavaScript. The main problem is that each new state will be at a different URL, so it can break the expected Back button functionality.	Not IE8 or earlier.

TABLE 1.3 CSS Selectors Reference *(continued)*

SELECTOR	EXAMPLE	DESCRIPTION	BROWSER SUPPORT
Structural pseudo-classes	`:root`	Styles the root element of the document, which is pretty much always `<html>`!	Not IE8 or earlier.
	`li:nth-child(2n+1)`	In a series of child elements, styles the elements specified by the formula in the parentheses. So, for example, this formula would select all odd-numbered list items (1, 3, 5, etc.). It's great for zebra striping to enhance readability.	Not IE8 or earlier.
	`li:nth-last-child(2n+1)`	Works the same as nth-child but starts at the last element and works backwards.	Not IE8 or earlier.
	`p:nth-of-type(3)`	Works the same as nth-child but ignores elements not of the type specified. I usually use this just to select a single child element or a certain type.	Not IE8 or earlier.
	`:nth-last-of-type(1)`	Works the same as nth-of-type, except that it counts backwards from the last child element.	Not IE8 or earlier.
	`p:first-child`	Selects the first child in a series of child elements, if it is of the type specified.	Not IE8 or earlier.
	`p:last-child`	Selects the last child in a series of child elements, if it is of the type specified.	Not IE8 or earlier.
	`p:first-of-type`	Selects the first child of that type in a series of child elements.	Not IE8 or earlier.
	`p:last-of-type`	Selects the last child of that type in a series of child elements.	Not IE8 or earlier.
	`li:only-child`	Selects the only child of an element if it is of the type specified. This is useful if, for example, you want to give list items a special styling only if there is one list item present. You might want to omit the bullet point because it is pointless and looks silly if there is only one bullet!	Not IE8 or earlier.

continues on next page

TABLE 1.3 CSS Selectors Reference *(continued)*

SELECTOR	EXAMPLE	DESCRIPTION	BROWSER SUPPORT
Structural pseudo-classes (continued)	`section p:only-of-type`	Selects the specified element if it is the only one of its type inside its parent.	Not IE8 or earlier.
	`:empty`	Selects an element only if it has no children.	Not IE8 or earlier.
Pseudo-elements	`p:first-letter`	Selects the first letter inside an element. It's perfect for making drop caps!	Not IE6 or earlier.
	`p:first-line`	Selects the first line of text inside an element. This is good for giving an intro paragraph an interesting look—for example, putting the first line in small caps.	Not IE6 or earlier.
	`a:before`	Allows you to generate content before the specified element—for example, adding icons before certain content.	Not IE7 or earlier.
	`a:after`	Allows you to generate content after the specified content—for example, placing a copyright symbol after certain pieces of content.	Not IE7 or earlier.

NOTES: The word All in Table 1.3 means all the browsers you'll likely need to support in most projects.

Some interesting new selector developments are in the CSS4 Selectors module, so keep checking www.w3.org/TR/selectors4 for the latest.

Let's move forward and look at a few cases in point to illustrate why CSS3 selectors are useful.

CSS3 ATTRIBUTE SELECTORS

CSS3 extends the basic attribute selector functionality by allowing you to select elements based on strings within attribute values. For example, you could select and style `<img src="alert.gif">` using the following:

```css
img[src^="alert"] {
    border: 1px solid #000000;
}
```

The ^ character dictates that this selector should select `<img>` elements only if they have the string `'alert'` at the start of the src attribute value.

`<img src="alert.gif">` could also be styled like this:

```css
img[src$="gif"] {
    border: 1px solid #000000;
}
```

The $ character dictates that this selector should select `<img>` elements only if they have the string `'gif'` at the end of the src attribute value. This is really useful for styling links that point to specific types of resources: You could perhaps add specific icons to different links depending on whether they link to PDFs, Word documents, and so forth.

You could also style `<img src="alert.gif">` like this:

```css
img[src*="ert"] {
    border: 1px solid #000000;
}
```

The * character dictates that `<img>` elements with the string `'ert'` anywhere within the src attribute will be selected.

THE NEGATION (NOT) PSEUDO-CLASS

The negation pseudo-class can be used to explicitly apply styles to elements that are not selected by a simple selector. Let's say you wanted to apply a specific width to a number of form elements but not the submit. You could do this:

```
input[type="text"], input[type="url"], input[type="email"],
 ⇢ select, textarea, etc, etc {
    width: 15em;
}
```

But this code is a total messy pain. The :not selector allows you to do this:

```
input:not([type="submit"]) {
    width: 15em;
}
```

You can put multiple simple selectors inside the parentheses separated by commas, like so:

```
input:not([type="submit"], [type="file"])
```

CSS3 PSEUDO-CLASSES

Pseudo-classes don't just select elements; they select elements in certain states—for example, a {} to select links, but then a:hover {} to select links only when they are being hovered over by the mouse.

CSS3 introduces some new pseudo-classes for you to sink your teeth into. My favorite, :target, allows you to select elements that are the target of the current page URL. This is very useful and allows for some cool effects, because it effectively lets you set styles to be applied when links are clicked. For example:

```
<a href="#target">Click me</a>
<div id="target">Woot!</div>
```

The page URL targets the `<div>` when the link is clicked. To style it in this state, you could use this:

```
div:target {

    ...

}
```

Note that you can see a real working example of CSS-only tabs using `:target` inside the target-demo folder in the chapter1 code download folder.

New pseudo-classes are also available for styling form inputs when the data is valid and invalid (see Chapter 2 for more about HTML5 forms). Funnily enough, they are:

```
input:valid { color: green; }
```

and

```
input:invalid { color: red; }
```

`:nth-child` allows you to select a repeating pattern of elements inside a continuous series—for example, several list items or several paragraphs or articles next to one another. Let's look at an example:

```
<ul>
    <li>First</li>
    <li>Second</li>
    <li>Third</li>
    <li>Fourth</li>
    <li>Fifth</li>
    <li>Sixth</li>
    <li>Seventh</li>
    <li>Eighth</li>
    <li>Ninth</li>
    <li>Tenth</li>
</ul>
```

To select list items, you'd do this, where n is a formula, number, or keyword:

```
li:nth-child(n)
```

To select just the odd or even list items, you'd do this (a very easy way to create the infamous zebra-striped table effect):

```
li:nth-child(odd)
li:nth-child(even)
```

Or, you could use this:

```
li:nth-child(2n+1)
li:nth-child(2n)
```

To create the same zebra stripes, let's look at some other formula examples:

- **li:nth-child(5)**. Selects the fifth adjacent list item.

- **li:nth-child(4n+1)**. Selects every fourth list item, and then adds 1 to each result. So numbers 5 and 9.

- **li:nth-child(3n-2)**. Selects every third list item, and then subtracts 2 from each result. So numbers 1, 4, and 7.

nth-last-child does the same thing as nth-child, but it counts backward from the last element in the sequence.

nth-of-type and nth-last-of-type are very similar but have one important difference: of-type ignores any rogue elements interspersed within the repeated sequence of elements because the selection is done by type of element, not child number. For example:

```
<div>
    1. <article class="abstract"> ... </article>
    2. <article class="abstract"> ... </article>
    3. <article class="abstract"> ... </article>
```

```
    4. <article class="abstract"> ... </article>
    5. <article class="abstract"> ... </article>
    6. <blockquote><p> ... </p></blockquote>
    7. <article class="abstract"> ... </article>
    8. <article class="abstract"> ... </article>
    9. <article class="abstract"> ... </article>
</div>
```

The `<blockquote>` is child number 6 out of 9. If you used `article:nth-child(2n)` as your selector to select all the even-numbered children of the `<div>`, you'd select the `<article>`s in positions 2, 4, and 8. The `<blockquote>` (position number six) wouldn't be selected because it is not an `<article>`.

If you used `article:nth-of-type(2n)` as your selector, you would select the `<article>`s in positions 2, 4, 7, and 9. The reason is that this selects by the type of element, not the child position. Therefore, in this case the `<blockquote>` is completely ignored and the even-numbered `<article>`s are selected. Yes, two of them are odd numbered according to my original numbering scheme, because in reality the `<blockquote>` exists and offsets their position. But `article:nth-of-type(2n)` ignores the `<blockquote>`, effectively counting positions 7 and 9 as 6 and 8.

Here are a few other pseudo-classes to quickly consider:

- **only-child**. Selects an element only if it is the only child of its parent—for example, `article:only-child` wouldn't select anything in the preceding example because there is more than one `<article>` child.

- **only-of-type**. Selects an element only if it is the only sibling of its type inside the parent element. For example, `blockquote:only-of-type` would select the `<blockquote>` in the preceding example because it is the only one of its type present.

- **empty**. Selects an element only if it has no children whatsoever (including text nodes). For example, `div:empty` would select `<div></div>` but not `<div>1</div>` or `<div><p>Hi!</p></div>` .

T LAST, I HAVE ASSEMBLED A GLORIOUS FORCE OF KNIGHTS, WORTHY OF BEING CALLED the knights of Camelot. We have the wisdom and intelligence of Sir Bevedere the Wise. We have the faith and devotion of Sir Galahad the pure. We have the power, courage and

FIGURE 1.4 first-letter and :first-line in effect!

PSEUDO-ELEMENTS

Pseudo-elements differ from pseudo-classes in that they don't select states of elements; they select parts of an element:

- **first-letter and first-line.** You can select the first letter inside a given element using the first-letter pseudo-element and the first line using first-line. In my King Arthur blog example (introduced in Chapter 2 and found in the king-arthur-blog-example code download folder), I've created a rather cool drop cap and first-line effect using both of these pseudo-elements in tandem (see **Figure 1.4** for the result):

```
#main>article>p:first-of-type:first-line {
    font-variant: small-caps;
}

#main>article>p:first-of-type:first-letter {
    font-size: 400%;
    float: left;
    /* loads more styling! */
}
```

- **Generated content using :before and :after.** You can use the :before and :after pseudo-elements to specify that content should be inserted before and after the element you are selecting. You then specify what content you want to insert or generate. As a simple example, you can use the following rule to insert a decorative image after every link on the page:

```
a:after {
  content: " " url(flower.gif);
}
```

You can also use the attr() function to insert the values of attributes of the elements after the element. For example, you could insert the target of every link in your document in brackets after each one using the following:

```
a:after {
  content: " " "(" attr(href) ")";
}
```

This is a great technique to use in a print stylesheet where you want to just show the URLs in the document rather than having them hidden inside links (useless on a printed page).

CSS3 PSEUDO-ELEMENT DOUBLE-COLON SYNTAX

Note that the new CSS3 way of writing pseudo-elements is to use a double colon—for example, a::after { ... }, to set them apart from pseudo-classes. CSS3, however, also still allows for single colon pseudo-elements for the sake of backward compatibility. This is what I'll be using throughout the book, although you might want to use double-colon syntax for better future proofing; it is really up to you.

GETTING THE NEW BREED OF SELECTORS TO WORK ACROSS OLDER BROWSERS

As you'll have gathered, many of the new selectors available don't work in those irksome older versions of IE that are still hanging around (like someone's rhythmically challenged dad on the dance floor at a wedding reception). So what hope do you have of using these selectors in the real world?

As luck would have it, for situations in which you really need old IE support, JavaScript can come to the rescue in the shape of Keith Clark's Selectivizr (http://selectivizr.com). It sits on top of an existing JavaScript library and adds support to IE 6–8 for many of the new selectors.

To add it in, download Selectivizr and apply it to your site. Then make sure you also have one of the compatible libraries detailed on the Selectivizr site applied to your page (I'm using NWMatcher in my example). The code will look something like this (again, check out my king arthur blog example in the chapter2 code download folder):

```
<script src="http://s3.amazonaws.com/nwapi/nwmatcher/
    nwmatcher-1.2.5-min.js"></script>
    <!--[if (gte IE 6)&(lte IE 8)]>
        <script type="text/javascript" src="script/
            selectivizr-min.js"></script>
<![endif]-->
```

And there you go! This CSS3 selector support for IE 6–8 works like a charm!

NOTE: Selectivizr works only on CSS contained in external stylesheets, not inline or internal CSS.

WRAPPING **UP**

By now I'm sure you've conceded that CSS3 is awesome, and that you should start to embrace it as soon as possible. You've read about the philosophy and general approach you'll be adopting for this book, reviewed the main CSS3 modules you'll be dipping into along the way, and learned about some general CSS features to whet your appetites. With all this information under your belt, you're ready for the next chapter, which focuses mainly on markup—riveting material.

2

BUILDING A SOLID CROSS-BROWSER TEMPLATE WITH HTML5 AND JAVASCRIPT

Before starting any creative work with CSS3, you should build up a rock-solid markup template to structure your data in and provide mechanisms to allow your content and layout to work in older browsers to an acceptable degree. Recall the discussion of progressive enhancement in the previous chapter.

Your resulting toolset will be akin to a cockroach—the sort of creature that could survive an ice age or a nuclear war.

In the interests of adopting efficient modern markup and future proofing your work, HTML5 should be your markup language of choice. In this chapter you'll explore the main features of HTML5 to ensure that you are up to speed. You'll also learn about the different mechanisms you'll use for enabling HTML5 and CSS3 support across older browsers.

STARTING WITH
SEMANTIC HTML5

The first part of your toolset for working with CSS3 will be clean, semantic HTML, also referred to as POSH (plain old semantic HTML). Not only is it advantageous in many ways (e.g., better for search engine optimization, more accessible, easier coding and maintenance), but it is essential for success when you start applying advanced CSS techniques to your content. Trying to work out a system for using advanced selectors to style copy or using multiple animations in a sane fashion is more difficult if all you have to play with is horrible, old-fashioned spaghetti code (to see an example of horrible spaghetti code, look at the source of pretty much any CMS or Wiki page).

And because one of this book's goals is to provide a forward-facing approach to web design, you'll use HTML5 for all the markup in this book.

WHY USE HTML5?

Before jumping into HTML5, let's consider HTML 4 for a minute. You'll probably agree that it does a pretty good job of marking up static documents that you can link between. This was the job it was originally written for. However, technology never stands still, and many developers quickly decided that they weren't happy just creating static documents. They wanted to start creating more dynamic sites that behaved like applications, and for such tasks, HTML 4 was missing a lot of native functionality. To implement video, animated graphics, and complicated form controls, developers turned to proprietary technologies like Flash, or complicated, inefficient kludges of HTML, CSS, and JavaScript if they wanted to create such functionality with open standards.

Originally termed "DHTML" (dynamic HTML), such kludges have more recently been handled in better ways using JavaScript libraries and the like. But the fact still remains that they are kludges for the following reasons:

- No better semantic elements are available to use for implementing features like video and complex form controls. The markup for such things tends to consist of loads of unsemantic nested `<div>`s and so forth. There is therefore no way for screen readers, search engines, or other automated user agents to work out what these constructs are supposed to be (although WAI-ARIA can help mitigate such problems), which is a problem for SEO and accessibility.

- Such implementations tend to add a significant amount of weight to the page.

- These kludges are used to create very common use cases: It seems ridiculous for you to have to resort to hacks and overcomplicated custom implementations to implement them.

HTML5 comes to the rescue in these regards while maintaining backward compatibility. It includes all of the features already available in HTML 4, plus it defines previously missing details and adds several new features into the mix for creating applications, such as:

- New semantic elements for defining common page regions, such as headers, footers, primary navigation, distinct articles of content, figures, and so on.

- `<canvas>` and its associated API for creating complex scripted graphics, like animations.

- `<audio>`, `<video>`, and associated APIs for working with AV content.

- Mechanisms for allowing applications to work offline.

- Error handling to define what should happen when badly formed markup is used (missing closing tags, etc.)

HTML5 ERROR **HANDLING**

Prior to HTML5, error handling was never defined in the specs, leaving browser vendors to decide how to handle markup errors. This has led to inconsistent error-handling implementations and different page rendering across browsers when errors are present. Now that more browsers are starting to get HTML5 parsers with consistent error handling as defined in the spec, a lot of cross-browser compatibility issues should go away.

It is really cool to be able to implement functionality like embedded video with native HTML rather than having to resort to Flash for a number of reasons:

- HTML plays nicely with other open standards, so you can style your video or other features with CSS or directly enhance their functionality with JavaScript. With Flash, you'd have to access and open the .fla file and update the code directly, because it doesn't communicate well with open standards. A Flash movie is just a black box as far as the browser is concerned: It doesn't understand the individual components inside the movie.

- An open standards solution is more accessible, generally speaking, and better for SEO. Text inside Flash can't be read using many screen readers and search engine robots. Flash video players aren't readily keyboard accessible, whereas keyboard accessibility is available out of the box with HTML5 `<video>`, at least in Opera, Firefox with JavaScript enabled, and IE (Safari and Chrome have some catching up to do here).

- Having to download a Flash plug-in before you can start using content is no big deal for tech-savvy geeks, but it can present a user-experience hurdle for someone like my grandma.

In addition, most of the important HTML5 features have good support across modern browsers, and you can provide alternatives and fallbacks for nonsupporting browsers in many cases. Therefore, much of HTML5 is usable now in real-world projects. What's good enough for youtube.com is good enough for you, right?

You'll look at HTML5 features in more detail later in the chapter.

BUILDING A TEMPLATE

At this point, let's start building a simple template that you can use to build your CSS3 examples in. Start by creating a blank HTML file (you can see the finished template in the example file template.html in the chapter2 code download folder).

HTML5 DOCTYPE

The first line you need to add, as always, is the DOCTYPE. The HTML5 DOCTYPE is a rather shorter proposition than you'll traditionally be used to in HTML 4.01 and earlier. Get ready for it, wait, go!

```
<!DOCTYPE html>
```

Well, that was easy, wasn't it? As you know, traditionally DOCTYPEs have been long shambling strings containing URLs, Klingon words, and other such unmemorables. For example, look at the HTML 4 Strict DOCTYPE:

```
<!DOCTYPE HTML PUBLIC "-//W3C//DTD HTML 4.01//EN"
    "http://www.w3.org/TR/html4/strict.dtd">
```

Why was it like this? Well, as far as I know the W3C had various interesting ideas about what DOCTYPEs might empower you and the browser to do. But in the end all DOCTYPEs really did was to put browsers in standards mode when rendering a page of markup. The writers of HTML5 recognized this and decided to whittle down the DOCTYPE to the shortest valid string of characters that would put browsers in standards mode.

LANGUAGE AND BASIC DOCUMENT OUTLINE

Next, you'll add the basic document outline below the DOCTYPE:

```
<html lang="en-gb">
    <head>
        <title>HTML5 template</title>
    </head>
    <body>
        ...
    </body>
</html>
```

This should look familiar, although I want to draw your attention to the `lang` attribute on the `<html>` element. It is good practice to set an overall language for the entire document like this for accessibility purposes: Screen readers will handle various languages differently. For example, "six" is pronounced "six" in English but "seees" in French.

You can also set the language of individual parts of the document by putting the `lang` attribute on any element that it makes sense to do so. For example:

```
<p>As the French say, <span lang="fr">c'est la vie</span>.</p>
```

Notice the two parts to the first language example you saw: en-gb. The first part is called the primary language code, which unsurprisingly sets the overall language. You can find a full list of over 8000 of these codes at the IANA Language Subtag Registry at www.iana.org/assignments/language-subtag-registry. The optional second part sets a dialect of the primary language. So, for example:

- **en-gb** is British English

- **en-us** is American English

- **en-ca** is Canadian English

You can set your own experimental languages using the x experimental primary code:

```
<html lang="x-millsian-nonsense"></html>
```

DEFINING YOUR DOCUMENT'S CHARACTER SET

You should also set a character set for your document, which specifies the range of text characters that can be used in your document: This has become much simpler in HTML5. Previously, the line you needed to use looked something like this:

```
<meta http-equiv="content-type" content="text/html; charset=UTF-8" />
```

In HTML5 this line has been reduced to the following, which older browsers will also understand: Add it just below the opening `<head>` tag:

```
<meta charset="utf-8">
```

All you are interested in is the character set; hence, the HTML5 spec has been written to allow this version. You don't need to specify that this is a content-type, and you don't need to specify the mime-type if you are working with HTML5.

> **NOTE:** Mime-types specify what type of content a file contains for the benefit of browsers trying to understand what content it is they are dealing with: in this case, `text/html` for HTML.

Here you've specified UTF-8, a universal character set that allows all characters from all languages, or just about. It is best to stick to this character set unless you have a very good reason not to.

XHTML5 AND CODING STYLES

In the HTML5 era there are no longer separate XHTML and HTML DOCTYPEs. You just use the same DOCTYPE, and then you really can stick to whatever coding style suits you, be it strict XML style or loose HTML style. It is possible to still use XHTML-style syntax in HTML5 (called XHTML5), as long as you use the correct mime-type, file extension, and so on. However this creates compatibility problems with older versions of Internet Explorer (IE), so I wouldn't recommend using it.

In terms of coding style for the book, I'll use a style first crystallised in my mind by fellow web education advocate and awesome Swede, Lars Gunther. He recommends the following guidelines:

- You'll be using HTML but sticking to some XHTML syntax rules. You'll be closing all open elements using lowercase for all elements and attributes, and including quotes around most attribute values.

- You don't need to write out attribute values in full for attributes whose values are the same as the attribute name—for example `<input type="text" required>`, not `<input type="text" required="required">`.

- You don't need to include trailing slashes to close empty elements, so you'll use the format `<meta charset="utf-8">`, not `<meta charset="utf-8" />`.

ADDING CROSS-BROWSER SUPPORT FOR HTML5 SEMANTIC ELEMENTS

Now you need to add some little helpers to be able to style unknown elements. Why? Because older browsers do not support the HTML5 semantic elements discussed later in the "Exploring HTML5 Elements" section.

This problem will diminish as time goes on, but for now you can add in support without too much trouble. To do this, you need to think about how browsers handle unknown elements.

By default, an unknown element is treated as an anonymous inline element. This includes all HTML5 elements that a browser doesn't recognize—for example, <section> and <footer>. You could even stick <banana> and <porcupine> elements in your page if you had a reason to do so.

The trouble is that the new HTML5 elements you'll be using are block-level elements. They are mostly more semantic containers to replace the slew of <div>s you've traditionally used to contain different parts of your pages. Therefore, you need to force nonsupporting browsers to treat them how you want. To do so, add the following inside your <head> element:

```
<style>
article, aside, audio, canvas, datalist, details, figcaption,
 → figure, footer, header, hgroup, menu, nav, section, video {
    display: block;
}
</style>
```

NOTE: Because the HTML5 spec is still not complete, it may change to include or remove various elements; therefore, the HTML5 element fix may well need to be updated to remove elements or include additional ones in the future.

This ensures that all browsers should basically do what you want with your CSS—well, except for IE. IE versions 6–8 need more help, because they won't style unknown elements at all! For IE versions 6–8 to recognize unknown elements, you need to create an instance of each unknown element in the DOM. Something like this will do:

```
<script>
    document.createElement('abbr');
    document.createElement('article');
    document.createElement('aside');
    document.createElement('audio');
    document.createElement('mark');
    // add more elements as required
</script>
```

Notice that here you're not only dealing with block-level HTML5 elements, but are also dealing with inline HTML5 elements like <mark> and HTML 4 elements that simply aren't supported in older versions of IE, such as <abbr>.

If you need to add a lot of these elements, there is a better way to deal with your script. Replace the preceding script block with the following:

```
<!--[if lt IE 9]>
    <script src="http://html5shiv.googlecode.com/svn/trunk/html5.js">
    </script>
<![endif]-->
```

This applies the "HTML5 shiv" to your code, which is a script written by the diminutively statured but huge-hearted Remy Sharp and hosted at Google Code. It does the work of all the JavaScript described earlier, and more. Because it is hosted at Google Code, you just have to link to it: You don't need to understand the contents or worry about hosting it yourself and upgrading to the latest version when it is updated.

To make the code even better, you've also put the `<script>` element inside an IE conditional comment, so that only IE8 and earlier versions will download the script (I'll talk a bit more about conditional comments later in the chapter). IE9 and 10 have much better HTML5 support; other browsers are unlikely to need it. So for all those browsers, you can skip downloading the script and avoid an unnecessary HTTP request.

NOTE: Remy's HTML5 shiv now also includes Jonathan Neal's IE Print Protector—a script that fixes IE's problems with printing HTML5 content.

VALIDATING HTML5

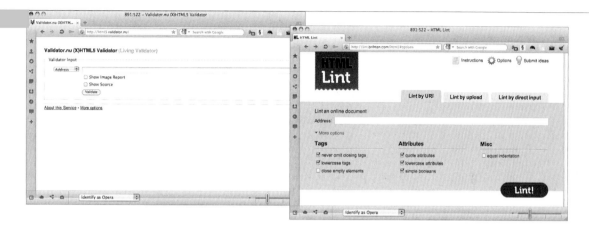

As you know, it is always a good idea to validate your finished HTML5 structure before going further in your work to catch any DOM errors and the like that may cause problems when you apply script and style to your content.

Henri Sivonen has created an experimental but perfectly usable HTML5 (+ WAI ARIA + SVG 1.1 + MathML 2.0) validator, which you can use to validate your HTML5 documents regardless of the markup style used. You can find this validator at http://html5.validator.nu. Unfortunately, it doesn't pick up on specific syntax styles—for example, the XHTML style I recommend in this book. It won't pick up on missing attribute quotes, attribute values, or closing slashes because that's all valid in HTML5!

To mitigate this problem, I recommend that you add an extra step to your validation for now until available validators catch up. Visit the HTML Lint site at http://lint.brihten.com (**Figure 2.1**) to check your markup against several style options. To check against the style I recommend in this book, check the following options:

- Never omit closing tags. All nonempty elements must have a closing tag (but empty elements don't need the trailing slash).

- Lowercase tags. All tags should be lowercase.

- Quote attributes. All attribute values should be in quotes.

- Lowercase attributes. All attributes and their values should be lowercase.

- Simple booleans. Minimised attributes are allowed (those with a value the same as the attribute name can be shortened to just the name: I showed the example `required` instead of `required="required"` earlier).

FIGURE 2.2 A simple HTML5 video example (see simple-video.html in the chapter2 folder).

Let's look at the HTML5 elements you'll be using in this book, plus a few more for good measure. An exhaustive treatment of HTML5 features is beyond the scope of this book because you'll be working with CSS3 styling, so most of the HTML5 APIs are pretty much irrelevant in this context. Yes, you could build a fully functional UI inside an HTML5 <canvas> element, but you won't be able to style it with CSS, and you'd be committing most of the same accessibility, usability, and SEO crimes that Flash developers used to when building full Flash websites and the like. So, don't even think about it!

In addition, most of the new elements you'll look at are pretty self-explanatory, and I know you are a clever bunch. All of the elements described in this section are supported across all modern browsers with the exception of the Form elements, which have been a bit slower to catch on.

NOTE: If you want a deeper treatment of HTML5, look no further than Bruce Lawson and Remy Sharp's excellent book, *Introducing HTML5*, 2nd Edition (New Riders, 2011). For free tutorials, check out the Opera developer community at http://dev.opera.com or the fantastic http://html5doctor.com.

<AUDIO> AND <VIDEO>

Two of the most important new elements in HTML5 are <audio> and <video>. These respectively allow you to add audio and video content to your sites as easily as you'd add images using <img>. Both elements are pretty self-explanatory. Here is a <video> example (**Figure 2.2**):

```
<video controls poster="ship-icon.png" width="640" height="360">
    <source src="video/boatride.mp4" type="video/mp4">
    <source src="video/boatride.webm" type="video/webm">
    <!-- fallback content here -->
</video>
```

The `<video>` element includes:

- A **controls** attribute, which tells the browser to include the default controls for the video. If you don't include this attribute, you can create your own controls instead using the media elements API.

- A **poster** attribute, which specifies the location of an image to use as a poster to display before the video starts to play. If not included, this defaults to the first frame of the video.

- **width** and **height** attributes to specify the width and height of the video. These work similarly to those for `<img>` except that if you specify different values to the video's intrinsic values, the video doesn't resize; instead, it letterboxes.

The `<source>` attributes point to the video files you want to play. You can instead put a single `src` attribute on the `<video>` element to just point to one video file to play, but this is currently a bad idea, because different browsers support different video formats (for reasons too boring to get into here.) IE and Safari prefer MP4, whereas Opera, Firefox, and Chrome prefer WebM. Therefore, you use two `<source>` elements to point to both formats, and the browser loads the one it recognizes. You don't have to include the `type` attributes, but it is a good idea to do so, because these tell the browser what type of video each element points to, and it can select the one it wants instantly. If you don't include the `type` attributes, the browser has to download a few bytes of each file to identify one it recognizes, which is a waste of time and effort.

NOTE: To easily convert between video formats, a good (and free) choice is Miro Video Converter (www.mirovideoconverter.com).

FIGURE 2.3 A simple HTML5 audio example (see simple-audio.html in the chapter2 folder).

`<video>` and `<audio>` both work in a similar way, however note that `<audio>` doesn't include the attributes not relevant to it, like `poster`, `width`, and `height`.

Here is an `<audio>` example:

```
<audio controls>
    <source src="audio/heavymetal.mp3" type="audio/mp3">
    <source src="audio/heavymetal.ogg" type="audio/ogg">
    <!-- fallback content here -->
</audio>
```

The audio example produces a display like the one shown in **Figure 2.3**.

The fallback content implied by the HTML comments in the preceding examples can be anything you like, whether it is a message telling users their browser doesn't support HTML5 video/audio with a direct link to download the media, or better, a Flash video/audio player fallback that can play the MP4/MP3 versions of your media.

Many other parts of HTML5 allow you to build in fallback content in this manner or will at least gracefully degrade to simpler content that people with older browsers will still be able to use.

NOTE: Check out "Simple HTML5 video player with Flash fallback and custom controls" by Bruce Lawson and Vadim Makeev (http://dev.opera.com/articles/view/simple-html5-video-flash-fallback-custom-controls) to see the Flash fallback technique in action. Or, check out "Everything you need to know about HTML5 video and audio" by Simon Pieters (http://dev.opera.com/articles/view/everything-you-need-to-know-about-html5-video-and-audio) for more details on `<video>` in general.

HTML5 `<video>` and `<audio>` represent a very exciting area that has many new features to keep an eye out for (coming soon in a browser near you!); for example, elements such as `<track>` for adding text tracks like subtitles, APIs for accessing web cams and microphones (`getUserMedia`), APIs for generating and manipulating sound (Web Audio API), and more.

<ARTICLE> AND <SECTION>

Now let's look at HTML5's improved semantics. First up, HTML5 provides two
elements—<article> and <section>—for separating your main content into
distinct pieces on your sites. They are often misunderstood, so let's tread carefully.
Let's consider a blog site, which has a main content column containing blog-post
summaries and a secondary content column containing the author's latest Tweets
(see blog-site.html in the chapter2 folder for the full code).

You would traditionally mark this up using something like the following:

```
<div id="main">

    <div class="post-summary">

        <!-- post summary -->

    </div>

    <div class="post-summary">

        <!-- post summary -->

    </div>

<!-- etc. -->

</div>

<div id="tweets">

    <div class="tweet"> ... </div>

    <div class="tweet"> ... </div>

    <div class="tweet"> ... </div>

</div>
```

This is all well and good, but all these <div>s are semantically anonymous; the browser doesn't see them as a main content column, different Tweets, and so on. It just sees them as "divs inside divs." You could upgrade this to HTML5, like so:

```
<section id="main">
    <article>
        <!-- post summary -->
        </article>
    <article>
        <!-- post summary -->
    </article>
<!-- etc. -->
</section>
<section id="tweets">
    <article> ... </article>
    <article> ... </article>
    <article> ... </article>
</section>
```

Here, a supporting browser immediately knows that this contains two distinct sections of content. Both contain distinct articles, which could quite sensibly be syndicated separately, for example, in an RSS feed. This gives you a hint as to the difference between <section> and <article>. Both elements are for containing content, but

- <section> is for containing conceptually different areas of content within the page—for example, stories about animals versus animal photos or stories about animals versus stories about underpants.

- <article> is for containing distinct pieces of content within a page or a <section>, whether they are new items, videos, Tweets, or whatever. Each group of <article>s will have similar, related functionality or purpose but will be self-contained entities. If you could happily take a piece of content and sensibly syndicate it as a separate entry in an RSS feed, it is probably a good candidate for an `<article>`. You shouldn't think of `<article>`s as being "news articles," because they can contain other items of content besides; think of them as being more like "articles of clothing on a clothing rail" and you'll have a better idea.

One thing to note is that it is perfectly reasonable to use multiple `<section>`s nested inside a single `<article>`. After all, you may have pages on your site in which the whole content of the page is an article, inside of which you might want to define separate sections of content, such as the introduction, summary, or different parts, perhaps (see full-post.html inside the chapter2 code download folder):

```
<article>

    <section id="introduction">

        ...

    </section>

    <section id="part1">

        ...

    </section>

    <section id="part2">

        ...

    </section>

    ...

    <section id="summary">

        ...

    </section>

</article>
```

For more details and examples covering these elements and other HTML5 semantics, read "New structural elements in HTML5" by Bruce Lawson and my bad self at http://dev.opera.com/articles/view/new-structural-elements-in-html5.

<HEADER> AND <FOOTER>

So, what about site headers and footers? You would traditionally mark these up using something like this:

```
<div id="header"></div>
<div id="footer"></div>
```

Pretty much every website or app has these. The header (or masthead) contains the site logo, title, and so on, and the footer contains site-wide content like copyright, accessibility statement, and so forth. The HTML5 creators recognized this and introduced the following unambiguous semantic elements to do the job:

```
<header></header>
<footer></footer>
```

If you refer back to my sample blog pages, you'll see some examples of <header> and <footer> usage. Note that there are some inside <article>s and <section>s. This is perfectly allowed: You can do this to specify headers and footers just for subsections of your content rather than the whole site. You can therefore have multiple <header>s and <footer>s in a single document.

<ASIDE>

The <aside> element is really a special kind of <section>, specifically tasked with containing secondary information related to the main content of the site that doesn't fit within the main flow. Good examples include a biography of the author of that page, a mini interview with the author, or a bibliography/references and further reading. It can, however, also be secondary content on the site, like a typical sidebar, a blogroll, or a list of other blog posts on the site you might be interested in (even if they are not posts related to the main content). The list of Tweets in my previous example is suitable as an <aside>.

You can also quite happily use an `<aside>` element inside an `<article>` too, as long as it contains content tangentially related to just that article. A biography of the author of just that article or further reading to go on to after you've finished that article would be suitable. The element simply looks like this:

```
<aside></aside>
```

<NAV>

The `<nav>` element was created to house the document's primary navigation, whether that is a standard "list-o-links" nav bar, a drop-down menu, or even a search box. It shouldn't be used for secondary navigation bars, related reading links, and so on. You can put it anywhere you like in your markup that makes sense. In my main blog site example, it's inside the `<header>`:

```
<header>
    <nav>
        ...
    </nav>
</header>
```

There are many advantages to having the document's primary navigation inside an unambiguous semantic element. For example, when browsers and screen readers start to recognize this element, it will make accessibility hacks like "skip to navigation" links a thing of the past.

<HGROUP>

<hgroup> has been created with one specific purpose—to allow you to put two (or more) headings right next to one another and have them count as only one heading for the purposes of the document structure/hierarchy (the group will be counted as a single heading of the same rank as the highest-ranked heading in the group). This is especially useful in a situation in which you want to mark up a heading with a subtitle or strapline above or below it, because you can now do so without breaking the document structure:

```
<hgroup>
    <h1>Cats and dogs</h1>
    <h2>Your local store for pets and pet supplies</h2>
</hgroup>
```

NOTE: Heading levels in HTML5 are determined not by the number after the h (<h1>, <h2>, etc.) but by their level of nesting inside so-called sectioning elements, worked out by the HTML5 outline algorithm. For more information about HTML5 sectioning and outlines, read Mozilla's excellent article "Sections and Outlines of an HTML5 Document" (https://developer.mozilla.org/en/Sections_and_Outlines_of_an_HTML5_document).

<FIGURE> AND <FIGCAPTION>

Another type of content you've previously had no decent, consistent way of marking up is figures with related captions. Prior to HTML5, you'd tend to do something similar to this:

```
<div id="figure">
    <p><img src="figure.png" alt="This is a picture containing
    → important content"></p>
    <p id="caption">This is a very important picture.</p>
</div>
```

But this feels a bit dirty, a bit grubby, and a bit amoral. It is almost completely semantically devoid, with nothing to let a browser or screen reader know this is a figure and caption, and certainly nothing to associate the caption with the figure! HTML5 offers a much better solution:

```
<figure>
    <p><img src="figure.png" alt="This is a picture containing
    → important content"></p>
    <figcaption>This is a very important picture.</figcaption>
</figure>
```

This code provides a consistent, semantic way of defining a figure and associating a caption with it. Note that the figure—the image in this case—can be anything you want. It could be a few images, videos, a <canvas>, or a combination of content types.

<TIME>

<time> quite simply provides you with a decent semantic way of marking up a date and time. Here's a simple example:

```
<time datetime="1978-06-27">27th June 1978</time>
```

The datetime attribute contains an ISO-standard date and time, which is unambiguous and machine-readable. The text inside the tags, on the other hand, can be any representation of the time and date you want and thus can be customized to suit the style of your site. You could also write:

```
<time datetime="1978-06-27">June 27 1978</time>
<time datetime="1978-06-27">My birthday</time>
<time datetime="1978-06-27">Nineteen seventy-eight, June the
→ twenty-seventh</time>
```

You can also add a time, as follows:

```
<time datetime="1978-06-27T23:58">Two minutes to midnight, on my
  birthday</time>
```

In addition, you can add a time zone adjustment. To make the previous example Central European Time (CET), you'd do this:

```
<time datetime="1978-06-27T23:58Z+01:00">Two minutes to midnight,
  on my birthday, CET</time>
```

There is one last bit of `<time>` syntax to discuss, which is particularly useful to the blog example: If you want to specify that a declared time is the publication date of the content it resides within, you can use the `pubdate` attribute, like so (although the removal of this attribute from the spec is being debated at the time of this writing, so it might disappear):

```
<time datetime="1978-06-27" pubdate>27th June 1978</time>
```

A number of people complained in the past that they were not able to mark up imprecise times using `<time>`, like you would in documents like museum catalogues. This has been updated to mitigate this problem somewhat: Now you can do things like this:

- `<time datetime="1983">The year 1983</time>`

- `<time datetime="1983-12">December 1983</time>`

- `<time datetime="12-25">25 November (any year)</time>`

- `<time datetime="1983-W23">Week 23 in 1983</time>`

- `<time datetime="P 20 D">A period of 20 days</time>`

<MARK>

The <mark> element is designed to highlight words inside a section of content that don't require emphasis in their meaning; for example, they aren't important key-words that need <strong> or technical terms that would typically be pronounced in an alternate voice. But they do require highlighting to indicate their significance in another context. A very good example is highlighting search terms in a list of search results, or tags on a site, or particularly useful parts of a set of quotes contained within some research documents. For example, if you were using a music search application, you might want to mark up a results page like this (see mark-example. html in the chapter2 code download folder):

```
<h1>Results for search term <mark>love</mark>:</h1>

<ul>

    <li><a href="/songs/allyouneedislove/">All you need is
    → <mark>love</mark></a> by The Beatles</li>

    <li><a href="/songs/lovewilltearusapart/"><mark>Love</mark> will
    → tear us apart</a> by Joy Division</li>

    <li><a href="/songs/lovehatelove/"><mark>Love</mark>, hate,
    → <mark>love</mark></a> by Alice in Chains</li>

</ul>
```

For more information about <mark>, read Mike Robinson's article "Draw attention with mark" (http://html5doctor.com/draw-attention-with-mark).

Range slider:

FIGURE 2.4 The range slider
input type.

Date picker:

Color picker: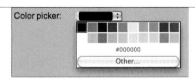

FIGURE 2.6 The color picker
input type.

FIGURE 2.5 The date picker
input type.

HTML5 FORM ELEMENTS

Let's now briefly look at the new form elements available in HTML5. Most of these were created to give you easier, semantically richer ways of implementing form controls that you already implement using kludges, because native mechanisms were not available in HTML 4. See simple-form.html in the chapter2 folder for a testable example.

NOTE: HTML5 forms are not supported as well across browsers as some of the other features discussed earlier. To determine which HTML5 form features your current browser supports, send it to Mike Taylor's "HTML5 inputs and attribute support" page at www.miketaylr.com/code/input-type-attr.html. I've referred you to this page rather than just listing the supported features, because they seem to change rapidly.

You can see examples in **Figures 2.4** through **2.6**.

```
<input type="range">
<input type="date">
<input type="color">
```

HTML5 also adds a few specialized text inputs, which expect more specific types of data:

```
<input type="url">
<input type="email">
<input type="tel">
```

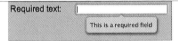

Required text:

This is a required field

FIGURE 2.7 Error message for the text input type when it is not filled in before submission.

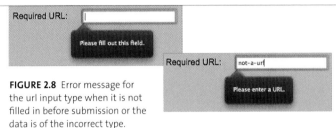

Required URL:

Please fill out this field.

Required URL: not-a-url

Please enter a URL.

FIGURE 2.8 Error message for the url input type when it is not filled in before submission or the data is of the incorrect type.

These don't look very interesting in desktop browsers until you combine them with HTML5's built-in data validation. Although if you try them on a mobile platform, such as iOS or Android, you'll notice that they give you special sympathetic keypads more tailored to filling in those types of data—a nice usability plus for your users.

You can specify that any form input must be filled in before the form can be submitted by adding the required attribute:

```
<input type="text" required>
```

The different types of text input will accept different types of data, automatically feeding back errors to the user when the data isn't correct for those inputs upon submission (as shown in **Figures 2.7** and **2.8**):

```
<input type="text" required>
<input type="url" required>
```

You can also narrow down the range of data that will be accepted in a form input using the min, max, and pattern attributes:

```
<input type="number" min="1" max="100">
<input type="text" pattern="[1-6]{3}">
```

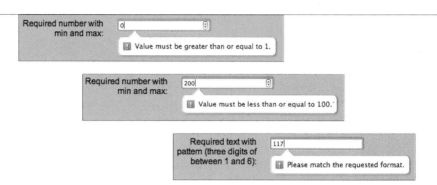

FIGURE 2.9 Error message for the number and pattern input type examples when they are not filled in with the correct data before submission.

Figure 2.9 shows usage of the new number input type and another simple text field. The first example will accept as valid data any number between 1 and 100, whereas the second one has a custom regular expression specified so that only three concatenated digits of between 1 and 6 will constitute valid data.

I added some rudimentary styling to my example so that it looks a bit less horrible than the standard HTML form looks. You'll notice as you play with it that when you enter data into the form, it turns green as it becomes valid but is black otherwise. I did this using the :valid CSS3 pseudo-class, which you'll learn more about in Chapter 9.

NOTE: For more information on HTML5 form elements, read "New form features in HTML5" by Patrick Lauke and me at http://dev.opera.com/articles/view/new-form-features-in-html5.

<CANVAS>

Last but not least in this section, you'll briefly explore HTML5 <canvas>, which allows you to manipulate bitmap graphics via script. The <canvas> element doesn't do much on its own. It creates a static space on the screen with dimensions that you specify (see simple-canvas.html in the chapter2 folder):

```
<canvas id="canvas" width="480" height="320">
    <!-- fallback content here -->
</canvas>
```

FIGURE 2.10 A simple HTML5 canvas example.

This code creates a blank bitmap image, which you can draw on and manipulate using the Canvas API. The magic comes when you target the canvas using JavaScript via its ID:

```
var c = document.getElementById('canvas');
```

You then get the drawing context of the canvas—in this case a two-dimensional image—using the following line (you can also draw 3D images in <canvas> using WebGL):

```
var context = c.getContext('2d');
```

You can then start using properties of the context you've created to draw onto the canvas. For example:

```
context.fillStyle = "rgb(0,0,200)";
context.fillRect (100, 50, 100, 150);
```

Here you select a blue color and draw a filled rectangle of that color that is 100px by 50px in size at coordinates (100,150) on the canvas. The top-left corner of the canvas (0,0) is the origin (**Figure 2.10**).

> **TIP:** Canvas has many more primitives available, such as full-text drawing capabilities and the ability to import images and video frames, among many others. Covering more of these primitives is beyond the scope of this book. For good <canvas> tutorials, hop on over to Mozilla's "Canvas tutorial" page (https://developer.mozilla.org/en/Canvas_tutorial). For more on WebGL, a good place to start is Luz Caballero's article "An introduction to WebGL" (http://dev.opera.com/articles/view/an-introduction-to-webgl).

CSS RESETS AND NORMALIZE.CSS

Many people favor the use of CSS resets in their work to get rid of the annoying differences between browser default styles. Such pieces of style are usually only tiny but still annoying when trying to get CSS layouts to work consistently. And some are not so tiny; for example, the differences between default form styling across browsers or margins and padding on the <html> and <body> elements, which you inevitably need to remove to get rid of unsightly spacing on the outside of your page.

CSS resets have traditionally been the answer to these style issues. CSS resets remove most or all default CSS styling, leaving you to add your own styles and be confident that you are much less likely to get weird behavior between browsers.

However, they are not perfect. CSS resets tend to be overzealous, removing every default style and leaving you with more work to add a lot of necessary styles back in. In addition, they inevitably clutter your styles: You can hide them in an external stylesheet, but you'll still see loads of crazy declarations when it comes to debugging your CSS using a debugging tool.

A much better option is to use normalize.css, which was written by Nicolas Gallagher (http://nicolasgallagher.com/about-normalize-css). Instead of removing everything, normalize.css makes default styles more consistent across browsers, fixes bugs, and makes subtle improvements.

You simply download the file from https://github.com/necolas/normalize.css, attach it to your page, and voilà! For those interested in learning more, the About page referenced previously and the CSS file contain extensive comments and examples.

I've included this file in the template, and it is used in most of the examples in this book.

JAVASCRIPT LIBRARY ROUNDUP

You've done a lot so far in the chapter in terms of building up a template you can use to write HTML5 and CSS3 into with confidence, and going on a quick tour of the new HTML5 elements available to you. Let's now return to further building up your toolkit for the coming events that shall unfold as you journey through the book. In this section you'll look at the different JavaScript libraries you'll be using to build in support for various CSS3 features that lack support in older browsers, most notably older IE versions. These libraries are often referred to as Polyfills.

> **NOTE:** I suggest that you consult the websites of these different projects, download the libraries so they are ready for you to start experimenting with (many of them have online copies available that can be linked to, but it is also useful to have them available for offline experimentation), and check out the available documentation. I won't include all of these in my default template, because you won't need all of them in each project.

CSS3-MEDIAQUERIES-JS

css3-mediaqueries-js is a nifty little library written by Wouter van der Graaf, which transparently adds support for Media Queries to browsers that don't have them natively. The transition is a bit clunky when you trigger a media query by resizing a browser window; but don't worry, users are very unlikely to ever do this or in fact know what a browser is (or care). For information about css3-mediaqueries-js, check out these sites:

- Home. http://code.google.com/p/css3-mediaqueries-js
- Download. http://code.google.com/p/css3-mediaqueries-js/downloads/list

Respond.js, written by Scott Jehl, is another library for adding in Media Query support to nonsupporting browsers. It specifically adds support for min-width and max-width Media Queries. Find out more about it at its Github page: https://github.com/scottjehl/Respond.

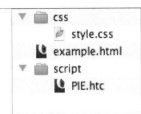

FIGURE 2.11 A typical, simple website directory structure.

CSS3PIE

CSS3PIE adds support for CSS3 "bling" features to older versions of IE that don't support them. It is part of Sencha Labs and was originally developed by Jason Johnston. The current feature support list includes:

- `border-radius`

- `box-shadow`

- `border-image`

- multiple background images

- `linear-gradient` as background image

Note that CSS3PIE includes a JavaScript version (read more at http://css3pie.com/documentation/pie-js), but the basic version that you will most likely use (at first, at least) is an `.htc` file (HTML component—an IE-specific script used to create custom display behaviors that can be applied to a page via CSS). Bizarrely, you need to reference the `.htc` file with a path relative to the HTML file, not the CSS file, even if you are including references to it in CSS that is contained in an external stylesheet!

For example, consider the directory structure shown in **Figure 2.11**.

To apply the CSS styling to the HTML file, you obviously need to reference it using the path `css/style.css`:

```
<link rel="stylesheet" type="text/css" href="css/style.css">
```

The `.htc` file works by being applied to the CSS properties you want to affect in the form of a behavior property. You'd think that you'd need to do this by going up a level and then down a level again to get from `.css` to `.htc`:

```
behavior: url(../script/PIE.htc);
```

But you don't. The `.htc` file is referenced from the CSS but actually acts on the HTML file after the CSS has been applied to it, so you need to reference it as if it were being referenced from the HTML file, like so:

```
behavior: url(script/PIE.htc);
```

This confused me at first.

For information about CSS3PIE, check out these sites:

- Home and download. http://css3pie.com

- About and support list. http://css3pie.com/about

- Documentation. http://css3pie.com/documentation

MODERNIZR

Modernizr is the daddy of all feature-detection libraries. It allows you to detect support for desired HTML5 and CSS3 features, and then serve up alternative styles and scripts to optimize the user experience in nonsupporting browsers. Created by Faruk Ateş, Paul Irish, and Alex Sexton, it has extensive documentation available, and Modernizr 2.0 and later allow you to download a customized version that only contains the feature tests you need for your particular project.

For information about Modernizr, check out these sites:

- Home. http://modernizr.com

- Documentation. http://modernizr.com/docs

- Download/customize. http://www.modernizr.com/download

SELECTIVIZR

Written by Keith Clark, and mentioned in the previous chapter, Selectivizr is a small utility that sits on top of an existing JavaScript library, such as jQuery or MooTools, and adds support for CSS3 selectors/pseudo-classes to nonsupporting versions of IE (6–8). The Home/Download page is at http://selectivizr.com.

IE CONDITIONAL **COMMENTS**

Many people saw IE conditional comments as bad, because they are a proprietary feature invented by Microsoft to allow developers to target HTML, CSS, and JavaScript just at specific versions of IE. These conditional comments could be used for all kinds of evil and represent the sort of "feature" that was probably originally invented by He-Man's arch nemesis, Skeletor (he also invented IE behaviors, the IE6 rendering engine, and soap operas).

But they are also very useful for modern web development practices if you need to target some CSS specifically at older versions of IE to fix rendering bugs and want to prevent browsers that don't need those fixes from wasting bandwidth or HTTP requests. Here is a reminder of what they look like. In my template I've included this code:

```
<!--[if lt IE 9]>
    <script src="http://html5shiv.googlecode.com/svn/trunk/html5.js">
    </script>
<![endif]-->
```

The entire structure is wrapped in a standard HTML comment, so any browsers that aren't IE will conveniently ignore the whole block. IE will treat it like an `if` statement, running the code if the browser matches the condition contained in the first line of the comment. In this example, the conditional logic is `if lt IE 9`, which means "if less than IE9"—so the script will be passed to any version of IE earlier than IE9. The [endif] part then marks where the conditional content ends.

Note that you can have as many of these IE conditional comments as you like inside your HTML. The most common ones you'll use are:

- **if IE**. Gives the content to all versions of IE.

- **if IE 6**. Gives the content to the specified version of IE only.

- **if lt IE 9**. Gives the content to all versions of IE earlier than the specified version of IE.

- **if lte IE 8**. Gives the content to the specified version of IE and all earlier versions.

You can also use gt and gte ("greater than" and "greater than or equal to") in the same way, but you will be much less likely to use these. Most likely, you'll use IE conditional comments to:

- Serve scripting only to specific IE versions, either to provide alternative mechanisms that will work in IE or to build in support for HTML and CSS features that don't have native support.

- Serve CSS to fix IE-specific CSS bugs that threaten to make your lovingly crafted layouts crumble. The most obvious fixes that spring to mind are serving older IE versions different width and height values to compensate from the broken box model and giving various layout features hasLayout to make those features behave properly in IE.

- Display abusive messages only to users of older IE versions while bullying them into upgrading their browser.

Bruce Lawson has written a great article that expands this topic further called "Supporting IE with conditional comments" (http://dev.opera.com/articles/view/supporting-ie-with-conditional-comments). There is also an article on MSDN called "About Conditional Comments" (http://msdn.microsoft.com/en-us/library/ms537512.aspx) that contains some pretty dreadful outdated web development ideas but provides a good reference for all of the IE conditional syntax available.

> **NOTE:** IE10 completely ignores conditional comments, so you can't use them to direct code only to IE10. This isn't as bad as it sounds: IE10 has really good standards support, worthy of a modern browser, so chances are you wouldn't need conditional comments anyway.

WRAPPING UP

After reading this chapter, you are up to speed on your markup structures and have built a toolkit you can rely on. Now you can stretch and relax a bit.

When you're ready to continue your work and start looking into CSS3 enhancements for text and fonts, turn the page when you hear the tone. (If you've not bought the interactive version of the book, invent your own tone and hum it to yourself.)

3

SPICING UP YOUR FONTS AND TEXT

Fonts and text have been pretty stable across browsers for a fairly long time in terms of CSS2 support, although the feature set has traditionally been a bit limited. But this is all changing, as you'll see as you travel through this chapter. CSS3 provides more powerful features for bending type to your will.

In this chapter you'll learn how to apply custom fonts to your web documents in a variety of ways, from hosting free fonts on your own server to using professional paid services. You'll also learn how to use some of the new CSS3 text features, such as controlling hyphenation and OpenType font features.

UP THE PYTHONS!

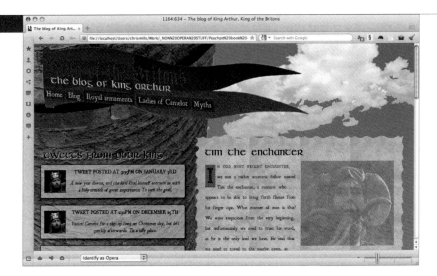

FIGURE 3.1 The *Holy Grail* tribute site.

In my quest to create examples for this book that were informative and entertaining, and at least remotely based in the real world, I created a tribute site for Monty Python's take on the familiar Arthurian legend, Monty Python and the Holy Grail (**Figure 3.1**).

You'll find a rather chaotic but entertaining finished version in the king-arthur-blog-example folder in the code download. Let's walk through how I applied custom fonts to the site.

USING **WEB FONTS**

For years, the lack of "web-safe fonts" available for web designers to use on their sites was a complete nightmare. Fonts like Times New Roman, Arial, Courier New, and Georgia can go quite a long way, but for custom headings or logos, you had to resort to tricky techniques like image replacement or even siFR or Cufon (which replaced text using Flash movies or SVG containing custom fonts).

Like a ray of sunshine, CSS2.1 introduced Web Fonts. Then it was dropped due to lack of agreement from browser vendors. Then it was reintroduced in the Web Fonts module, which was later subsumed into the Fonts module (www.w3.org/TR/css3-fonts), and lo, there was much rejoicing. This module contains functionality that allows you to specify custom font files to download along with your website, and then use them in the same way as any other font. You first need to specify the font to download using a @font-face block, like so:

```
@font-face {
    font-family: myfont;
    src: local("myfont"),url(myfont.ttf),url(myfont.woff);
    font-weight: bold;
    font-style: italic;
}
```

Inside the curly braces, you can include:

- A **font-family** declaration to specify the name of your font, which is how you will refer to it in your CSS. You can pretty much use any term you like here, as long as you use it consistently throughout your CSS. Use font-family: 'monkey butt'; if you really think your boss or client will be cool with it.

- A **src** declaration to point to the actual font(s) you want to use. This can point to a single font file or a comma-delimited list of as many different fonts as you want. The browser will go through the list until it can find a format it recognizes. The fonts can be local, such as local("foo"), or external downloadable fonts, such as url(http://example.com/path/to/foo.ttf).

- A **font-weight** declaration to specify usage of a bold version of the font if it's available. If the font file you are pointing to contains a bold version, it will be used; otherwise, setting bold will have no effect, and you should set it to normal instead or not include it.

- A **font-style** declaration to specify usage of an italic version of the font if it's available. If the font file you are pointing to contains an italic version, it will be used; otherwise, setting italic will have no effect, and you should set it to normal instead or not include it.

Of course, nothing is ever this simple in web design. Those dastardly browser vendors haven't been able to agree on a single font file format to support until recently, and you also need to think about older browsers, which use older font formats. **Table 3.1** gives you an idea what current font format support looks like across browsers.

TABLE 3.1 Browser Support Matrix for Font Formats

BROWSER/ FONT FORMAT	SUPPORT @ FONT-FACE	TRUETYPE (.TTF)	OPENTYPE (.OTF)	EMBEDDED OPENTYPE (.EOT)	SVG	WEB OPEN FONT FORMAT (.WOFF)
Opera	Since 10	Yes	Yes	No	Yes	Yes
Firefox	Since 3.5	Yes	Yes	No	No	Yes
Safari	Since 3.1	Yes	Yes	No	Yes	Yes
Chrome	Since 4	Yes	Yes	No	Yes	Yes
Internet Explorer	.eot since 4, .woff since 9	No	No	Yes	No	Yes
iOS	SVG up to 4.1	Yes	Yes	No	Yes	Yes
Android	Since 2.2	Yes	Yes	No	Yes	No
Chrome Mobile	Since beta	Yes	Yes	No	Yes	Yes
Opera Mobile	Since beta	Yes	Yes	No	Yes	Yes

Fortunately, all browser vendors have now agreed on supporting the new W3C WOFF standard (www.w3.org/TR/WOFF), which is a container/compression format for OpenType and TrueType fonts that can also contain licensing information and suchlike. It is a winner all around, resulting in smaller file sizes and happier font foundries. It has been supported for ages in Firefox and Chrome, Safari since version 5.1, Opera since version 11, and Internet Explorer (IE) since version 9.

Older versions of most browsers don't matter as much anymore because they tend to be updated regularly. However, older versions of IE still need to be supported; many IE installs won't be updated anytime soon (49 percent of the world's computers still run Windows XP, which can only run IE version 8 and earlier).

The good news is that IE has supported Microsoft's proprietary Embedded OpenType format since version 4, meaning that old versions of IE can work with custom fonts quite well.

ADDING WEB FONTS TO THE EXAMPLE

To chronicle the adventures of Arthur and the Knights of Camelot—and their fights against such denizens as the Knights who say Ni and The Temptresses of Castle Anthrax—I decided to try to find some old-world fonts to communicate the right sort of look for a blog written by a medieval king. To find what I wanted, I looked at a few free font sites:

- dafont.com

- myfonts.com

- fontsquirrel.com

I eventually settled on three from Font Squirrel that would work out for this demo:

- Ugly Qua (www.fontsquirrel.com/fonts/UglyQua)

- kells sd (www.fontsquirrel.com/fonts/Kells-SD)

- Genzsch Et Heyse (www.fontsquirrel.com/fonts/Genzsch-Et-Heyse)

You might think that creating syntax and different font formats to provide cross-browser support would be a nightmare, given what I said earlier. But Font Squirrel provides two great features that will help you out here. The first one is the ready-made @font-face kits page (www.fontsquirrel.com/fontface), which contains all the font files and code you'll need to get fonts working cross-browser.

But what if you want to customize one of Font Squirrel's fonts or make one of your own fonts work cross-browser? The second feature—the @font-face generator—will come to your rescue. Just follow these steps to create what you need.

1. Download some fonts you want to use. Generally, they will be in .otf or .ttf format, but either will do.

2. Go to the @font-face generator at www.fontsquirrel.com/fontface/generator.

3. Click the Add Fonts button, and select one of your font files. Repeat this step until you've added all the fonts you need to the list.

4. Select the "Yes, the fonts I'm uploading are legally eligible for web embedding" check box. The fonts I chose from Font Squirrel are free for commercial web use, but you'll find many that are not, so be careful here.

5. Click the Download Your Kit button, and save the resulting ZIP download to a location you'll remember.

At this point you'll have a ZIP file full of different format fonts, HTML, CSS, and other shizzle. For each font you want to use, copy the font files (.eot, .svg, .ttf, and .woff) to a fonts subdirectory in your working directory. Then open stylesheet.css and copy all the CSS from there to the top of your CSS. It needs to be at the top so the fonts will be available when you apply them later on. At the top of main-style. css in my King Arthur example, you'll find one of these structures for each font:

```
@font-face {
    font-family: 'GenzschEtHeyseRegular';
    src: url('genzschetheyse-webfont.eot');
    src: url('genzschetheyse-webfont.eot?#iefix')
    ⇢ format('embedded-opentype'),
        url('genzschetheyse-webfont.woff') format('woff'),
    url('genzschetheyse-webfont.ttf') format('truetype'),
        url('genzschetheyse-webfont.svg#GenzschEtHeyseRegular')
        ⇢ format('svg');
    font-weight: normal;
    font-style: normal;
}
```

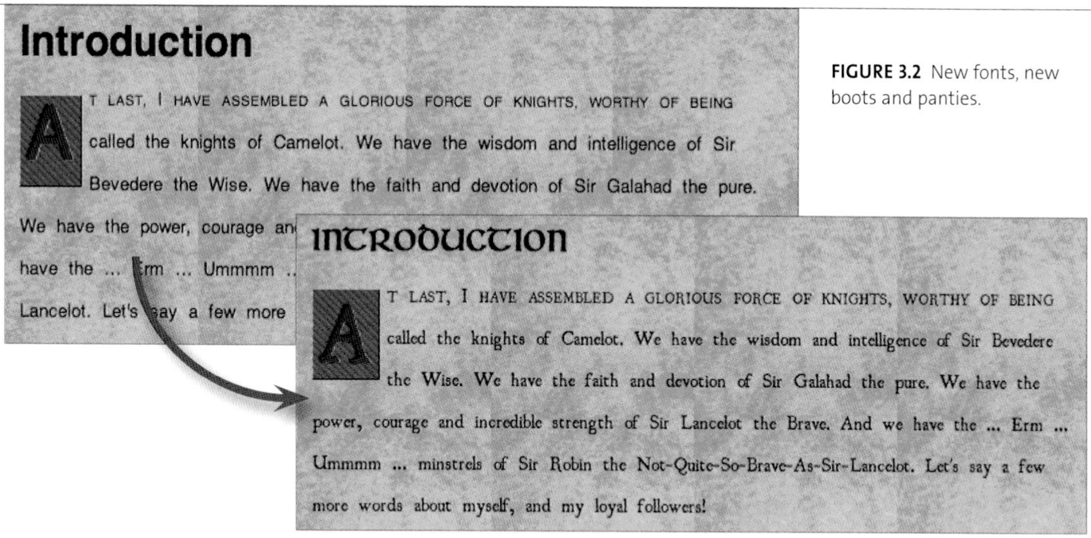

Introduction

T LAST, I HAVE ASSEMBLED A GLORIOUS FORCE OF KNIGHTS, WORTHY OF BEING called the knights of Camelot. We have the wisdom and intelligence of Sir Bevedere the Wise. We have the faith and devotion of Sir Galahad the pure. We have the power, courage an[d] ... have the ... [E]rm ... Ummmm ... Lancelot. Let's [s]ay a few more

INTRODUCTION

T LAST, I HAVE ASSEMBLED A GLORIOUS FORCE OF KNIGHTS, WORTHY OF BEING called the knights of Camelot. We have the wisdom and intelligence of Sir Bevedere the Wise. We have the faith and devotion of Sir Galahad the pure. We have the power, courage and incredible strength of Sir Lancelot the Brave. And we have the ... Erm ... Ummmm ... minstrels of Sir Robin the Not-Quite-So-Brave-As-Sir-Lancelot. Let's say a few more words about myself, and my loyal followers!

FIGURE 3.2 New fonts, new boots and panties.

This looks slightly scary compared to the simple @font-face example you saw earlier, but don't worry; you don't really need to know exactly what is going on here. It is termed the "Bulletproof font syntax," and it is guaranteed to support most if not all browsers you'd need to support. If you want more details on why this structure works, read "Bulletproof @font-face syntax" by Paul Irish at http://paulirish.com/2009/bulletproof-font-face-implementation-syntax.

With the font specified in this manner, you can then use it in your code in the standard way:

```
h1 {
    font-size: 6em;
    font-family: GenzschEtHeyseRegular, serif;
}
```

Figure 3.2 shows the updated look.

WEB-FONT PROBLEMS

Unfortunately, web fonts are not without their problems. If you really want a professional look to your site's text, you need to consider your font choices carefully and test them thoroughly. The following problems need considerable thought.

FLASH OF UNSTYLED TEXT (FOUT)

FOUT refers to the way some browsers behave (namely Opera, Firefox earlier than version 4, and IE earlier than version 10) when they encounter a web font; that is, they first render the text without the font applied. Then they download the font file and apply it to the text. This can create a rather jarring and unsightly effect, which you've probably witnessed at some point.

There are a couple of solutions to this problem. One solution is the webfont loader from Google (http://code.google.com/apis/webfonts/docs/webfont_loader.html), which is a JavaScript API with quite a few features available. You can include it in your page using the following script:

```
<script src="//ajax.googleapis.com/ajax/libs/webfont/1/
    webfont.js"></script>
```

You then need to point to the fonts in question by putting scripts like the following in your document's <head>; the scripts need to be included before your style declarations:

```
<script>
    WebFont.load({
        custom: {
            families: ['MEgalopolisExtraRegular',
                'SansationRegular'],
        }
    });
</script>
```

The JavaScript targets the fonts and the stylesheets that refer to them. It adds classes to the document's <html> tag to indicate different stages of web-font loading. Before a web font has loaded, the class wf-loading is included. During this stage, you could hide the text using a descendant selector:

```
.wf-loading h1, .wf-loading p {
    visibility: hidden;
}
```

When the font has finished loading and is ready to be used, the wf-loading class is removed, and a series of -active classes are included instead. Now you can include the fonts as desired, like so:

```
.wf-megalopolisextraregular-n4-active h1 {
    visibility: visible;
    font-family: MEgalopolisExtraRegular, arial, sans-serif;
}
.wf-sansationregular-n4-active p {
    visibility: visible;
    font-family: SansationRegular, arial, sans-serif;
}
```

If the font fails to load for some reason, a class of wf-inactive is included instead, and you can point to a fallback font:

```
.wf-inactive body {
    visibility: visible;
    font-family: sans-serif;
}
```

NOTE: Google also has a free Fonts service at www.google.com/webfonts, which is worth checking out if you are looking for some decent quality free fonts and want an easy-to-use service. The fonts are also hosted by Google, so you'll save some bandwidth.

ADDED BANDWIDTH

Web fonts have many advantages over image replacement in terms of flexibility and the power you have to control your designs. They can also result in a smaller file size, depending on your situation. But you really need to think carefully about using them if, for example, you are only using a single font for a single heading at the top of your site.

In King Arthur's blog I only used the Genzsch Et Heyse font for the <h1> on each page. The EOT and TTF versions are 66 kb; the WOFF version is 41 kb; and the SVG version is a whopping 209 kb (although this is only needed by users of old versions of iOS). Some single font files can range in size from 300 to 400 kb. And this is made worse by the fact that some browsers erroneously download more fonts than they need (see the "Browser bugs" section later in this chapter).

This problem will be mitigated as time goes on—as old IE versions die out and all browsers support WOFF. But it won't go away completely. Some font files will just be very big, especially when you consider CJK (Chinese, Japanese, Korean) languages, which can feature literally thousands of characters; such fonts can weigh in at several megabytes.

NOTE: If font file size is a problem in your situation, you could create a font file containing just the characters you need using a program called Fontforge (http://fontforge.sourceforge.net). In addition, a property in the spec called unicode-range allows you to specify which characters you want to load from the font file, making the bandwidth problem even easier to solve. But at the time of this writing, unicode-range was only supported in WebKit, so I decided not to talk about it in detail.

So determine whether you really need a web font or if you'd be better off with image replacement, or even a web-safe font, such as Times New Roman. Just because you can use web fonts doesn't mean you have to!

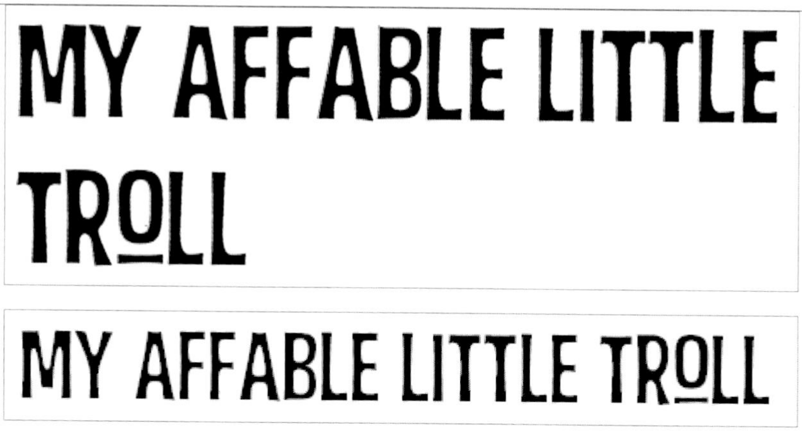

MY AFFABLE LITTLE TROLL

MY AFFABLE LITTLE TROLL

FIGURE 3.3 A web-font example with the `<h1>` set to 48px in Firefox 8 on the Mac (top) and in IE6 (bottom). The IE6 rendering, as well as getting the sizing wrong so it looks a lot smaller, is more jagged and fuzzier looking.

WINDOWS RENDERING PROBLEMS

Another problem you'll come across with web fonts fairly frequently is that web-font rendering can be pretty awful with certain fonts on certain browsers, especially IE on Windows.

Windows uses a technology called ClearType, which uses subpixel rendering to make font rendering appear smoother. If this option is not enabled, the font will look worse on Windows, and it's not something you can control. That said, this technology has been around forever (it is turned on by default in most modern Windows systems but not XP, unfortunately), but it still doesn't look appealing for larger font-size rendering compared to Apple's anti-aliasing on Mac OS X (**Figure 3.3**). For more on this rendering problem, be sure to read Jon Tan's excellent post "Display type and the raster wars" (http://jontangerine.com/log/2008/11/display-type-and-the-raster-wars).

Some modern browsers do font anti-aliasing as well, which can help when rendering. Chrome, IE, and Safari use the operating system default, whereas Firefox seems to use its own font-smoothing system. Opera doesn't do any anti-aliasing of its own.

Because there are so many variables, the only way to approach this rendering problem is to do a decent amount of testing across Windows XP, Vista, Windows 7 and later versions, including the full gamut of modern browsers, as well as IE6–8. See if the quality of the font rendering is acceptable to you and your clients, and explain the potential problems with Windows.

FIGURE 3.4 Glyphs that don't appear inside your web font will be rendered in the system default, if you've specified it as a fallback in your font stack.

FIGURE 3.5 There's nothing worse than seeing horrible blank spaces in your text! Always specify a fallback font stack, even if it is just the system default sans-serif or serif font!

If your headings look ghastly, one potential solution is to set the heading font sizes in pixels just on the problem browsers. This has been known to help. You could do this via an IE conditional comment perhaps or by using browser sniffing.

Another tip is that when you generate your @font-face kit in Font Squirrel, as you saw earlier, you should click the Expert option, and then choose Rendering > Apply Hinting > Improve Win rendering.

QUALITY AND WIDESPREAD USAGE

Free fonts are all well and good, but the really decent fonts are few and far between. Many free fonts have a small range of glyphs included in them, which is not too bad if you are using the glyphs for headings that you can control, but it can be disastrous if you are using them on user-generated content, like a blog. If you have specified a fallback font, the characters that don't appear in your web font will appear in the fallback font. For example, in Figure 3.4 I've replaced the "K" in Knights in my example's <h1> with a registered trademark symbol that doesn't appear in the GenzschEtHeyseRegular font.

If you don't specify a fallback font stack, certain characters could easily be rendered as horrible little blank spaces or ugly squares (**Figure 3.5**), because the web font does not contain those glyphs.

Museo AaBbCcDdEeFfGgHhIiJjKk

ChunkFive AaBbCcDdEeFfGgH

In addition, the good free fonts are likely to be used a lot. For example, Museo and Chunk Five (**Figure 3.6**) have been used so many times that they are becoming tiresome, which is a shame because they are great fonts.

If font quality and overuse are problems in your work, you could consider using a paid font service for better quality and more varied fonts (see the later section "Commercial Font Services"). That old adage of you get what you pay for was never truer than today.

BROWSER BUGS

At the time of this writing (and perhaps for a good while after), browser bugs can impair the efficiency of web-font usage, so you should be mindful of them as you work with @font-face. Let's quickly look at the bulletproof @font-face syntax again:

```
@font-face {
    font-family: 'myfont';
    src: url('myfont.eot');
    src: url('myfont.eot') format('embedded-opentype'),
        url('myfont.woff') format('woff'),
        url('myfont.ttf') format('truetype'),
        url('myfont.svg#myfont') format('svg');
    font-weight: normal;
    font-style: normal;
}
```

If you are experiencing strange blips in font performance or rendering quality, it could be due to one of the following:

- IE9 and later support the WOFF format, but they also support EOT. If you are using syntax like that in the preceding code, IE9 and later will download the EOT file and use it (browsers go through the list and use the first font they recognize). You can find a more detailed reference for fixing IE9 font problems at www.fontspring.com/blog/fixing-ie9-font-face-problems.

- If your web fonts are failing in Firefox or IE and you are serving your fonts from a different domain, it might be because they have a stricter same-origin policy than most. A workaround is to serve the fonts using the `Access-Control-Allow-Origin` HTTP header defined in CORS (see http://dev.opera.com/articles/view/dom-access-control-using-cross-origin-resource-sharing for more details).

- If you are using WOFF and your fonts are being served from IIS, you'll need to add a MIME type: WOFF doesn't have a MIME type, but `font/x-woff` will work.

- Never declare `@font-face` rules for fonts you don't end up using: IE 6–8 will download them all anyway.

- Opera 11.5 and earlier on the Mac, unfortunately, download the EOT font as well as the WOFF font that it actually uses, wasting some bandwidth. Let's hope this will be fixed soon.

COMMERCIAL FONT SERVICES

Commercial font services tend to give you better quality fonts on average, although there are some great free fonts available. You have two options for commercial font services:

- Buying fonts outright
- Using a hosted font service

If you want to buy fonts outright and host them yourself, there are a number of different shops to visit, but the ones I'd recommend are:

- Myfonts.com

- Fontspring.com

- Fontshop.com

The three best options for commercial-hosted font services at the time of this writing are

- Typekit (https://typekit.com). Started off as an independent company by some very clever folks in the United States and recently acquired by Adobe.

- Fontdeck (http://fontdeck.com). Created by designers in the UK.

- WebType (www.webtype.com). Another quality font service set up in collaboration between a number of type experts.

All the hosted font services work in roughly the same way: You sign up for the service, specify which domain(s) you want the fonts used on, paste some custom JavaScript and/or CSS into the <head> of the pages you want the fonts used on, and then choose the fonts you want to use on the web interface of the service.

You'll then be given all the CSS you need; they are very easy to use. Another useful feature of all three is that you are free to test them to a certain degree. Fontdeck gives you full access to all font services free of charge, but only the first 20 IP addresses that access your sites will see your fonts. Typekit allows you to use a limited set of its fonts on one website with limited page views. WebType gives you a 30-day free trial with each font.

When you start using these services, the benefits become very clear: You have access to high-quality fonts with full glyph sets and multiple weights and variants. For example, you can make proper use of the following and more:

```
font-weight: 200;
font-weight: 300;
font-weight: light;
font-weight: black;
```

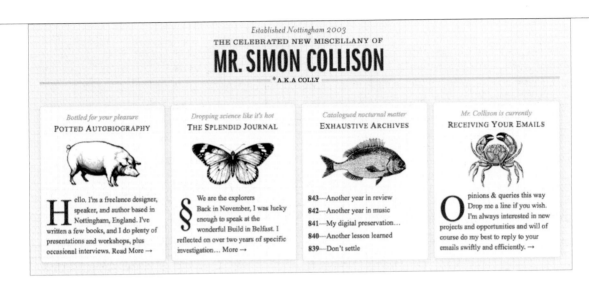

Established Nottingham 2003

THE CELEBRATED NEW MISCELLANY OF

MR. SIMON COLLISON

✦ A.K.A COLLY

Bottled for your pleasure
POTTED AUTOBIOGRAPHY

Hello. I'm a freelance designer, speaker, and author based in Nottingham, England. I've written a few books, and I do plenty of presentations and workshops, plus occasional interviews. Read More →

Dropping science like it's hot
THE SPLENDID JOURNAL

We are the explorers
Back in November, I was lucky enough to speak at the wonderful Build in Belfast. I reflected on over two years of specific investigation... More →

Catalogued nocturnal matter
EXHAUSTIVE ARCHIVES

843—Another year in review
842—Another year in music
841—My digital preservation…
840—Another lesson learned
839—Don't settle

Mr. Collison is currently
RECEIVING YOUR EMAILS

Opinions & queries this way
Drop me a line if you wish.
I'm always interested in new projects and opportunities and will of course do my best to reply to your emails swiftly and efficiently. →

FIGURE 3.7 Colly.com is entirely typeset in Times New Roman. Would you believe it?

You can achieve a lot using different weights of just one typeface, as evidenced by excellent sites, such as Simon Collison's personal site, colly.com (**Figure 3.7**).

All the fonts have agreed licenses for using them on the web. The font files are optimized as much as they can be to reduce file size, and although your users will still have to download them to use them, you can place the server burden on the font service, which reduces your bandwidth burden.

Each service has advantages and disadvantages: I prefer Fontdeck because it is slightly more intuitive to use than the others. Also, the restrictions are not as limited for testing purposes; you pay per font, and it doesn't require JavaScript like Typekit does. It might work out to be slightly more expensive, but the costs are pretty minor either way.

NOTE: You can see some examples of Typekit and Fontdeck in action at http://people.opera.com/cmills/css3book/typekit_example.html and http://people.opera.com/cmills/css3book/fontdeck_example.html. I've also included these examples in the chapter3 code download folder, but you'll only see the font examples working on the preceding URLs, because my Fontdeck and Typekit examples were tied to that domain at the time.

CSS3 **TEXT WRANGLING**

Now that you've gone through @font-face in some detail, including cross-browser support and mitigation of potential problems, and looked at commercial and free font supply options, let's have even more fun and look at some of the rather cool text effects CSS3 offers. (I'll cover the CSS3 typography details at the end of the chapter, because typography is a bit more experimental and cutting edge.) Table 3.2 shows the browser-supported CSS3 text features.

TABLE 3.2 Browser Support Matrix for CSS3 Text Features

BROWSER	TEXT-SHADOW	TEXT-OVERFLOW	WORD-WRAP	HYPHENATE
Opera	Since 9.5	Since 9 with -o-	Since 10.5	No
Firefox	Since 3.5	Since 7	Since 3.6	Since 6 with -moz-
Safari	Since 3.1	Since 3.2	Since 3.1	Since 5.1 with -webkit-
Chrome	Since 4	Since 4	Since 4	No
Internet Explorer	Since 10	Since 6	Since 5.5	Since 10 with -ms-
iOS	Since 3.2	Since 3.2	Since 3.2	Since 4.2 with -webkit-
Android	Since 2.1	Since 2.1	Since 2.1	No
Chrome Mobile	Since beta	Since beta	Since beta	No
Opera Mobile	Since 10	Since 10 with -o-	Since 10	No
Opera Mini	No	Since 5 with -o-	Since 5	No

TEXT SHADOWS

The CSS3 text-shadow property allows you to programmatically create drop shadows on text and is supported across all modern browsers without prefixes. It is very useful to be able to create a flexible drop shadow on text without relying on JavaScript, text duplication, or any other such silliness. You can use drop shadows for a variety of effects but generally for highlighting text, giving it depth, and making it stand out.

FIGURE 3.8 A simple text-
shadow highlight.

The syntax is pretty intuitive:

```
h2 {
    text-shadow: 1px 1px 1px white;
}
```

The first two unit values set the horizontal and vertical offset of the shadow from the original text, respectively. Positive values move the shadow right and down, whereas negative values move the shadow left and up. You can pretty much use any CSS units for these values. But generally, using pixels is recommended, because ems and percentages can make shadows move, and you probably don't want the effect varying with the font size in most cases.

The third unit value sets the amount of blur applied to the shadow. You can set this to a large value to produce an indistinct shadow below the text or set it to 1px to just make it act as an outline highlight (in which case you could just delete the third value altogether, because it defaults to 1px when not specified explicitly). Let's run through a couple of examples. The preceding code is used in my King Arthur blog example to give the <h2>s not appearing in a background a contrasting highlight to make them more visible (**Figure 3.8**).

FIGURE 3.9 A more "embossed" effect.

FIGURE 3.10 The text is now really flying off the page!

You can also use a more subtle color that blends better with the background behind the text to give the text an embossed effect, and use negative offset values to change the light direction (**Figure 3.9**):

```
h2 {
    text-shadow: -1px -1px 1px gray;
}
```

Or perhaps create a much bigger blur and offset the text to make it look like it is about to fly off into space (**Figure 3.10**):

```
h2 {
    text-shadow: 5px 5px 10px black;
}
```

MULTIPLE TEXT SHADOWS

You'll be ecstatic to know that you can also use multiple text shadows on the same selector, like so:

```
text-shadow: 0 0 2px #000,
             0 0 2px #aaa,
             0 0 4px #999,
             0 0 6px #888,
             0 0 8px #666,
             0 6px 6px rgba(0,0,0,0.5),
             0 8px 20px rgba(0,0,0,0.5);
```

You just write each additional text shadow one after the other inside the same property separated by commas. The preceding example produces a rather pleasing, raised 3D text effect (**Figure 3.11**), which blends in well with any backgrounds behind it because RGBA colors are used for the outermost shadows.

CONTROLLING TEXT OVERFLOW

The text-overflow property can be used to control the display of text, which overflows its containing box (when overflow: hidden; is set on it). It is included on the <p> element in my text-overflow.html example in the chapter3 code download folder:

```
p {
    overflow: hidden;
    -ms-text-overflow: ellipsis;
    text-overflow: ellipsis;
}
```

I deliberately included a very long word in this example so it would overflow the <body> box, which was set to 400px wide. text-overflow: ellipsis; can replace the usual unsightly clipping behavior with slightly nicer-on-the-eye ellipses. **Figure 3.12** shows the result.

text-overflow: ellipsis; is not an essential new addition to your toolkit, but it is a useful addition when you want potential text overflow to look a bit less unsightly. It is supported across all major modern browsers.

FIGURE 3.12 The progression you can achieve with `text-overflow: ellipsis;`.

When not out helping those in need, my troll likes to kick back and relax. His favourite hobby is the delicate art of antidisestablishmentarialism.

+ `overflow: hidden;`

When not out helping those in need, my troll likes to kick back and relax. His favourite hobby is the delicate art of antidisestablishmentarialisr

+ `text-overflow: ellipsis`

When not out helping those in need, my troll likes to kick back and relax. His favourite hobby is the delicate art of antidisestablishmentaria...

When not out helping those in need, my troll likes to kick back and relax. His favourite hobby is the delicate art of antidisestablishmentarialis m.

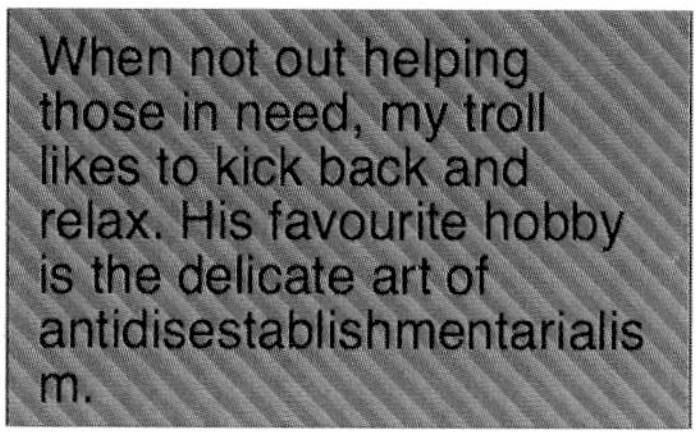

FIGURE 3.13 The effect of `word-wrap: break-word;`.

BREAKING LONG WORDS WITH WORD-WRAP

The new `word-wrap` property offers another potential solution to the problem of words overflowing narrow containers. It's included on the `<p>` element in my word-wrap.html example in the chapter3 code download folder:

```
p {
    word-wrap: break-word;
}
```

Instead of providing a nicer look to the clipped overflowed text, `word-wrap` forces the word to break so that it fits inside the container, as shown in **Figure 3.13**.

Again, this property is supported across all major modern browsers.

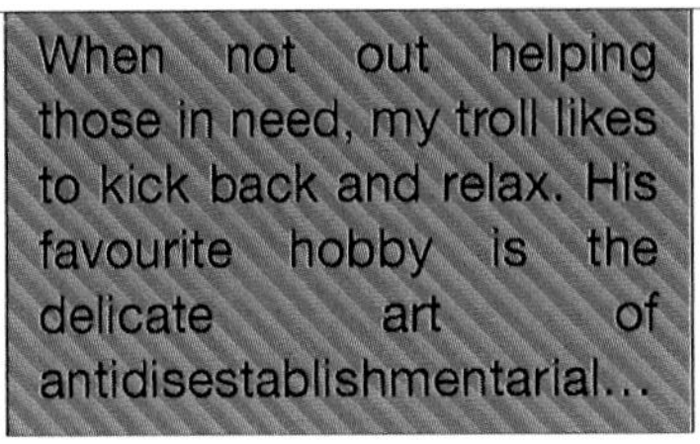

FIGURE 3.14

text-align: justify
usually results in lots of
nasty big gaps in your text.

When not out helping those in need, my troll likes to kick back and relax. His favourite hobby is the delicate art of antidisestablishmentarial...

CONTROLLING HYPHENATION

Hyphenation has long been a sore point on the web. If you want a body of text to sit neatly in a containing box, the obvious solution in print would be to justify the text and hyphenate words as required to make the column work without too many long gaps. This is standard fayre, especially in newspapers and magazines.

But on the web, this treatment is difficult to achieve: You can't just hyphenate words and add line breaks as needed unless you can control the exact copy, font-size, font, containing box, and so forth. And this will almost never be the case; it just isn't how the web works! Instead, you have to settle for left, right, or centred text; text-align: justify usually looks terrible, especially if you have lots of big words in your copy. **Figure 3.14** illustrates this perfectly.

CSS3 comes to the rescue with the hyphens property. The three possible values include:

- **none**. No hyphenation occurs. This could be used to turn off inherited hyphenation set on a parent element.

- **manual**. Words are hyphenated onto separate lines, only there are line-breaking characters present within them (like a hyphen character or a soft hyphen—for example, ­).

- **auto**. Words are automatically broken at appropriate hyphenation points. To work successfully, browsers need to recognize the language to be hyphenated. Therefore, hyphens only works on markup with a correct language declared on a parent element via the lang attribute.

When not out helping those in need, my troll likes to kick back and relax. His favourite hobby is the delicate art of antidisestablishmentarialism.

Let's look at my `hyphens.html` example, which has the following properties set on the paragraphs:

```
p {
    overflow: hidden;
    text-overflow: ellipsis;
    text-align: justify;
    hyphens: auto;
}
```

I've hidden the overflowing text and set `text-overflow: ellipsis` as with previous examples. However, this time I've also set the text to be justified and set automatic hyphens. This produces an effect like that shown in **Figure 3.15**.

> **NOTE:** In the future you'll be able to specify exactly which character the browser uses for its automatic hyphens using the `hyphenate-character` property; for example, `hyphenate-character: "\2010";`. The values are unicode references to glyphs.

HYPHENATION IN OLDER BROWSERS

To use automatic hyphenation in nonsupporting browsers, you can build it in with JavaScript. The Sweet Justice library (see https://github.com/aristus/sweet-justice) provides this script for you. You just need to include the JavaScript file at the bottom of your markup along with jQuery or YUI3. Yes, it works on top of another JavaScript library, which could result in some page bloat. Other disadvantages include the fact that you must include a specific class on each element that you want justified.

Let's turn our attention to the typographic control features detailed in the CSS3 Fonts module that's starting to become available across browsers. The following features are not available everywhere yet, but I'm including them because none of them will cause any major disruption in browsers that don't support them. You'll also get to see some attractive flourishes in browsers that do! It is a breath of fresh air to start to see web browsers directly supporting the advanced features contained inside font files, although some would say it is long overdue. Table 3.3 shows browser support for the font features discussed in this section.

TABLE 3.3 Browser Support Matrix for CSS3 Text Features

BROWSER	TEXT-RENDERING: OPTIMIZELEGIBILITY	FONT-FEATURE-SETTINGS
Opera	No	No
Firefox	Since 8	Since 8 with -moz-
Safari	Since 5.1	No
Chrome	Since 13	Since 17 with -webkit-, only on Windows
Internet Explorer	Since 10	Since 10 with -ms-*
iOS	No	No
Android	No	No
Chrome Mobile	Since beta	No
Opera Mobile	No	No
Opera Mini	No	No

*IE10 platform preview 6 saw the prefix removed

NOTE: Other properties inside the CSS3 Fonts module support programmatic creation and control of features like ligatures and kerning, but none of them seem to have any concrete browser support at the time of this writing (a recent Chrome Beta has support for font-variant-ligatures and font-kerning). At least this section of the chapter can act as a taster for things to come.

FIGURE 3.16 Compare the words on the left to those on the right.

LIGATURES AND OPTIMIZING TEXT RENDERING ON THE WEB

It is common in typography to join the strokes of certain sequences of characters to make them more legible and pleasing to the eye. **Figure 3.16** shows some examples.

These are called ligatures, and decent font files will contain separate glyphs to handle them. When a specific sequence of characters is found, such as "ffl," the separate glyphs of the letters are replaced with the special glyphs containing the ligatures. In CSS this can be controlled using the text-rendering property (which was actually first defined in SVG—see www.w3.org/TR/SVG11/painting.html#TextRenderingProperty):

```
text-rendering: optimizeLegibility
```

This turns on ligatures, which are very attractive but require a bit of extra processing power to render. Keep this in mind if you are desperate to tweak performance as much as possible.

In terms of browser support, you'll be able to see the ligatures in Safari 5.1+, Firefox 4.0+ (uses ligatures automatically anyway, regardless of this property), IE10+, and Chrome 13+.

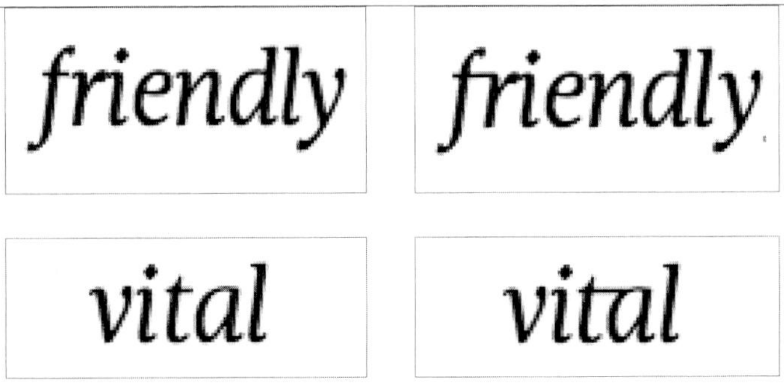

FIGURE 3.17 **FIGURE 3.17** Words rendered without ligatures (left) and with (right).

Figure 3.17 shows further examples. You can also see them at http://people .opera.com/cmills/css3book/fontdeck_example.html.

One detail to note is that the point of the `text-rendering` property is not just to control ligatures, but to dictate how special font features are rendered in the interests of legibility versus speed and geometric precision. The intended values for `text-rendering` include:

- **optimizeLegibility**. Legibility is favored over speed and geometric precision. Generally, ligatures and other font hints will be turned on.

- **optimizeSpeed**. Speed is favored most. Generally, ligatures and other font hints will be turned off. This has no effect in Firefox due to it using ligatures automatically.

- **geometricPrecision**. Geometric precision will be favored most. Ligatures and other font hints will be turned on, depending on what produces the best shape forms.

- **auto**. The browser makes the rendering decision, depending on the current rendering context (e.g., What device am I on? What processing power do I have available?).

ENABLING ADVANCED FONT FEATURES ON THE
WEB WITH FONT-FEATURE-SETTINGS

The web typography story does not end with "a bit more line-height" (commonly known as leading) or even some of the features explored earlier, like ligatures and hyphenation. Oh no! OpenType fonts often contain many alternative letter forms, flourishes, fractional number glyphs, and other such goodies that are just crying out to be utilized. Fortunately, these can be turned on in supporting browsers (at the moment IE10 and later, Chrome 17 and later on Windows, and Firefox 8 and later, and currently only with vendor prefixes) using the font-feature-settings property, which takes as its value a comma-delimited series of features you want to use. For example, to specify that you want to use discretionary ligatures, kerning, and fractions in Firefox, you'd use this:

```
-moz-font-feature-settings: "dlig=1, kern=1, frac=1";
```

IE and Chrome use a slightly newer version of the syntax, which hopefully Mozilla and other browsers will adopt soon after this book is published:

```
-webkit-font-feature-settings: "dlig" 1, "kern" 1, "frac" 1
-ms-font-feature-settings: "dlig" 1, "kern" 1, "frac" 1;
```

> **NOTE:** Microsoft's "Use the whole font" showcase provides some very good examples of font feature usage at http://ie.microsoft.com/testdrive/Graphics/opentype/Default.html.

Fonts will often have different sets of the same feature available—for example, multiple different styles of kerning. You can access these by changing the number after the declaration—for example, "dlig" 0 (in some cases), "dlig" 1, "dlig" 2, "dlig 3".

With that, let's go forward and explore the different font features available to you!

FIGURE 3.18 Discretionary ligatures (font is Magneta Book Italic from Fontdeck).

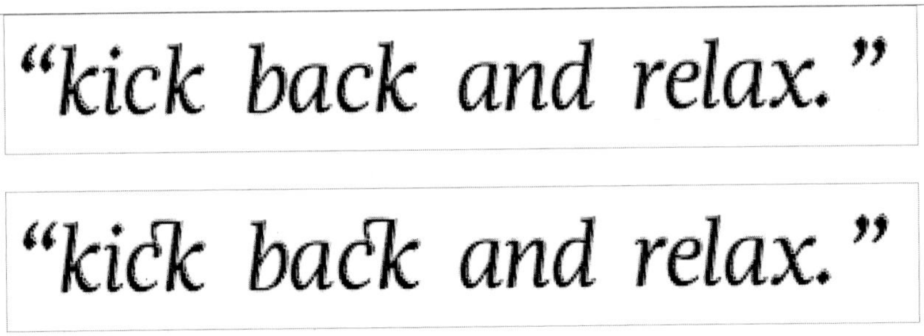

LIGATURES AND DISCRETIONARY LIGATURES

You've already met ligatures, but there are also discretionary ligatures—extra flourishes that can make your text look more attractive. These features are enabled like so:

```
-webkit-font-feature-settings: "liga" 1, "dlig" 1;
-moz-font-feature-settings: "liga=1, dlig=1";
-ms-font-feature-settings: "liga" 1, "dlig" 1;
```

liga basically just acts as a different way to enable ligatures than using text-rendering, although at the time of this writing, the latter had better browser support. dlig produces effects like those shown in **Figure 3.18**.

NUMERALS, FRACTIONS, AND ORDINALS

OpenType fonts often contain some great features for numbers. Consider the following example:

```
-webkit-font-feature-settings: "onum" 1, "tnum" 1, "frac" 1;
-moz-font-feature-settings: "onum=1, tnum=1, frac=1";
-ms-font-feature-settings: "onum" 1, "tnum" 1, "frac" 1;
```

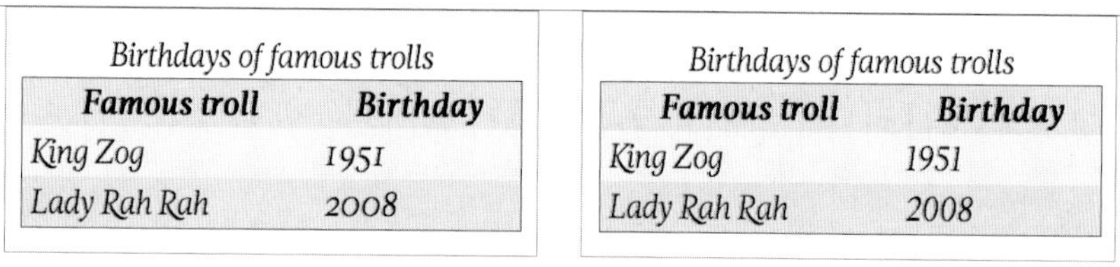

	Birthdays of famous trolls	
Famous troll	**Birthday**	
King Zog	1951	
Lady Rah Rah	2008	

	Birthdays of famous trolls	
Famous troll	**Birthday**	
King Zog	1951	
Lady Rah Rah	2008	

FIGURE 3.19 Tabular numerals (font is Magneta Book Italic from Fontdeck).

0123456789

0123456789

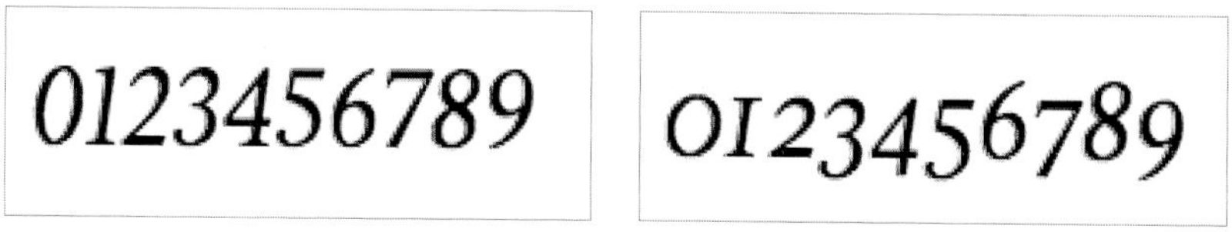

FIGURE 3.20 Old-style numerals (font is Magneta Book Italic from Fontdeck).

ORGANIC INGREDIENTS

✓ 99 44/100 Pure sweetness
✓ All the taste with 1/2 the effort
✓ 2/3 Less sweat
✓ 7/8 Creative inspiration

ORGANIC INGREDIENTS

✓ 99 $^{44}/_{100}$ Pure sweetness
✓ All the taste with ½ the effort
✓ ⅔ Less sweat
✓ ⅞ Creative inspiration

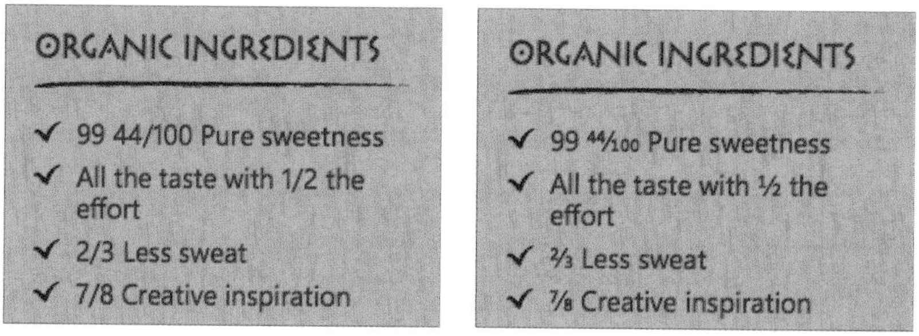

FIGURE 3.21 Fractions (font is Segoe UI Regular from http://ie.microsoft.com/ testdrive/Graphics/opentype/ opentype-monotype/ index.html).

These different declarations mean the following:

- **tnum**. Tabular numerals swap out numbers (and other text, in fact) for the most legible ones available. This generally means they are evenly spaced, uniform height, and not old style (**Figure 3.19**).

- **onum**. These are either ordinals—numerals that denote a position of ranking, for example, 1st or 3rd—or old-style numerals, which are not always the same height and don't always fit exactly on the baseline. (I've found websites that claim one or the other is true) (**Figure 3.20**).

- **frac**. When used, these fractions automatically allow you to use fraction glyphs instead of three separate characters—for example, ¾ instead of 3/4. As **Figure 3.21** shows, this looks a lot more attractive and less clumsy.

FIGURE 3.22 Browser-calculated small caps are on the left; proper small caps are on the right and are much better! (Font is Magneta Book Italic from Fontdeck.)

FIGURE 3.23 Petite caps (font is Ernestine from http://ie.microsoft.com/testdrive/Graphics/opentype/opentype-fontfont/index.html).

SMALL CAPS AND PETITE CAPS

You can use font-variant: small-caps and text-transform: uppercase to control capitalization of your text, but small caps tend to be just shrunken capitals. Some fonts include dedicated small caps glyphs, which look better than just using text-transform. To use these in your page, you'd do this (see the result in **Figure 3.22**):

```
-webkit-font-feature-settings: "smcp" 1;

-moz-font-feature-settings: "smcp=1";

-ms-font-feature-settings: "smcp" 1;
```

You can also use another variant called "petite caps," which is basically just more stylized capitals (**Figure 3.23**):

```
-webkit-font-feature-settings: "pcap" 1;

-moz-font-feature-settings: "pcap=1";

-ms-font-feature-settings: "pcap" 1;
```

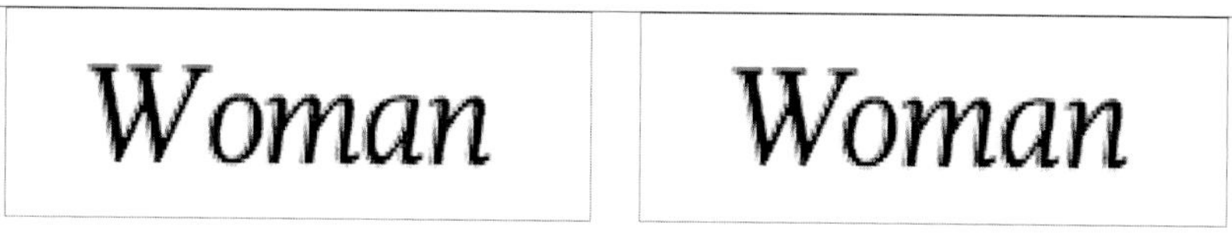

FIGURE 3.24 Kerning (font is Magneta Book Italic from Fontdeck).

KERNING

Kerning refers to altering the horizontal spacing between characters to make it look more even. Kerning is turned on using a single declaration:

```
-webkit-font-feature-settings: "kern" 1;
-moz-font-feature-settings: "kern=1";
-ms-font-feature-settings: "kern" 1;
```

The need for kerning is most evident when you have a curved capital with a compact lowercase letter and no ascender or descender follows it—for example, in the word "Woman" (**Figure 3.24**).

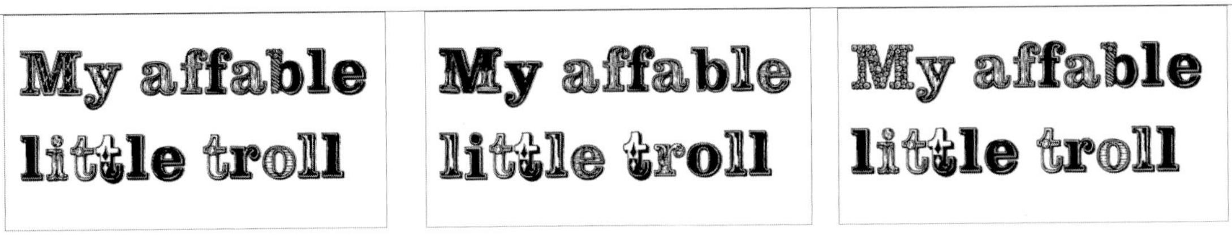

FIGURE 3.25 Stylistic set examples (font is Majestic Mishmash Regular from Fontdeck—standard, ss01, and ss02).

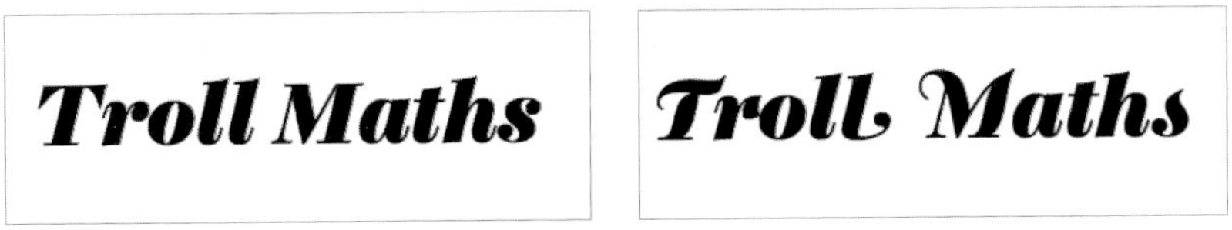

FIGURE 3.26 Stylistic swashes (font is Trilogy Fatface Regular from Fontdeck).

STYLISTIC SETS AND OTHER ASSORTED EFFECTS

Here are a few stylistic sets and other text effects that I've lumped into one final section. Consider the following examples:

```
-webkit-font-feature-settings: "ss01" 1, "swsh" 1, "cswh" 1, "calt" 1;
-moz-font-feature-settings: "ss01=1, swsh=1, cswh=1, calt=1";
-ms-font-feature-settings: "ss01" 1, "swsh" 1, "cswh" 1, "calt" 1;
```

Explanations of the different declarations used here are as follows:

- **ss01**. Stylistic sets specify the usage of an alternative set of glyph styles for the standard glyphs (**Figure 3.25**).

- **swsh**. Stylistic swashes specify the use of stylistic swashes where available, which are often similar to stylistic sets, although the latter tend to be more wide-ranging in terms of the kinds of changes they include (**Figure 3.26**).

FIGURE 3.27 Contextual swashes (font is Nexus Serif from http://ie.microsoft.com/testdrive/Graphics/opentype/opentype-fontfont/index.html).

FIGURE 3.28 Contextual alternatives (font is Mister K from http://ie.microsoft.com/testdrive/Graphics/opentype/opentype-fontfont/index.html).

- **cswh**. Contextual swashes are similar to stylistic swashes except that these flourishes are used only in certain contexts (**Figure 3.27**).

- **calt**. Contextual alternatives are alternative letter forms available for use, an example of which is shown in **Figure 3.28**.

TIPS FOR FONT-FEATURE USAGE

For more successful usage of advanced typographical font features, consider the following tips.

BUILD UP TEST FILES

Missing from the typographical puzzle seems to be how to determine which fonts include the font features I've been discussing in this section so that you can use them. At this time, it will take a bit of trial and error. When looking for a font to use, my advice is to create a sample type template that includes all the potential letter sequences you might want, and then apply a simple stylesheet to it that includes all available ligatures and other font features. Then try applying different fonts to it and observe the results. A service such as Fontdeck makes this very easy to do. In Firefox 8 or IE10, try viewing the following example: http://people.opera.com/cmills/css3book/fontdeck_example.html.

USE DIFFERENT SELECTORS AND FONT SUBSETS
FOR APPLYING FONT FEATURES

You'll probably not want to use advanced font features on all of your type. It would just be overkill! Most likely, you'll just apply such features to headings, single characters, or small strings of characters near the start or end of your lines of text.

In addition, you could consider using a subset of your fonts that just contains the font features you want to style your headings and other text elements. This will reduce bandwidth as well:

```
h1, .flourish {
    font-family: 'my posh font subset', fallback, fallback;
    -webkit-font-feature-settings: "dlig" 1, "swsh" 1;
    -moz-font-feature-settings: " dlig=1, swsh=1";
    -ms-font-feature-settings: "dlig" 1, "swsh" 1;

}
```

WRAPPING **UP**

In this chapter you investigated the new text and font features available in CSS3 and learned about usage and common problems you'll encounter. You also looked at free and commercial font solutions. By now, you should be comfortable making good choices for fonts and text styling on your site.

For more in-depth information on fonts and to keep up with the latest on web fonts and text, be sure to read the blogs of such talented typography fanatics as Rich Rutter (clagnut.com), Jon Tan (jontangerine.com), and Mark Boulton (markboulton.co.uk).

4

ENHANCING BOXES WITH **CSS3 BLING**

One of the overriding general problems that CSS3 works toward solving is reducing the number of images (and the inflexibility of those images) you are called upon to use to prettify your websites. This chapter groups together all such CSS3 features (like box shadows, gradients, and border images) that have strong browser support under the moniker "bling boxes."

In this chapter you'll learn new ways to (tastefully) add graphical effects to your sites programmatically without having to use millions of background images. You'll start by looking at some basic isolated examples and then advance to more involved implementations. So put on your sequined disco clothes, jangle your change, and prepare to strut your funky stuff.

A **BRIGHT FUTURE**
WITH **CSS3 BLING**

Most of you will have a good idea of the kinds of CSS3 features I'm referring to by bling boxes: Drop shadows, rounded corners, linear and radial gradients, and alpha transparency are exemplary examples. Also, a number of properties still require the use of images but allow you to use them in a more flexible way!

The advantages of such features should be obvious, but just in case, let's briefly review them before moving on:

- Less downloading. Programmatically creating bling effects allows you to decrease the number of images you need for your designs and therefore the number of HTTP requests and download sizes involved.

- Easier maintenance of graphical effects. You can now vary colors, dimensions, and so on by just changing some CSS syntax rather than having to open Photoshop and manually alter image files.

- Less spaghetti code. Back in the day, so-called "bulletproof CSS" solutions typically involved multiple images and multiple nested <div>s—a double disappointment of extra complexity of design time and unsemantic cruft code. If you wanted to create bulletproof rounded corners on a content box to allow it to flex horizontally and vertically, you'd need three extra nested <div>s for holding all the necessary images. If you had only one container available, you'd have to settle for an inflexible, one-size box, which was usually rendered useless when content changed. CSS3 features, such as rounded corners and multiple background images, change all this.

- Fewer Photoshop ninja skills required. Creating such bling effects in code is a lot easier and more intuitive for non-Photoshop experts.

Of course, the main disadvantages at this time are that some of these CSS3 features are not supported in older browsers (usually meaning Internet Explorer 6–8), and they are often used with vendor prefixes. Table 4.1 gives you an at-a-glance reference of browser support for the properties covered in this chapter.

TABLE 4.1 Browser Support Matrix for CSS3 "Bling Box" Features

BROWSER	RGBA/HSLA	Border-radius	Box-shadow	Multiple backgrounds	Gradients	Background-size	Border-image	Background-clip	Box-decoration-break
Opera	version 10.5	version 10.5	version 10.5	version 10.5	11.6 with -o-	version 10.5	11 with -o-	version 10.5	version 10.5
Firefox	version 3	3 with -moz-, 4 prefixless	3.5 with -moz-, 4 prefixless	version 3.6	3.6 with -moz-	version 4	3.5 with -moz-	version 4	Exact details unknown
Safari	version 3.1	3.1 with -webkit-, 5 prefixless	3.1 with -webkit-, 5 prefixless	version 3.1	5.1 with -webkit-	version 5	3.1 with -webkit-	version 5	Exact details unknown
Chrome	version 4	4 with -webkit-, 5 prefixless	4 with -webkit-, 10 prefixless	version 4	10 with -webkit-	version 4	15 with -webkit-	version 4	Exact details unknown
Internet Explorer	version 9	version 9	version 9	version 9	10 with -ms-*	version 9	10 with -ms-	version 9	Exact details unknown
iOS	version 3.2	version 4	3.2 with -webkit-, 5 prefixless	version 3.2	5.0 with -webkit-	version 5	3.2 with -webkit-	version 5	Exact details unknown
Android	version 2.1	2.1 with -webkit-, 2.2 prefixless	2.1 with -webkit-	version 2.1	4 with -webkit-	version 2.1	2.3 with -webkit-	version 2.1	Exact details unknown
Opera Mobile	version 10	version 11	version 11	version 10	11.5 with -o-	version 10	11 with -o-	version 10	Exact details unknown
Opera Mini	version 5	no	no	version 5	no	version 5.0	no	version 5	Exact details unknown

*IE10 platform preview 6 saw support without the prefix

BORDER-RADIUS: GOD BLESS THOSE ROUNDED CORNERS

FIGURE 4.1 A simple container with equally rounded corners.

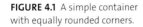

Rounded corners are vital for street cred, critical for keeping with the Web 2.0 cool school, and essential if you want to impress your significant other.

These elements are such a commonly requested design feature that the spec writers added the border-radius property to the Borders and Backgrounds module (www.w3.org/TR/css3-background). The syntax is very simple to use (see border-radius-examples.html in the code download for many examples). You can specify a single value for the radius size of all the rounded corners. For example:

```
border-radius: 10px;
```

You can use pixels or any other CSS unit that makes sense. The preceding line of code results in corners like those in **Figure 4.1**.

FIGURE 4.2 The container on the left has four values set; the one on the right has two values set. I've not included a three-value example, because I find it a bit pointless.

FIGURE 4.3 Setting different horizontal and vertical radii on a container.

As you'd logically expect, you can also specify two, three, or four values. For example:

- **border-radius: 0px 0px 20px 20px;** These relate to top-left, top-right, bottom-right, and bottom-left values, respectively.

- **border-radius: 0px 10px 20px;** These relate to the top-left value, top-right and bottom-left, and bottom-right values, respectively.

- **border-radius: 10px 20px;** These relate to the top-left and bottom-right, and top-right and bottom-left values, respectively.

- A couple of examples are shown in **Figure 4.2**.

Using border-radius, you can also specify two sets of values separated by a forward slash to indicate separate horizontal and vertical corner radii. For example, the following line sets every horizontal radius to 10px and every vertical radius to 20px (**Figure 4.3**):

```
border-radius: 10px/20px;
```

FIGURE 4.4 Specifying the horizontal and vertical radii separately.

The x and y values can follow the same rules as the single set of values you saw in the first couple of examples. You can set a different value for each radius, like this:

```
border-radius: 5px 10px 15px 30px/30px 15px 10px 5px;
```

Or, you can set separate values for the horizontal radii and one value for all four vertical radii:

```
border-radius: 10px 20px 30px 40px/30px;
```

These examples produce the results shown in **Figure 4.4**.

ADDING SUPPORT FOR OLDER BROWSERS: CSS3PIE!

All modern browsers support rounded corners, but older versions of IE, of course, don't. So what can you do here? The simple answer in this case is to use CSS3PIE, which you first looked at in Chapter 2. You can download CSS3PIE from http://css3pie.com. Unzip the file and save PIE.htc to your working directory.

Next, you need to apply the following property line to all elements in your CSS that use properties you want to add support for:

```
behavior: url(path/to/PIE.htc);
```

The easiest way to do this for the border-radius-examples.html file was to just apply this line to all `<div>`s, which works well even though the actual border-radius properties are applied via different classes on the different `<div>`s:

```
div {

    ...

    behavior: url(PIE.htc);

}
```

> **NOTE:** I tried applying the PIE behavior property to all elements on a complex site using `* { behavior: url(PIE.htc); }`, but it resulted in some very weird behavior, so it's best not to try this strategy. The `*` selector is expensive to render anyway, at the best of times.

The path you specify to the PIE.htc file must be relative to the HTML file the CSS is applied to, not the CSS, if you are using an external CSS file. This sounds very odd, but it is due to the way HTC file works: It alters the behavior of the CSS after it is applied to the HTML!

The other major part of using the CSS3PIE technique comes when you use it to add support for gradients. To do so, you need to add a special `-pie-` prefixed version of the property. For example:

```
-pie-background: linear-gradient(rgba(0,0,0,0), rgba(0,0,0,0.2));
```

You'll notice that when using the `-pie-` prefix on a gradient, the prefix is put on background, not `linear-gradient`, which is where the vendor prefixes would go.

There is an added complication: the limitation of CSS3PIE's RGBA support. You see, CSS3PIE will add support, but it won't render the alpha bit. Instead, it will drop the alpha channel and render the equivalent RGB color. This is certainly better than nothing and is probably not disastrous in many situations, but it could also cause content to be rendered unreadable or just look shocking, especially if you're relying on a color with a low alpha value to just add a faint shadow or tint to a container on your page. To remedy this problem, it is a good idea to change the `-pie-` prefixed version of the property to a sensible fallback color or even remove it in some situations:

```
-pie-background: linear-gradient(#ff0000,#A60000);
```

FIGURE 4.5 A basic box shadow (left).

FIGURE 4.6 Box shadow and rounded corners together (right).

Next on the whistle-stop tour is box-shadow (also in www.w3.org/TR/css3 -background), which allows you to add drop shadows to containers. This property is very useful for adding depth to a design, highlights, and user feedback when used in conjunction with pseudo-classes and transitions, as you'll see in later examples (buttons, link highlights, etc.)

The basic box-shadow syntax is as follows:

```
box-shadow: 2px 2px 1px black;
```

The first two unit values specify the horizontal and vertical offset of the shadow from the container. Positive values offset the shadow right and down, whereas negative values offset the shadow left and up. The third unit value specifies the amount of blur radius the shadow has (this is optional and defaults to 0 if not explicitly declared). Increase the value for more blurry, spread-out shadows. The color is, as you'd expect, the color of the shadow.

This basic shadow creates the effect shown in **Figure 4.5**.

Using a subtle shadow like this is ideal for implying just a bit of depth or texture, making the container look slightly raised.

Now let's add some rounded corners into the mix:

```
border-radius: 10px;
```

```
box-shadow: 2px 2px 1px black;
```

As you can see in **Figure 4.6**, the shadow follows the shape of the rounded corners, which is rather convenient.

Using more offset and blur produces a more striking effect:

```
border-radius: 10px;
box-shadow: 5px 5px 10px black;
```

The box now looks like it has truly been lifted into the air (**Figure 4.7**):

But something about the box just doesn't look right. The shadow is rather unnatural. Usually, shadows have a tint of the color of whatever is below them peeking through. But never fear; you can achieve this look easily using an RGBA color (**Figure 4.8**):

```
border-radius: 10px;
box-shadow: 5px 5px 10px rgba(0,0,0,0.5);
```

Multiple box
shadows in action. (left)

FIGURE 4.10 An inner, or inset,
box shadow. (right)

You next need to know that you can include multiple box shadows on a single
container. You just write the different shadows you want one after another, delim-
ited by commas:

```
border-radius: 10px;
box-shadow: 2px 2px 5px rgba(0,0,0,0.5),
            10px 10px 15px rgba(0,0,0,0.5),
            -1px -1px 30px rgba(0,0,0,0.2);
```

This trio creates some immediate depth, plus the suggestion of multiple
light sources (the very faint shadow is offset left and up using negative values)
(**Figure 4.9**).

Now let's look at inner box shadows. You can make any box shadow an inner
box shadow by adding the `inset` keyword at the start. For example:

```
border-radius: 10px;
box-shadow: 2px 2px 5px rgba(0,0,0,0.5),
            inset 5px 5px 8px rgba(0,0,0,0.5);
```

Figure 4.10 shows the result. This technique is useful for creating nice "button
being pushed in" type thingamajigs (technical term).

FIGURE 4.11 A box shadow with a spread value.

Finally, let's look at one more possible unit value you could include: spread. I'm not talking about middle-aged spread or marmalade but the fact that you can add a fourth unit value to specify an amount that the shadow size will increase by in all directions. It's like "padding" for shadows. For example:

```
border-radius: 10px;
box-shadow: 5px 5px 10px 10px rgba(0,0,0,0.5);
```

See the effect in **Figure 4.11**. I've never found a use for adding a spread value, but you probably will.

> **NOTE:** Use box shadows responsibly! Used subtly they can produce a great effect and lift a design. However, if you use them a lot on the same site and on large containers, they can make the site look cluttered and horrible. They can also cause a significant performance impact, especially if you combine them with animations. They are expensive to render in terms of processing power required.

ADDING BOX SHADOW SUPPORT TO OL' IE

Adding CSS3PIE into the mix, as you did earlier, also adds box-shadow support for older versions of IE. But remember CSS3PIE's limited support for RGBA: It is often better to provide an alternative style with a nontransparent color that might be more effective. You could provide this in a conditional-commented stylesheet.

BRING THE BLING WITH CSS GRADIENTS

Gradients are one of the most hotly anticipated features to become native to CSS. Gradients are vital for design in general to reproduce the effects of light falling on curved/shiny surfaces and create interesting patterns. The number of developers who use them in web design is staggering, if not unsurprising. What is a surprise is that until CSS3 came along, web developers never had the ability to create gradients programmatically in any sane way that would work across browsers. SVG had gradients for a long time before that, but IE never supported SVG until IE9.

All this time you've been stuck with either faking SVG in IE using a Polyfill solution like SVGWeb or using repeated background images for those gradients or repeating patterns you desired. This last technique works OK-ish but is an inflexible pain and can become cumbersome very quickly, especially if your boss keeps changing his mind about the gradient colors (more playing with Photoshop; oh goody) or if you are trying to create any kind of complicated layered effect.

Again, CSS3 comes to the rescue with linear and radial gradients, which are defined in the CSS Image Values and Replaced Content module (http://dev.w3.org/csswg/css3-images). To see how flexible CSS gradients are, just have a good play with the examples in this section.

Let's review the two different gradient types separately.

LINEAR GRADIENTS

Linear gradients are the simpler of the two types; these are smooth color progressions that start at one side or corner of an area and cycle smoothly between two or more color stops, ending at the other side or corner.

In CSS they work the same. CSS gradients are basically a special kind of background image. You can set them in place of an image in most places that it would make sense to do so; for example, background-image and border-image (see the "Box Clever: border-image" section later in this chapter for more on border images).

FIGURE 4.12 A basic linear gradient.

FIGURE 4.13 A linear gradient direction can be varied via the use of keywords or degree values.

The most common place you'll want to use them is on standard, commonplace backgrounds. Here is a simple syntax example:

```
background: linear-gradient(#ff0000,#007700);
```

Figure 4.12 shows the result, taken from an example file in the chapter4 code download folder called linear-gradient-test.html. The two colors are the start color in the gradient and the end color, and by default the gradient runs from the top to the bottom of the container.

LINEAR GRADIENT DIRECTION

If you want to vary the direction of your gradient, you can add a direction value at the start of the gradient, like this:

```
background: linear-gradient(to bottom right, #ff0000,#007700);
```

This direction value makes the gradient travel from the top left to the bottom right (**Figure 4.13**).

As you'd expect, you can use a whole range of logical keywords for gradient direction: to top, to top right, to right, to bottom right, to bottom, to bottom left, to left, to top left.

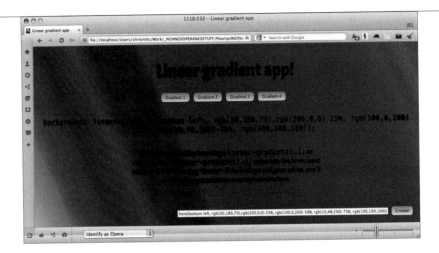

FIGURE 4.14 My gradient app allows you to quickly experiment with gradients.

You can also specify the direction you want the gradient to travel in using an angle. Zero degrees (0deg) is the equivalent of to right; as you increase the angle, it travels around counterclockwise. So the subsequent equivalents would be 90deg = to top, 180deg = to left, 270deg = to bottom. Bear in mind that 135deg will not be the equivalent of to top left (as you might expect) unless the container is a perfect square: The diagonal keywords will change the angle so the gradient will always run from one corner to the other. As a result, you can choose keywords or angles, depending on the effect you want to create.

Note: The spec states that 0deg is the equivalent of the keywords *to top*, but browsers don't follow this currently. This could change in the future.

NOTES: If you look at the code for the linear gradient example, you'll notice that I've included five lines for the gradient—a prefixless line and one for all four major rendering engines. (Opera, Chrome, Firefox, Safari, and IE all support linear and radial gradients now with vendor prefixes.)

Check out my linear-gradient-app.html file in the chapter4 code download folder (which looks like **Figure 4.14**). It is a simple little page I put together using some JavaScript that allows you to dynamically apply different gradients to the page, either by clicking the preset buttons or entering your own linear-gradient(...); value into the form input and clicking the Create! button. You need to include the semicolon, but you don't need to include all the vendor prefixes—just one single nonprefixed version is all you need.

FIGURE 4.15 A gradient with multiple color stops.

FIGURE 4.16 Italiano, pasta, meatballs, Roma Roma (well, not quite).

LINEAR GRADIENT COLOR STOPS

You can also add multiple color stops between the start and the end point by putting them between the start and end color stops, like this:

```
background: linear-gradient(to right,#ff0000,#0000ff 40%,
  #000000 70%,#007700);
```

The result is shown in **Figure 4.15**.

The unit values specify the distance away from the start of the gradient. Note that the percentage values are optional: If you don't specify them, the color stops will be evenly spaced along the gradient.

Instead of percentages, you can use any units you like that would make sense in the circumstances. By default, the first and last values are at 0% and 100%, but you can alter their positions too. For example:

```
background: linear-gradient(#ff0000 66px, #ffffff 67px,
  #ffffff 133px, #00ff00 134px);
```

This effect creates three solid color bands from left to right (**Figure 4.16**). The green color stop is set at 66px down from the top, and everything before it adopts the same color. The red color stop is set at 134px, and everything after it adopts the same color. I also inserted two white color stops in the middle to force the middle band to be completely white. This technique is very useful, especially if you want to start creating more intricate and interesting repeating background patterns, as you'll read about later in the "Multiple Backgrounds" section.

You can even use negative unit values if for some reason you want the linear gradient to start or end outside the container. (You might want to change the gradient on hover. Unfortunately, you can't smoothly animate a gradient, at least not at the time of this writing. Believe me, I've tried.)

Again, I'll extol the awesomeness of transparent colors by providing a very simple gradient with a vital difference (**Figure 4.17**):

```
background: linear-gradient(to top right,
  rgba(0,0,0,0.6),rgba(0,0,0,0));
background-color: #ff0000;
```

Here the gradient is a transparency gradient overlaid onto a solid background color to create the different gradient colors. This is a very powerful technique because it means you can control the look of an entire site section just by varying the background color. It's perfect if you want to vary the look of different pages on a site with minimum effort. Try it!

TIP: It's a good idea to always include a suitable background color in a separate property alongside your gradient, even if the gradient is not transparent. It acts as a good fallback mechanism for a browser that doesn't support CSS gradients, ensuring that content is still readable.

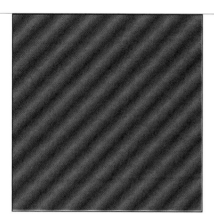

FIGURE 4.18 A simple repeating gradient.

REPEATING LINEAR GRADIENTS

Repeating linear gradients have a similar syntax to linear gradients. Look at the following example and the result in **Figure 4.18**:

```
background: repeating-linear-gradient(to top right, rgba(0,0,0,0.4)
→  10px ,rgba(0,0,0,0) 20px, rgba(0,0,0,0.4) 30px);
background-color: #ff0000;
```

Only 30 pixels' worth of gradient has been specified, but it is repeated over and over again until the end of the container is reached.

UPDATED **LINEAR GRADIENT** SYNTAX

The linear gradient syntax was updated at the time of this writing—the keywords used to not include the to keyword, and mean the opposite direction. For example, to right used to be left. All browsers supported this at the time of publication, but you might come across an older browser that doesn't support the new syntax at some point.

FIGURE 4.19 A simple radial gradient.

RADIAL GRADIENTS

Radial gradients work a bit differently than linear gradients. Instead of traveling across a container from one side to another, they radiate outwards from a single point. Here is a simple example:

```
background: radial-gradient(50% 50%, 60% 60%, rgb(75, 75, 255),
→ rgb(0, 0, 0));
```

This produces the result shown in **Figure 4.19** (if you want to experiment with this code, download the radial-gradient-test.html file in the chapter4 folder).

UPDATED **RADIAL GRADIENT** SYNTAX

The syntax of radial gradients has also been recently changed in the spec. Although this new syntax is much further behind that of linear gradients—it has no current browser implementations—it may well be implemented in the not-too-distant future. Explore http://dev.w3.org/csswg/css3-images/#radial-gradients for more details. As an example, the first example shown in this section would be rewritten as:

```
background: radial-gradient(60% circle at 50% 50%, rgb(75, 75, 255), rgb(0, 0, 0));
```

NOTE: Radial-gradient-app.html is also included in the code download: This works in the same way as linear-gradient-app.html but with different radial gradient presets plugged in. Use it to play!

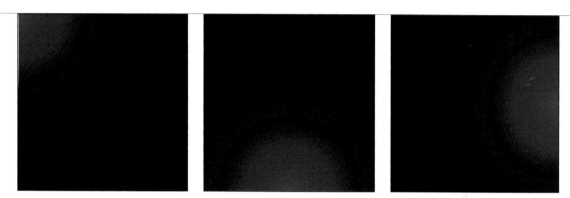

FIGURE 4.20 From left to right: top left, bottom center, and right positioning of a gradient. When only one keyword is supplied, it is assumed to be the horizontal keyword, and the vertical one is given a value of center.

The syntax is a little different than that of linear gradients, so let's go through the radial gradient syntax step by step.

RADIAL GRADIENT POSITION

The first two values in the syntax (50% 50% in the preceding code) dictate the location of the origin of the radial gradient: The first value is the horizontal position inside the container, and the second value is the vertical. In the preceding example, the radial gradient equates to 50% across from the left side and 50% down from the top, which places it slap bang in the middle of the container. As with linear gradients, you can use any unit values that make sense, even negative unit values.

You can also use keywords in place of unit values in the same manner as you learned earlier but with the addition of center if you want the horizontal or vertical position to be centered in the container (this doesn't make sense for linear gradients, but it does for radial gradients). **Figure 4.20** shows a few examples.

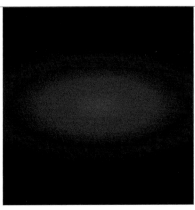

FIGURE 4.21 background: radial-gradient(50% 50%, 100% 100%, rgb(75, 75, 255), rgb(0, 0, 0)); swamps the container.

FIGURE 4.22 Creating an ellipse using different vertical and horizontal radius values. Neo's amphetamine lunch?

RADIAL GRADIENT SIZE AND SHAPE

The second set of values in the radial gradient syntax (60% 60% in the example) dictates the size of the gradient—the horizontal and vertical radius size. Because you are working with the radius rather than the diameter, 50% or 60% will produce a nice spread across a container. 100% would be double the width/height of the container, swamping it entirely, which may or may not be the effect you want (**Figure 4.21**).

NOTE: Firefox has never implemented size percentage values, so they won't work in Firefox. For this reason, it is better to use keyword values.

Again, to set these values, you can use any units that make sense. You can also use different values for the horizontal and vertical radii, for example:

```
background: radial-gradient(50% 50%, 70% 40%, rgb(75, 75, 255),
    rgb(0, 0, 0));
```

This effect is shown in **Figure 4.22**.

 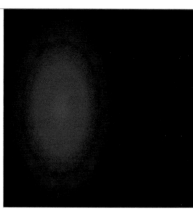

But as usual, there are more ways to set the radii: CSS3 supplies several keywords for setting the radii, which need explaining because they are a bit confusing. Consider the following examples (**Figure 4.23**):

```
background: -o-radial-gradient(30% 50%, circle closest-side,
  rgb(75, 75, 255), rgb(0, 0, 0));
background: -o-radial-gradient(30% 50%, ellipse closest-side,
  rgb(75, 75, 255), rgb(0, 0, 0));
```

So, what's going on here? By using `circle` and `ellipse`, you specify that you want your gradient to be a circle or an ellipse, respectively. `closest-side` means that the shape will expand so that it just touches the container side closest to the point of origin of the radius in the case of a circle and the horizontal and vertical container sides closest to the point of origin of the radius in the case of an ellipse.

TIP: You can use the keyword `contain` in place of `closest-side`.

FIGURE 4.24 The effects of
circle closest-corner and
ellipse closest-corner.

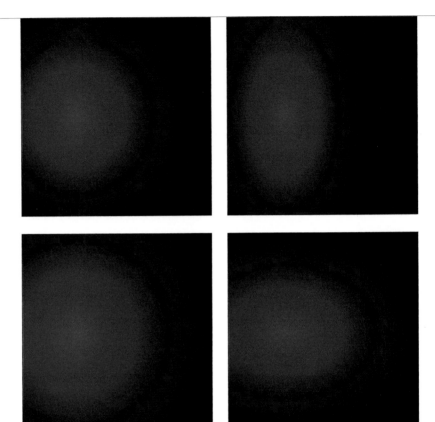

FIGURE 4.25 The effects of
circle farthest-side and
ellipse farthest-side.

Other keyword combinations available to you include:

- **closest-corner** positions the gradient so that its edge just touches the corner of the element closest to the origin (**Figure 4.24**).

- **farthest-side** positions the gradient so that its edge touches the side of the element farthest from its centre in the case of a circle or the farthest horizontal and vertical sides in the case of an ellipse (**Figure 4.25**).

- **farthest-corner** positions the gradient so that its edge just touches the corner of the element farthest from the origin. You can use the keyword cover in place of farthest-corner (**Figure 4.26**).

FIGURE 4.26 The effects of circle farthest-corner and ellipse farthest-corner.

I've not used these implicit shape values very much, preferring instead to control the shape using explicit unit values. But this doesn't mean you won't.

RADIAL GRADIENT COLOR STOPS

Color stops work in the same way as the color stops in linear gradients except that the units you specify denote distance from the center of the gradient, not distance from the starting corner/edge.

I encourage you to experiment with different color values with the examples I've provided and otherwise. Try creating a sun's rays or a shadow or flashlight moving across the top of your site. Again, use RGBA colors for the win! You'll see more exciting examples throughout the book.

FIGURE 4.27 A simple repeating radial gradient.

REPEATING-RADIAL-GRADIENT

As with linear gradients, you can also create repeating radial gradients by adding repeating values into the syntax (**Figure 4.27**):

```
background: -o-repeating-radial-gradient(50% 50%, 60% 60%,
→ rgba(75, 75, 255,0.5) 10px, rgba(0, 0, 0,0.5) 20px);
background-color: #ff0000;
```

PROVIDING GRADIENT SUPPORT FOR OLD VERSIONS OF IE

CSS3PIE also adds support for CSS gradients. But again, you need to be careful of its limited RGBA support. To use CSS3PIE, target a separate, nontransparent color gradient to IE using a special -pie- prefixed background property (bear in mind that CSS3PIE doesn't add support for background-image, just the shorthand). Look at the following example from the Monty Python blog (I've removed all the less interesting and prefixed properties for brevity):

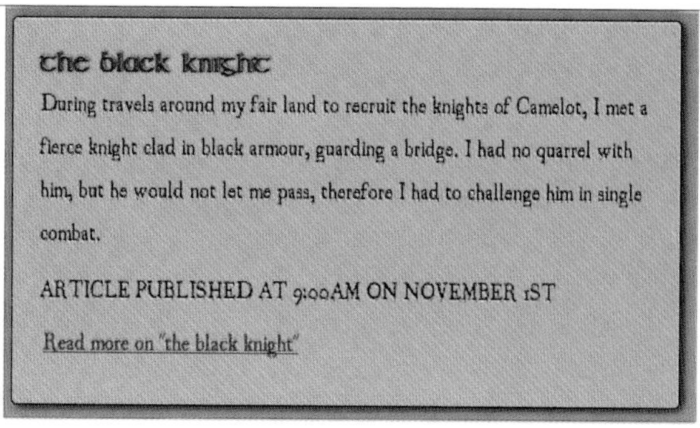

FIGURE 4.28 An attractive bling box.

FIGURE 4.29 A pleasing alternative set of styling provided for older versions of IE.

```
aside article {

    ...

background: repeating-linear-gradient(45deg, rgba(0,0,0,0.1) 1px,
→ rgba(0,0,0,0.05) 2px, rgba(0,0,0,0.1) 3px, rgba(0,0,0,0) 4px,
→ rgba(0,0,0,0) 5px);

background-color: rgba(255,255,255,0.4);

border-radius: 4px;

box-shadow: 2px 2px 10px black;

}
```

The result is a rather nice container with a shadow, rounded corners, and a textured repeating gradient pattern (**Figure 4.28**).

To add IE support after you've placed the PIE.htc file, you can add the following two lines, which include a far simpler gradient without an alpha channel that is still in keeping with the color scheme (**Figure 4.29**):

```
-pie-background: linear-gradient(45deg, #6988af, #a6b9cf);

behavior: url(/cmills/arthur/script/PIE.htc);
```

FIGURE 4.30 Multiple backgrounds rock!

CSS3 gives you the ability to attach multiple backgrounds to a single element, which is très cool. For so long, if you wanted to have multiple background images on a container, you had to have a number of extraneous wrapper `<div>`s for the extra background images, which was a very lame hack to have to use.

The multiple backgrounds are simply added in a comma-delimited list. Let's look at a simple example to illustrate the point; you'll revisit multiple backgrounds a number of times throughout the book.

If you again consult the Monty Python example in the king arthur blog example folder, you'll find the following in the main-style.css file (multiple vendor prefixed versions have been omitted here for brevity):

```
body {

    ...

    background: url(../images/castle.png) top left no-repeat,
    →  url(../images/clouds.png) top right no-repeat,
    →  linear-gradient(top right, #3B6498, #C1CDDB);

    background-color: #C1CDDB;

}
```

Notice that I've used two background images here and a gradient as well. The ability to include CSS gradients in the list of multiple backgrounds makes them even more awesome! I've also included a separate background color as a fallback for nonsupporting browsers (**Figure 4.30**).

FIGURE 4.31 A great effect created with multiple gradients.

The castle is positioned at the top left, the clouds are positioned at the top right so they flow nicely behind the castle, and a subtle blue gradient has been added behind both for the sky. If you resize the browser with this demo open, it will immediately become evident how awesome and flexible multiple backgrounds are!

However, you need to bear in mind that the images later in the property value appear behind those earlier on, which is rather contrary to the way CSS usually works. In CSS, elements drawn later appear on top of those drawn before, so you'd expect it to work the same way with background images. Occasionally, you'll wonder what the spec writers were thinking when they wrote certain parts of the spec.

Multiple backgrounds are also very cool for using multiple gradients together to create complex background patterns. In the Monty Python example (full-post. html/full-post.css), I've used positioning to lay the figure captions over the top of the images. I then used two gradients to apply a grainy texture to the images and added a highlight to each one (**Figure 4.31**).

NOTE: At the time of this writing, there are differences between browser implementations of multiple gradients, but these should be ironed out by the book's release.

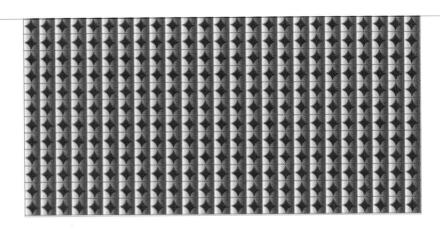

FIGURE 4.32 A rather interesting pattern created with multiple gradients and background-size.

Another interesting effect to explore is combining a gradient effect with background-size to force it to repeat as a single, small, square unit (rather than along the gradient, as is the case with normal repeating gradients). You'll see this in action again later on in the book, too. Consider this example:

```
background: radial-gradient(transparent 10px, #A60000 11px,
    #A60000 12px),
repeating-linear-gradient(transparent, transparent 20px,
    rgba(255,0,0,1) 21px, rgba(255,0,0,1) 21px) 0 -10px,
repeating-linear-gradient(left, transparent, rgba(255,0,0,1) 19px,
    transparent 21px) 12px 0;
background-size: 21px 21px, 100%;
```

The effect is shown in **Figure 4.32**. This example is in the file gradient-background-size.html.

The radial gradient creates a simple, small, transparent circle with red on the outside. The background-size property was used to force this circle into a 22-pixel square, which then repeats. A couple of simple line patterns are then placed over the top and spaced so they perfectly bisect the circles, horizontally and vertically. This is a rather complex bit of code to write for a simple repeating pattern, but it does show what is possible. You can find more aesthetically pleasing examples at Lea Verou's fantastic CSS3 patterns gallery at http://lea.verou.me/css3patterns.

MULTIPLE BACKGROUNDS IN IE?

Unfortunately, CSS3PIE's supremacy collapses when you consider multiple background support in past versions of IE. There isn't a decent way to add support for multiple backgrounds to older IE versions without resorting to those nasty old nested <div>s. And you don't want to go down that road!

So, the only way around this limitation is to provide alternative styling, either via a conditional comment or via Modernizr, which you'll explore in Chapter 5.

> **TIP:** Providing multiple background image fallbacks is difficult if you need the flexibility the multiple backgrounds provide in a liquid layout, as in the Monty Python example. To make IE fallback styling easier to work out, it's best to make the layout fixed in IE by serving a style in your IE-targeted CSS, such as: body { width: 1024px; }.

FIGURE 4.33 A sample border image.

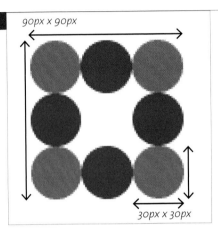

FIGURE 4.34 The image has been carefully dressed around the example container. Cool!

CSS3 provides you with more powerful properties to control borders. The most interesting of these properties is border-image, which in effect allows you to divide an image into different slices and dress the edges around any box you'd like. This sounds a bit complicated, so let's walk through a simple example. To demonstrate border-image, I first created a simple image to grab a border from (**Figure 4.33**).

Next, I applied the border image neatly to the border of a larger box in a flexible manner (**Figure 4.34**). Check out the border-image.html file in the chapter4 code download folder. So, how do you do that?

Try increasing and decreasing the width of the browser, and you should see the border flexibly adjust. The following lines of code are doing the heavy lifting here (border-image is currently supported across all major browsers using vendor prefixes, but I've omitted them here for brevity):

```
border-image: url (border.png) 30 30 30 30 round round;
                              A  B  C  D
```

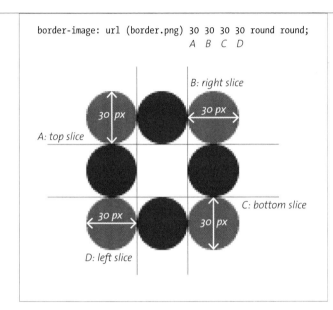

FIGURE 4.35 Slicing up the image samurai style.

```
border-image: url(border.png) 30 30 30 30 round;
border-width: 30px;
```

As you'd expect, the url() syntax points to the image you want to use for the border.

The four numbers after that specify the widths of the border slices (be mindful that these are numbers of pixels, even though they have no units) you want to chop the image into. In order, they refer to the top slice, the right slice, the bottom slice, and the left slice, as indicated in **Figure 4.35**.

You can set the slices to any size you like, but it obviously makes sense to divide the image so the slices in the border contain the parts of the image you want. As logic would suggest, because in this case all four slices are the same size, you could write the border-image line using two values or one value, like so:

```
border-image: url(border.png) 30 round;
```

NOTE: You can also use percentage values to specify the slice sizes; note that the pixel values shouldn't have px units. If you include these (e.g., 30px), it won't work.

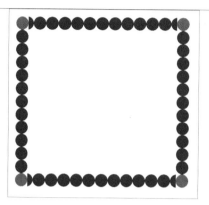

FIGURE 4.36 `border-image` fragments look shoddy.

FIGURE 4.37 `stretch` is OK for very small variations in container size but looks terrible if your containers greatly differ in size from the original image.

After slicing the image, it is applied to the borders of your container: The four corners remain the same. The four sides all tile in one dimension to fill up the borders, however long they are (although see the end of this section for browser differences). The center of the image tiles in both directions to fill up the remaining background space.

How do you control the manner in which the tiling of the sides is handled? You use the `round` keyword. `round` specifies that the browser should always show a whole number of repeated border segments and no incomplete fragments, adjusting the size of each segment to maintain the desired result. If you try increasing or decreasing the browser window width in Opera, Firefox, and IE, you'll see that the size of the balls adjust slightly. Unfortunately, WebKit-based browsers treat `round` the same as `repeat`, another value that just tiles the side slices until they fill up each side without rounding. You are therefore left with fragments at each end of the sides, which don't look great (**Figure 4.36**).

Fragments might look OK as long as you plan the shape of your slices carefully and make sure they don't differ much in height along their course. Another value to be aware of is `stretch`, which is the default. If you swap `round` for `stretch` in this example or omit it altogether, you'll get the result shown in **Figure 4.37**.

Again, note that I've specified one value here for the repeating behavior of all four sides. If you want to specify different behavior for different sides, you could use two or four sides as logic would suggest; for example, `round stretch` or `round stretch round stretch`.

FIGURE 4.38 Border images at half the size—very funkalistic.

And there's one more detail you should know about the basic syntax. To actually provide space for your border image, you need to specify a border width, which is why `border-width: 30px;` was included in the code example. If you don't do this, you won't see anything. The `border-width` property offers additional interesting possibilities: If you make the `border width` bigger or smaller than the slices within the `border-image` property, the slice size will scale up or down to suit. So, if you make the border half as big, like so:

```
border-width: 15px;
```

the border image slices will be displayed in half dimensions, as shown in **Figure 4.38**!

BORDER-IMAGE PROBLEMS

Using `border-image` is not all plain sailing, of course, as with most things in web design. Aside from the fact that WebKit-based browsers currently don't use the round value properly, there are a couple of other issues to keep in mind.

First, you need to determine if you want your central slice to be discarded or not. You might want the central slice to act as the background for your container content, or you might just want to put the border image only in the border. Unfortunately, the default behavior according to the spec is to discard it, but most browsers do the opposite, except for Chrome (try comparing border-image-2.html in Chrome and Opera). You are supposed to be able to control this behavior with `border-image-slice`, but this property is currently not supported in any browser,

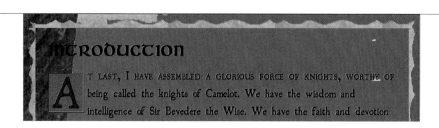

so your only option is to fill in your background explicitly with a background-color or repeated background-image, and try to make it match the border-image.

Second, older versions of IE do not support border-image, so you should test to make sure your content is still readable and looks OK in these older IE browsers.

With these two issues in mind, this border-image won't work at all in old versions of IE, and it looks dreadful in Chrome (**Figure 4.39**).

To fix these issues, I added a repeated background image to my containers, which is basically just the center slice of the border image with the rough edges removed. Initially, this looked ghastly because the background image extended into the border. But I sorted out the problem with a nifty little property called background-clip. The code additions are as follows:

```
background: url(../images/parchment-bg.jpg);
background-clip: padding-box;
```

This snippet of code made the background look better again in Chrome, although it wasn't perfect, and it made the content readable in Internet Explorer's decrepit old ancestors. This example is difficult because I am using a complicated background image on a variable width container. Getting a seamless look would be a lot easier to do in a simpler, fixed-width case!

NOTE: background-clip, defined in www.w3.org/TR/css3-background, allows you to specify that you want background content to be rendered all the way out to the edges of the browser (border-box, which is also the default), to the edges of the padding (padding-box), or to only the edges of the content (content-box). This property comes in handy in certain situations and is supported across all modern browsers.

These limitations mean that border-image usage will be slightly more restricted than is ideal for the moment, but it is already usable to great effect in many situations.

BOX-DECORATION-BREAK

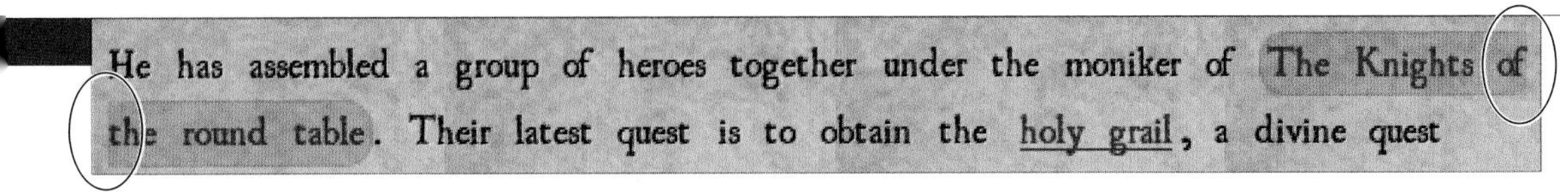

He has assembled a group of heroes together under the moniker of The Knights of the round table. Their latest quest is to obtain the holy grail, a divine quest

FIGURE 4.40 An ugly box break across lines.

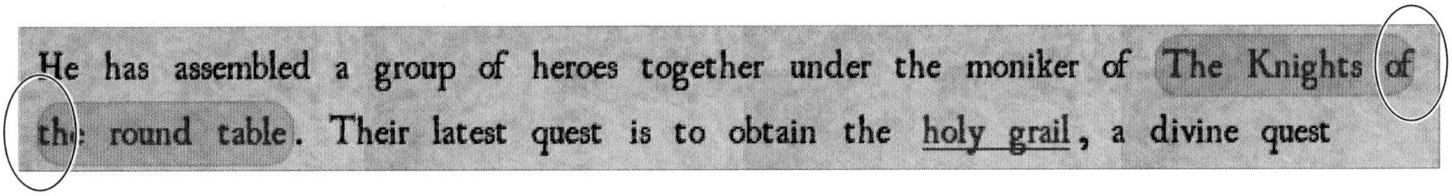

He has assembled a group of heroes together under the moniker of The Knights of the round table. Their latest quest is to obtain the holy grail, a divine quest

FIGURE 4.41 The broken ends of the box are now filled in and are cloned from the start and end of the box. This looks a lot better!

Let's finish the CSS bling tour with a simple little fix for those ugly breaks you get when a nicely styled element wraps across lines (or columns or pages). **Figure 4.40** shows a styled link as an example.

This break is easily remedied by a new CSS property called box-decoration-break (in www.w3.org/TR/css3-background). If you add the following to the link properties:

```
box-decoration-break: clone;
```

you'll produce a better-looking result (well, in Opera anyway; other browsers should catch up soon) (**Figure 4.41**).

To round off the chapter, let's build an ad example using some of the cool properties you learned about earlier. You'll make it look good, albeit different across older browsers, and make it sing with a minimum of images (and a video). Later in the book you'll explore how to make the ad responsive and add some cool animated effects.

The ad will be for a fictional metal band called Dead Hamster. The band is making a comeback, and its management wants to move forward with an online advertising campaign that is going get the band noticed! And what better way to get people to notice than by using thrills, spills, moving pictures, and raw exciting content? OK, so they don't have Bieber or Jedward, but they would only serve to draw the wrong kind of attention.

To make a big splash, the ad will work on mobile devices, so the poster needs to work at different sizes and on different devices. And the band also has a huge following in developing countries due to their freedom anthems. Therefore, the ad needs to work across less-capable browsers.

Let's rock!

NOTE: I got the idea for creating a responsive advertising example from Mark Boulton's rather interesting "Responsive advertising" article at www.markboulton.co.uk/journal/comments/responsive-advertising.

BASIC SETUP

The basic idea is to create a set ad size: the Internet Advertising Bureau (IAB) has semistandardized sizes for web ads, as you'll see at http://en.wikipedia.org/wiki/Web_banner. Let's start off this example by creating a 730 x 300 pixel "pop-under ad."

But let's take it even further and make an eye-catching ad to show that many of the tasks you used to do with Flash are now possible using only CSS3. In this chapter you'll just build up the basic ad. (Animation will come in Chapter 5, and responsiveness in Chapter 8.) You'll also learn how to provide a reasonable alternative in older browsers and what improvements you can and should make if you were to do something similar in a production environment.

FIGURE 4.42 The rocking heavy metal ad.

The background of the entire advertisement is a short looping video clip that shows off the energy of the band. Over the top of this the most important information is displayed, and on hover/focus another pane of information is shown containing more info. The final product as it stands at this point is shown in **Figure 4.42**.

The basic markup structure is as follows:

```
<section id="ad">
    <video></video>
    <div id="video-frame"></div>
    <div id="frame1"></div>
    <div id="frame2"></div>
</section>
```

One section contains the entire ad and includes a `<video>` element to render the rocking Dead Hamster footage, a `<div>` to apply an effect over the top of the video (more on this shortly), and then a couple more `<div>`s to contain the two panes of information.

> **NOTE:** JavaScript has been used to mute video: I fire the JavaScript on the `onloadedmetadata` event to make sure mute is fired before the content starts playing; otherwise, a clip of sound might be heard before the mute kicks in.

Most of the content is absolutely positioned so the layers stack on top of one another, and most of the containers are set to 720 x 300 px, the same dimensions as the outer container, to keep everything inside the ad working well. Most of the code should be pretty simple to understand for anyone with previous CSS experience, so I'll just explain the CSS3 code. You can find my code in the poster folder in the code download.

ADDING THE CSS3 SPARKLE

Let's walk through the different layers of this example in turn so it'll make more sense. You first have the video, and the `video-frame` div is positioned on top of it. This "superfluous" div is annoying to have to include, but it is necessary at the moment because currently `border-image` doesn't work correctly across all browsers. Recall that in all browsers except Chrome the middle slice is wrongly included, and you can't get rid of it. If you could, then you could add the ripped edges using `border-image`, but at present you can't. So instead you'll add the ripped edges on this div using multiple background images:

```
#video-frame {
    width: 720px;
    height: 300px;
    background: url(left-edge.png) top left repeat-y,
        url(right-edge.png) top right repeat-y;
}
```

This is a rather useful technique in many ways: Imagine if you had lots of elements, such as headers or articles, and you wanted them to have a background image at either end and have a flexible width and height. This code is all you'd need.

Next, you'll set a uniform black text shadow on all text, apart from the interesting flaming effect I've put on the word "hell": This is suitable for increasing the latent cheese factor to be appropriate for the average heavy metal band. This can be done like so—add this now to your text:

```
#ad #hell {
    font-size: 150%;
    text-shadow: 0 0 4px white,
                 0 -5px 4px #FFFF33,
                 2px -10px 6px #FFDD33,
                 -2px -15px 11px #FF8800,
                 2px -25px 18px #FF2200;
}
```

Also, you'll include a repeating radial gradient using various transparent blacks for a bit of background texture, plus a background color to provide a faint blue tint:

```
#ad #frame1 {
    background-image: repeating-radial-gradient(top left,
                      rgba(0,0,0,0) 9px,
                      rgba(0,0,0,0.05) 10px,
                      rgba(0,0,0,0.05) 15px,
                      rgba(0,0,0,0.1) 16px,
                      rgba(0,0,0,0.1) 20px);
    background-color: rgba(16,8,115,0.2);
}
```

And finally, you'll use cool, very metal web fonts! These all result in a great set of components that blend well into one another.

SUPPORTING OLDER BROWSERS

To support older browsers, instead of using clever Polyfilling of content, you'll include a simple image fallback for non-<video> supporting browsers:

```
<img src="poster.jpg" alt="">
```

You'll do this because Flash content tends to dominate the area of the page it is put on, so rollovers on top of the video content won't work on a Flash fallback.

In the end, let's opt for the coward's option of not displaying the hover effect in the second frame because IE6, 7, and 8 tend to prove troublesome when you are trying to get hover effects to work on positioned content. You'll use text-indent to push the text far off the screen, so it will still be available to screen readers.

In addition, you'll include some quick box model and positioning fixes for IE6 and 7. The box shadows, text shadows, gradients, and RGBA colors all degrade well.

ADDING AD IMPROVEMENTS

I think you've created a fairly effective basic ad in this example. The ad is all contained within a single container, so it is fairly easy to transplant in whichever page you want it in, and then position it where you want it.

But why not just create the ad in Flash? It would potentially be simpler to deal with, but the point is that you are trying to create components with open standards, which includes all the advantages they bring to the project, plus the text would not be accessible if you put it in a Flash video. The advantages open standards have over Flash in this context will be even more obvious when you start to add animated effects in Chapter 5.

Of course, before you really use this ad, you might want to make a few improvements:

- Optimize video files. The video files as they stand are a fairly heavy addition to a page, so you should optimize them.

- Pare down fonts. The fonts are also quite heavy. In a real production environment, you could use Fontforge (as mentioned in Chapter 3) to reduce the size of the font files and just include the glyphs you need.

- Add a link. You should also wrap the final version in a link (HTML5 allows block-level linking) to click through to wherever you want the ad to lead to.

WRAPPING **UP**

Hopefully, you've come away from this chapter with an understanding of the great new tools CSS3 offers for making your visuals less image-dependent and therefore more flexible and lightweight. Although having the ability to programmatically create web graphics does make web design a lot easier for non-Photoshop ninjas (like me), I hope you're committed to using those features in a responsible way rather than just spamming all the relevant properties onto every container on your site!

And, you also now know how to get these CSS3 features working in a reasonable manner across older, less-capable browsers.

5

ANIMATED EFFECTS
USING **CSS3**

Traditionally, the web was a very static place. Achieving animations was not possible in any sane way until JavaScript, animated GIFs, and Flash came along, at which point everyone rejoiced and applauded the ensuing slew of skip intros and horrible obtrusive animations that crashed onto the web.

Using these newer technologies was all well and good, but there was still no way for nondevelopers to create animations using open standards—until now! With CSS3, you can animate elements of your web documents. As a result, standards-based web design has become even more fun!

In this chapter you'll learn how to create useful animated effects for your web pages using CSS3 Animations, Transforms, and Transitions.

Combined, the following four specs provide you with several possibilities for creating more responsive interfaces, animated effects, and presentational enhancements, which previously were only available through JavaScript:

- **CSS Transforms (www.w3.org/TR/css3-2d-transforms and www.w3.org/TR/css3-3d-transforms).** These two specifications define mechanisms for transforming the size, position, and shape of elements in two and three dimensions, and are in the process of being superseded by a single updated spec; see http://dev.w3.org/csswg/css3-transforms.

- **CSS Transitions (www.w3.org/TR/css3-transitions).** Transitions give you a way to smoothly animate changes in state, such as a change in link color. Transitioning changes in Transform properties is also very effective in many circumstances.

- **CSS Animations (www.w3.org/TR/css3-animations).** CSS Animations are similar to Transitions but don't rely on state changes. Instead, you define different property values inside @keyframes blocks that relate to different stages of an animation (e.g., color: red at the start of the animation; color: blue at the end of it). You then apply these animations to any element you want; the browser then applies the starting property values to the element and smoothly cycles them through to the end property values (so color: red at the beginning smoothly animates to color: blue at the end).

Support for all four specs is good across modern browsers. In any case, for non-supporting browsers it is simple to provide alternative styling using the Modernizr library, which you'll learn about in detail later in the "Providing Alternatives with Modernizr" section.

So let's explore these interesting new features. You should experiment and have fun with these features but also use them responsibly. You don't want every new website to turn into a crazy animated nightmare!

NOTE: The appearance of animations/transitions inside CSS has led a number of web developers to complain about CSS-based animations breaking the "separation of structure, presentation, and behavior layers" best practice. And they are technically right. However, you can spout all the religious arguments you want about animation belonging in the behavior layer rather than the presentation layer, but animation definitely falls in the realm of design.

TRANSFORMS

Let's first walk through CSS Transforms. The idea with transforms is that you can change the shape and size of the area an element takes up. As a simple contextual example, I used a skew transform to rotate the angle of the top-level header in the Monty Python example, as illustrated in **Figure 5.1**.

The full code block I used to achieve this follows:

```
body>header {

    ..

    transform: skew(4deg,6deg);

}
```

As you can see, transforms take the form of the `transform` property with a value consisting of a transform function (in this case skew) and associated values in parentheses (in this case `4deg, 6deg`).

FIGURE 5.1 A skewed header created using a CSS Transform.

The two specs define two- and three-dimensional transforms. I'll cover the features they offer in two separate sections and will be brief, because transforms are a lot more interesting when combined with animations and other effects. Browser support for transforms is summarized in **Table 5.1**. I've not broken them down into detailed references because generally this data works for all properties associated with the 2D and 3D varieties of transforms.

TABLE 5.1 Browser Support for Transforms

BROWSER	2D TRANSFORMS	3D TRANSFORMS
Opera	10.6 with -o-	No
Firefox	3.5 with -moz-	10 with -moz-
Safari	3.1 with -webkit-	4 with -webkit-
Chrome	4 with -webkit-	12 with -webkit-
Internet Explorer	9 with -ms-	10 with -ms-
iOS	3.2 with -webkit-	3.2 with -webkit-
Android	2.1 with -webkit-	3 with -webkit-
Mobile Chrome	Since beta with -webkit-	Since beta with -webkit-
Opera Mobile	11 with -o-	No
Opera Mini	No	No

Note that in IE10 platform preview 6, support for non-prefixed transform properties has been added.

FIGURE 5.2 A simple container example.

FIGURE 5.3 A 2D translate transform in action.

2D TRANSFORMS

Generally, websites are thought of as working in two dimensions, so to start this discussion, I'll keep it flat and simple. The functions and properties you have for transforming elements in two dimensions are discussed in the following sections.

In the chapter5 code download folder, you'll find a series of transform- files demonstrating different transforms applied to a simple container. You can find the example without any transforms applied in transform-template.html (**Figure 5.2**); the others are named intuitively.

TRANSLATE, TRANSLATEX, TRANSLATEY

translate simply moves the element it is applied to by the amount you specify in the value. If you look at transform-2dtranslate.html, you'll see the following declaration applied to the container:

```
transform: translate(200px,100px);
```

This makes the element move 200 pixels to the right and 100 pixels down, as shown in **Figure 5.3**. Note that in each of these examples, I've included a "ghost" version of the element to show the original position, so it is easy to see exactly what's happened.

You can use any distance units that make sense; percentage values will be a percentage of the width or height of the container you are transforming, not its parent container. If you use negative units, you will translate the container left instead of right and up instead of down.

If you want to move the container in only one direction, you could set the other value to 0, for example; use the following line if you want to just move the container 200 pixels to the right:

```
transform: translate(200px,0);
```

or simply omit it altogether:

```
transform: translate(200px);
```

Be warned, however: If you specify only one value inside a translate transform, the browser will assume that it is an X transform and assume Y and Z are 0. It is therefore better to be more explicit about the direction you want to translate in, and use this:

```
transformX: translate(200px);
```

or this:

```
transformY: translate(200px);
```

if you want to move it along the vertical axis.

X, Y, AND Z AXES

X, Y, and Z are talked about a lot in this chapter. They refer to the X, Y, and Z axes of the web page, which transforms, transitions, and animations move elements along. X is the horizontal axis, moving from left to the right on the page (so a negative X value would mean movement from right to left). Y is the vertical axis, moving from top to bottom (a negative Y value would mean movement from bottom to top). The Z axis moves out of the screen "toward the viewer," so from farther away to closer in distance; negative Z would do the opposite.

FIGURE 5.4 Rotating the example container.

ROTATE

As you might expect, the rotate transform allows you to rotate an element. In the transform-2drotate.html file you'll find the following line:

```
transform: rotate(15deg);
```

which produces the effect shown in **Figure 5.4**.

As you can see from this example, a positive deg (degree) value rotates the element clockwise. You can use a negative degree value for counterclockwise rotations. For the mathematically minded, you can use radians instead of degrees (e.g., 1rad), although this is of limited use, because there is no way to accurately represent PI in CSS values, which working with radians heavily relies on.

Try altering the values to see what you get!

A **NOTE** ABOUT **TRANSFORM-ORIGIN**

In the "rotate" section, notice that the rotation happens around the center of the element, which may or may not be what you want. The good news is that you can alter the position of the point the transform happens around using the transform-origin property. Return to the transform-2drotate.html file and uncomment the following property (+ prefixed versions) to see what effect it has on the result:

```
transform-origin: top left;
```

You'll find transform-origin's possible values easy to understand if you are already experienced in CSS2. They work the same as background-position values. Therefore, you can set values using:

- Any standard CSS distance units, such as px, em, rem, cm, and so on
- Percentages
- Keywords, such as center, top left, bottom right.

You can mix and match different values for the horizontal and vertical if you like, for example, top 35%. If you set only one value, it is assumed to be the horizontal value with a vertical value of 50%.

Finally, you can set negative values to set the rotation point somewhere outside the element you are transforming.

Note that transform-origin can also affect other types of transforms, such as scale, and the effect is more noticeable when you start combining transforms with transitions. Do you want your element to grow from the top-left down and to the right, or do you want it to grow from the center outwards?

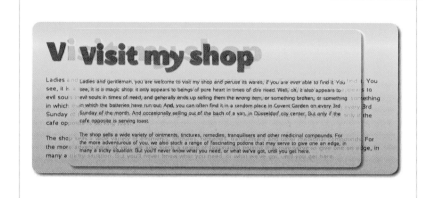

FIGURE 5.5 Scaling the example container—the smaller version over the top is the original; the larger version behind is the scaled version.

SCALE, SCALEX, SCALEY

scale allows you to grow your elements horizontally and vertically, in a similar manner to width and height, except that it treats the element and its child content as one static entity; text won't be reflowed and so on. In the transform-2dscale.html file in the chapter5 code download folder, you'll find the following line:

```
transform: scale(1.25,1.1);
```

which produces the effect shown in **Figure 5.5**.

This line scales the example by 25% horizontally and 10% vertically. scale takes unitless values called *scale factors*, which indicate the amount to grow or shrink by. So, 1.1 means "grow by 10%," 1.25 means "grow by 25%," 2 means "grow by 100%," and so on.

You can also use values less than 1 to shrink the affected element: 0.9 means "shrink by 10%," 0.4 means "shrink by 60%," and so on. You can even use negative values with scale , which invert the elements they are applied to; all the points on the element will go down past 0 and take a position on the opposite side from where they started.

In the previous example, two values are provided for scaling along the X and Y axes. If you specify only one value, it will be applied to both dimensions, for example:

```
transform: scale(1.25);
```

would scale the element by a factor of 1.25 horizontally and vertically.

FIGURE 5.6 Skewing the example container.

If you want to scale only in a single direction, you could set the direction you don't want to scale to 1, for example:

```
transform: scale(1.25,1);
```

But it is more efficient and intuitive to specify a single value for scaling—either horizontally:

```
transform: scaleX(1.25);
```

or vertically:

```
transform: scaleY(1.25);
```

Try experimenting with different values to see the results!

SKEW, SKEWX, SKEWY

skew is rather fun because you can use it to squish an element, changing it from a square or rectangular box into a rhombus or parallelogram. This transform is rather handy if you want to transform certain elements to create some sort of perspective effect—for example, an isometric view—or fit text onto a background shape that isn't flat.

To see how this transform works, open the transform-2dskew.html example. In it you'll find the following line:

```
transform: skew(10deg,13deg);
```

which produces the effect shown in **Figure 5.6**.

FIGURE 5.7 Applying multiple transforms to the example.

skew accepts the same unit values as rotate, but it works in a different way. Instead of the whole element being rotated but looking the same, it is deformed by three degrees horizontally and ten degrees vertically. In real terms, this might seem a bit illogical, because the three degrees x value is applied to the vertical sides (they are slanted three degrees off vertical) and the ten degrees y value is applied to the horizontal sides (they are slanted ten degrees off horizontal). Just think of it this way: *The x and y values refer to the axes the shape is distorted along.*

If you want to skew an element in only one direction, use skewX or skewY. For example:

```
transform: skewX(3deg);
transform: skewY(10deg);
```

> **TIP:** As you'd expect, you can use negative values to skew the element in the other direction, vertically/horizontally.

MULTIPLE TRANSFORMS

You can apply multiple transforms in the same rule by including them all in the same property separated by spaces.

In the example file multiple_2dtransform.html, you'll find the following transform line:

```
transform: skew(-3deg,-10deg) translateX(-200px) scale(0.7)
   rotate(10deg);
```

The effect is shown in **Figure 5.7**.

MATRIX

I won't discuss the `matrix` transform function in any great detail, because it is very complicated. If you have years of experience with SVG, and/or are a math geek, you'll be familiar with these so-called transform matrices: They take the form of algebraic expressions. For example, the equivalent of `transform: rotate(30deg);` as a matrix would be:

`transform: matrix(cos(30), sin(30deg), -sin(30deg), cos(30deg), 0, 0);`

Transform matrices are very powerful because you can effectively use a single matrix to apply multiple transforms at once. However, they are unreliable and overcomplicated. In my opinion, you are better off just using multiple transform functions as explained in the previous section.

NOTE: If you want to read more details on matrix transformations, read http://dev.opera.com/articles/view/understanding-the-css-transforms-matrix/ by Tiffany Brown. The website www.w3.org/TR/SVG/coords.html#TransformMatrixDefined also provides a pure matrix explanation.

3D TRANSFORMS

Now let's pop up from the flat world of 2D and look at transforms that work in three dimensions. These are slightly more limited in support (at the time of this writing, Opera didn't yet support them), but it definitely won't be long before you see support across the full gamut of modern browsers!

Let's explore the properties you have to work with.

TRANSLATE3D, TRANSLATEZ

3D translations work in the same way as 2D translations (see the earlier "translate, translateX, translateY" section for full details) except you can move elements along the Z axis as well—that is, into and out of the screen. You would think that if you translate elements along the Z axis, they would move closer and farther away from you, making them appear bigger and smaller.

However, in practice it doesn't quite work that way. Look at the transform-3dtranslate.html example. As in previous examples, this contains the example container along with a ghost. However, this time the two containers are inside a wrapper <div>.

FIGURE 5.8 A 3D translation in effect!

```
<div id="wrapper">
    <article id="real"></article>
    <article id="ghost"></article>
</div>
```

The wrapper `<div>` has `transform-style: preserve-3d;` and a 3D rotation applied to it: You'll learn more about both later in the chapter. These are needed to demonstrate the effect of 3D translations. The #real container has the following transform applied to it:

```
article#real {
    transform: translateZ(100px);
}
```

This produces the effect shown in **Figure 5.8**. The #real element appears to have been moved 100 pixels in front of the #ghost element in the 3D space.

translate3D produces a very similar effect to what you've already seen with translation functions; however, translate3D allows you to translate elements along the X, Y, and Z axes at the same time:

```
transform: translate3D(100px, 200px, 300px);
/* 100 pixels along the X axis, 200 pixels along Y, 300 pixels
→ along Z */
```

ROTATEX, ROTATEY, ROTATEZ

Moving on to 3D rotations, the rotateX, rotateY, and rotateZ properties are a bit confusing at first, because they produce quite different results than what you might expect. rotateX and rotateY rotate the element they are applied to around the X and Y axes, respectively, which actually transforms them in the Z axis direction! rotateZ rotates the element around the Z axis, which produces a similar effect to the 2D rotation you saw in the earlier "rotate" section!

Let's look at an example to smooth out this confusion: Open the transform-3drotate-x-y-z.html file in the chapter5 code download folder. In this file you'll see three copies of an example with a 180 degree rotateX, rotateY, and rotateZ applied to them, respectively. I've also applied a basic transition to each one; as you hover over the example's #wrapper <div>, each <article> will animate, so you can easily visualize the effects of these transforms. The rotation along the X axis looks like this:

```
transform: rotateX(180deg);
```

The Y axis rotation looks like this:

```
transform: rotateY(180deg);
```

And the Z axis rotation looks like this:

```
transform: rotateZ(180deg);
```

I've not included images here, because it is much easier to see the full effects of these examples by viewing the code example in your browser.

ROTATE3D

I've included rotate3D in a separate section because it works in a different manner than the other 3D rotate functions. In the transform-3drotate-rotate3D.html file, you'll see three copies of an example with the same rotations applied to them as in the previous example! The difference is that this time I used rotate3D in each case, not rotateX, rotateY, and rotateZ. Let's look at equivalents:

- **transform: rotateX(180deg);** is equivalent to rotate3D(1,0,0,180deg);

- **transform: rotateY(180deg);** is equivalent to rotate3D(0,1,0,180deg);

- **transform: rotateZ(180deg);** is equivalent to rotate3D(0,0,1,180deg);

So how do these work? Notice that the rotate3D function takes four arguments. The fourth one is the number of degrees (or radians) you want the element to rotate through. The first three unitless values specify a direction vector for the element to rotate around. So 1,0,0 is one rotation along the X axis, and none in the Y or Z directions. So, in the first example, the element rotates around the X axis.

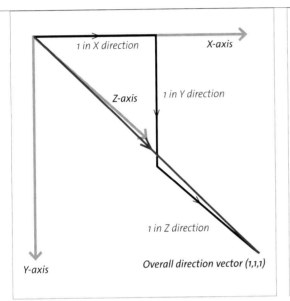
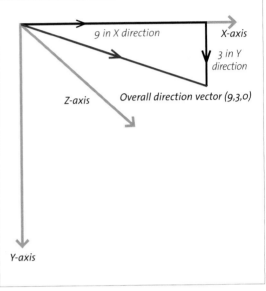

FIGURE 5.9 Visualizing direction vectors.

Now it's your turn: Try adjusting the vector values in this example to make the elements rotate in all sorts of weird and wonderful directions! For example, using a vector of 1,1,1 would cause the element to rotate around a line that travels downward at 45 degrees between the X, Y, and Z axes. A vector of 9,3,0 would cause the element to rotate around a line traveling down and right 30 degrees from the X axis and 60 degrees from the Y axis but not traveling at all in the Z direction. You can see visualizations of these values in **Figure 5.9**.

Note that the individual numbers in the vector values don't matter; it is the proportions that matter. So, for example, 78,78,78 will result in the same direction vector as 1,1,1. You can also use negative vector values to make your direction vector travel in the opposite direction. For example, -1,-1,0 makes the element rotate around a line that is 45 degrees between the X and Y axes but runs left and up, not right and down, as positive values would produce.

NOTE: Be clear on the way the axes travel! As I've said before, positive X is right; negative X is left. Positive Y is down; negative Y is up. Positive Z is out of the screen; negative Z is into the screen.

SCALE3D, SCALEZ

The scale3D and scaleZ transform functions don't do much in real terms; they imply the ability to grow elements along the Z axis, for example, increasing their height. But HTML elements intrinsically don't have any thickness in this direction—they are wafer thin. In actual fact, scaleZ will act as a multiplier for the translateZ function; transform: translateZ(10px) scaleZ(20); would have the same effect as transform: translateZ(200px). But you'd be better off just using translateZ or translate3D instead, as discussed earlier. If you want to give the impression of an element increasing in size and/or getting closer to the user, setting a simple 2D scale is often best.

MATRIX3D

As discussed earlier in the "matrix" section, matrix transforms are very powerful but very complicated and pretty much not within the realms of understanding for designers and other nontechies! And 3D matrices are even more complicated: They have 16 values for each function, as opposed to six for 2D matrices! Therefore, I won't discuss them here (refer to the "matrix" section for links to more information).

PERSPECTIVE, TRANSFORM: PERSPECTIVE, AND PERSPECTIVE-ORIGIN

The transforms you've learned about so far can be used in a 3D space, but the elements exist on a flat plane, as if they are all right in front of your eyes. In real life, this is not the case. You see objects in different positions around you in different perspectives. To simulate this a bit more accurately on the web, you can use the transform: perspective(); function, the perspective property, and the related perspective-origin property to make your elements look more three dimensional, even if they don't have other transforms applied.

Let's first look at the `perspective` function. Open the perspective-transform.html file in the code download folder. It contains three copies of an example container; they all have a transform of `rotateX(10deg)` applied to them, which gently transitions to `rotateX(30deg)` on hover/focus. The difference between them is that different amounts of perspective are applied to each one. Their default states are as follows:

```
#x {
    transform: perspective(250px) rotateX(10deg);
}

#y {
    transform: perspective(800px) rotateX(10deg);
}

#z {
    transform: perspective(2000px) rotateX(10deg);
}
```

These result in the different perspectives you see in **Figure 5.10**.

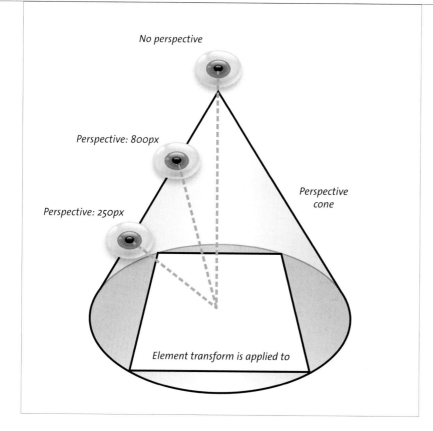

No perspective

Perspective: 800px

Perspective: 250px

Perspective
cone

Element transform is applied to

FIGURE 5.11 A visualization of how perspective works in CSS Transforms.

As you can see, a small pixel value produces a very large perspective—this equates to your point of view being closer to the element—which possibly looks a bit over the top and unrealistic. A value of 800 pixels is very visible but a bit more realistic, and a value of 2000 pixels is much more subtle.

So how does perspective work?

The `perspective` value defines how far away the viewpoint of the element is from the closest side of the element. OK, that might not make much sense, so I'll use a diagram and provide some more explanation. Imagine that the element you are applying the transform to is being viewed by a big eyeball, like your own Eye of Sauron but without the bad-ass attitude. And imagine that a giant invisible cone sits on top of the element. The apex of the cone is right above the middle of the element, and the base of the cone sits on the flat plane of the element (**Figure 5.11**).

With no perspective applied, the Eye of Sauron will be right at the apex of the cone looking directly toward the element, which will therefore be seen straight on and totally flat. If you apply perspective values, the Eye of Sauron still looks directly at the element, but its position is shifted down the side of the cone. The perspective value is the distance the Eye of Sauron is from that edge; therefore, smaller values produce more dramatic distortions in the viewing of the element, whereas bigger values produce more subtle effects.

You can use pretty much any distance units that make sense for defining the amount of perspective, although pixels provide the most exact control and are probably the best to use. If you don't include any units, the units default to pixels.

TIP: You need to put the perspective transform before other transforms you want it applied to. If you use rotateX(10deg) perspective(800px), for example, the perspective would have no effect.

Now let's turn to the separate perspective property: Look at the perspective-property.html file. In this example I've added an extra wrapper <div> around the three <article> elements identified with an ID of perspective-wrap and applied perspective to the whole lot using the following:

```
#perspective-wrap {
    perspective: 800;
}

#x, #y, #z {
    transform: rotateX(30deg);
}
```

Looking at the example you'll see that the rotation transforms are applied to the <article> elements, but the perspective is applied to all the children of the <div>, as if they are all in the same 3D space. Because of the perspective, even though all the child elements have the same amount of rotation applied, they appear differently (**Figure 5.12**).

FIGURE 5.12 The perspective property in effect.

Finally, let's look at `perspective-origin`. The `perspective-origin` property allows you to change the position of the perspective viewpoint. Returning to the awesome Eye of Sauron and cone metaphor, changing to `perspective-origin` effectively changes the positioning of the cone apex.

The default value of `perspective-origin` is center, and you can use the same values for it as you can for `transform-origin` (units, keywords, percentages; see the earlier sidebar "A Note About transform-origin" for more details). To get an idea of the effect this property has, look at the perspective-origin.html file. This file is similar to the perspective-property.html file, but it has some extra properties/rules added:

```
#perspective-wrap {
    perspective-origin: 0% center;
    perspective: 800px;
    transition: 3s all;
}

#perspective-wrap:hover {
    perspective-origin: 100% center;
}
```

FIGURE 5.13 From top to bottom, the perspective-origin values are 0% center, 50% center, and 100% center.

If you try this code in a supporting browser, you'll see that when the container is hovered over, the viewpoint changes, making it look as though the camera (or Eye of Sauron in this case) is panning around the scene. For those of you who don't have a computer in front of you, **Figure 5.13** indicates the effect the change in perspective-origin has.

Using the perspective-origin property is quite fun, but rather annoyingly, it only works for the perspective property; you can't apply it to transform: perspective();.

FIGURE 5.14 A rather funky little 3D notepad.

TRANSFORM-STYLE

transform-style is used when you have multiple 3D transformed elements that appear next to or on top of one another. It has two possible values: flat, the default, and preserve-3d.

When the default value is in effect, 3D transforms will be rendered, but they will all be rendered in the same flat 2D plane. This means that when multiple 3D transforms appear in the same space, some of the detail may get lost because they all appear at the same position along the Z axis.

If you use transform-style: preserve-3d;, the different positions of the elements will be preserved along the Z axis. To see this property in action, look at the preserve-3d.html example file.

In this example I've created a rather nifty little 3D notepad (**Figure 5.14**) that rotates toward you when moused over and allows you to pull out the first page to read it when you mouse over the edge of it.

So how does this example work? Well, the only image used is the repeating image tile for the front and back covers of the notepad; the rest of the graphics were created using box-shadow, text-shadow, gradients, and web fonts. You learned about these in previous chapters, so I won't explain them here. I'll also not discuss the animated elements I've created using transitions, because you'll look at those in detail later in this chapter. Here I'll just concentrate on the transforms. To start, the markup is just some <article>s wrapped by a wrapper <div>:

```
<div id="wrapper">
    <article id="front"></div>
    <article id="p1"></div>
    <article id="p2"></div>
    <article id="back"></div>
</div>
```

To create the basic book, all of the pages are absolutely positioned on top of one another. The book is then rotated in three dimensions using the following:

```
#wrapper
    transform: perspective(1200px) rotateY(-9deg);
    transform-style: preserve-3d;
}
```

The pages are then moved into different positions in 3D space using the following:

```
#front {
    transform: translateZ(5rem);
}

#p1 {
    transform: translateZ(0rem); /* Explicitly setting this is
    → needed; Firefox does weird things with this example if
    → you don't.*/
}
```

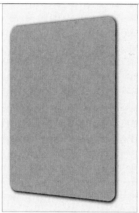

FIGURE 5.15 Comparing the difference between transform-style: preserve-3d; (left) and transform-style: flat; (right).

```css
#p2 {
    transform: translateZ(-5rem);
}

#back {
    transform: translateZ(-10rem);
}
```

This is where `transform-style: preserve-3d;` comes into play. I used `translateZ()` to move the pages into different places along the Z axis, and preserve-3d forces them to maintain their positions in 3D space (**Figure 5.15**, left). If I didn't use preserve-3d, the default—`transform-style: flat;`—would come into play, and the `translateZ()` functions would have no visual effect because all the transitions would stay on the same flat plane (Figure 5.15, right). It is worth noting that setting `overflow: hidden;` on the wrapper makes everything go flat as well.

The page that flies out for you to read when moused over is handled using a simple :hover state:

```css
#p1:hover, #p2:hover {
    transform: translateX(20rem) rotate(0deg) scale(1.1);
}
```

This example isn't perfect. It would be better handled by a series of CSS Animations triggered by links using JavaScript, because it would mean you could handle multiple pages flying out and it would be easier to make it keyboard accessible. (You'll look at triggering animations with JavaScript later in the "Animations" section.)

Also, it doesn't work in Opera and older browsers because they don't support 3D transforms, so you'll need to provide an alternative representation of the data for those browsers. You'll find out how to do that later in the "Providing Alternatives with Modernizr" section.

BACKFACE-VISIBILITY

backface-visibility serves a single function: to specify whether an element's backface (i.e., the reverse view of its content) is visible when the element is rotated in 3D so that its front is facing away from the viewer. To demonstrate using this property, let's look at how to create a business card that flips over with a 3D transform (with realistic dimensions sized in millimeters!). You can find a finished example in the file two-faced-cheek.html.

Again, I'll ignore the details that aren't directly relevant to the example. The markup is again pretty simple:

```
<div id="wrapper" tabindex="0">

    <div id="inner-wrapper">

        <div id="front">

        </div>

        <div id="back">

        </div>

    </div>

</div>
```

TIP: Adding the tabindex="0" attribute is an old trick to make any element appear in the page's tabbing order and therefore be keyboard focusable.

Here, the inner wrapper is used for the sizing and positioning, and the design work is applied to the two front and back <div>s for the front and back of the card. The outer wrapper <div> is there to add hover and other state change effects to, so that you don't get that unwanted behavior in some browsers that was discussed earlier (see the "Firefox Bad Hover?" sidebar). The <div> contents are unimportant for the purposes of this example, although for a real business card you'd probably want to mark up the contact details in a more useful way by using an hCard microformat, for example.

You'll first set a transition on the inner wrapper and then tell it to preserve the 3D space:

```
#inner-wrapper {
    ...
    transition: 1.5s all;
    transform-style: preserve-3d;
}
```

Next, set backface-visibility: hidden; on both the front and back <div>:

```
#front, #back {
    ...
    backface-visibility: hidden;
}
```

Then set up the default state of the business card:

```
#front {
    transform: rotateX(0deg);
    z-index: 2;
}

#back {
    transform: rotateX(180deg);
}
```

FIGURE 5.16 The default card state (left) and when hovered over (right).

The front of the card doesn't need to be rotated for its default state. However, I've applied a rotateX(0deg); transform to it, because it seems to solve a problem in Firefox in that some of the content on the front of the card is displayed in reverse when the card flip is triggered, even with backface-visibility: hidden; applied. Weird but true. The back of the card is rotated around the X axis by 180 degrees and set to backface-visibility: hidden, because you'll want it to be invisible and upside down by default. z-index is also needed on the front to make it appear at the front. By default, it would appear behind the back because the back comes later in the source order.

The last step is to rotate the whole business card by 180 degrees when it is moused over/focused:

```
#wrapper:hover #inner-wrapper, #wrapper:focus #inner-wrapper {

    transform: rotateX(180deg);

}
```

which produces the result shown in **Figure 5.16**.

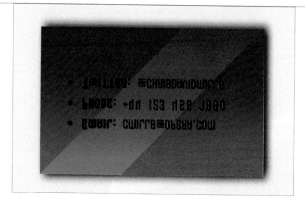

FIGURE 5.17 Without backface visibility: hidden;, the result will generally be a mess.

To see why backface-visibility: hidden; is essential in such situations, try removing the line from the code and reloading. If backface-visibility: hidden; is not employed, the effect is spoiled, resulting in the content of both sides being visible at all times or something unexpected happening (**Figure 5.17**).

USING HARDWARE ACCELERATION

Across many browsers, 3D animations are hardware accelerated; that is, they are rendered using the GPU of the device, not just the browser. To take advantage of the smoother rendering this produces, some developers have started doing 2D transforms using 3D functions. For instance, look at the following simple example:

```
transform: rotate(45deg);
```

You could force the browser to use hardware acceleration for this by adding a 3D function at the end of the transform list that does nothing to the element, like so:

```
transform: rotate(45deg) translate3d(0,0,0);
```

This is useful if animations are running too slow on a certain device, for example, an Android phone or iPhone. However, be careful not to change all the prefixed versions of the property, because you might stop some browsers from using the property (for example, Opera doesn't support 3D transforms at the time of this writing). So until support is more consistent, you could do this:

```
-webkit-transform: rotate(45deg) translate3d(0,0,0);
-o-transform: rotate(45deg);
```

THE **TROUBLE** WITH **3D CSS** AND **HTML**

All in all, the 3D transforms are great fun and provide you with some interesting possibilities for more dynamic, responsive user interfaces. But they are not perfect by any means and need to be used sparingly and subtly.

The kinds of effects involving transforms, animations, and transitions that I present in this chapter will not change the entire web paradigm, but these kinds of effects are what work while still remaining inside the realms of accessibility, usability, and good taste. Many of the more flashy 3D CSS demos I've seen are fun demos but would probably not fly in the real world.

The trouble is that HTML and CSS form an inherently flat, 2D delivery mechanism. You can imply some depth and perspective, sure, but there is no way you can build an immersive, real, 3D world with such technologies. In addition, HTML elements have no inherent depth; the transforms and transitions required would be very processor-intensive, and HTML really isn't the right technology to choose.

For a proper 3D environment, you would be much better served with HTML5 <canvas>/WebGL, which is beyond the scope of this book. And of course, such technologies have issues of their own. Text inside <canvas> is just drawn onto an image, so is inaccessible.

A combination of all these technologies is needed for more ambitious 3D work, methinks.

TRANSITIONS

With a run-through of CSS3 Transforms complete, let's now turn to pastures new, namely transitions. As you've seen in some of the transform examples, transitions allow you to smoothly animate properties that change upon a state change (for example, when a link is hovered over) rather than the usual on/off rollover that would occur otherwise.

Table 5.2 summarizes the browser support for transitions.

TABLE 5.2 Browser Support for Transitions

BROWSER	TRANSITIONS
Opera	10.5 with -o-
Firefox	4 with -moz-
Safari	3.1 with -webkit-
Chrome	4 with -webkit-
Internet Explorer	10 with -ms-
iOS	3.2 with -webkit-
Android	2.1 with -webkit-
Mobile Chrome	Since beta with -webkit-
Opera Mobile	10 with -o-
Opera Mini	No

Note that in IE10 platform preview 6, support for non-prefixed transition properties has been added.

NOTE: It makes very little sense to try to demonstrate a transition using static images, so I'll not include many in this section. I'd advise that you have the code download files close at hand while reading this section.

FIGURE 5.18 A simple, well-styled button.

SELECTING WHAT TO TRANSITION

To demonstrate transition basics, let's walk through building up a very simple button example (see transition-button.html in the chapter5 folder). The button is simply a link styled to produce depth and shadowing using a combination of box shadow, linear gradients, text shadow, and more (**Figure 5.18**). There is nothing remarkable here except perhaps to say that I've used an inset box shadow to give the gradient a bit more shape.

When the link is moused over or focused via the keyboard, the background color changes (as dictated by the :hover/:focus states), and when the link is clicked/activated, another stronger, inset box shadow is applied to give the button the look of being pressed in. This is standard fare on the web, but I'm sure you'd agree that the experience could be better if the state changes were a bit smoother.

You can do this very easily by setting a transition on the link, as follows:

```
a {

    ...

    transition-property: background-color;

}
```

You must set the transition on the element you want the transition to occur on. transition-property takes as its value the property you want to transition upon state change.

NOTES: Notice from the code examples in this section that the transition properties currently need prefixes.

Not all CSS properties are animatable via CSS Transitions and Animations, but most of the ones you'd conceivably want to animate are. A list of animatable properties is available in the CSS Transitions spec in the Animatable Properties section at www.w3.org/TR/css3-transitions/#animatable-properties.

SELECTING TRANSITION LENGTH

So far so good, but you need one addition to get the basic example working: You need to set a duration over which the transition will occur. This is done using the transition-duration property:

```
a {

    ...

    transition-property: background-color;
    transition-duration: 0.5s;
}
```

This property can take values with any CSS time units, but you'll pretty much always use seconds.

DELAYING TRANSITIONS

If you want to set up a delay between the state changing on the element to be transitioned and the transition occurring, you can use the transition-delay property, like so:

```
transition-delay: 2s;
```

This property is useful if you want to fire multiple transitions but want them to happen one after the other in a staggered fashion.

ALTERING THE RATE OF TRANSITIONS

By default, transitions occur at the same rate throughout their duration. This is OK for many uses, but in some cases you'll want to vary the transition rate to emulate concepts such as acceleration, friction, or gravity. To apply such variations to your transitions, you can use the transition-timing-function property.

CUBIC BÉZIER CURVES

Transition/animation timing functions are modeled on cubic Bézier curves (Figure 5.19), which you'll be familiar with if you have studied math(s) to a high level. For us nonmathematicians, the actual maths is complicated (see http://en.wikipedia.org/wiki/Bézier_curve). But basically, in the context of transitions and animation, Bézier curves site on a graph with time on the X axis and progression on the Y axis. The start and end of the graph have control handles attached to them, which control the

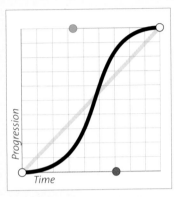

FIGURE 5.19 A cubic Bézier curve.

shape of the curve. Shallower parts of the curve equate to slow movement, and steeper parts produce faster movement.

If this is hard to visualize, head over to http://cubic-bezier.com by Lea Verou, which is a fantastic site that allows you to create your own curves by dragging the control handles around, playing sample animations to give you an idea of the effect these curves have, and importing, exporting, and sharing your curves.

The available values you can use (modeled on cubic Bézier curves) are:

- **linear.** The transition happens at the same rate from beginning to end.

- **ease.** The default value; the transition starts quickly and then gradually slows down.

- **ease-out.** The transition starts quickly, stays quick for longer than ease, and then slows down more abruptly at the end.

- **ease-in.** The transition starts off slowly and then speeds up toward the end.

- **ease-in-out.** The transition starts off by accelerating, is quite fast for most of the duration, and decelerates toward the end.

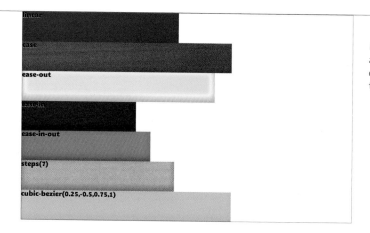

linear

ease

ease-out

ease-in

ease-in-out

steps(7)

cubic-bezier(0.25,-0.5,0.75,1)

FIGURE 5.20 A funky animated bar graph that demonstrates the different transition-timing-functions.

- **steps().** Instead of giving a smooth transition throughout, this value causes the transition to jump between a set number of steps placed equally along the transition. For example, steps(10) would make the transition jump along in ten steps. You can also set an optional second parameter with a value of start or end—for example, steps(10, start) or steps(10, end). This specifies whether the change in property value should happen at the start or end of each step. You won't find much use for this optional parameter, but it is worth a mention.

- **cubic-bezier().** You can use cubic-bezier() to specify your own custom cubic Bézier curve to use for the transition. This function takes four arguments: the X and Y coordinates of the beginning control handle, and the X and Y coordinates of the end control handle. For example, cubic-bezier(0.25, 0.1, 0.25, 1.0) is equivalent to the ease preset value.

To make the difference between these timing functions easier to appreciate, I've created an animated bar graph example that shows several different bars transitioning across the screen when the display is hovered over (**Figure 5.20**). Each one has a different timing function applied, so all will reach the end of their course at the same time, but their rates will vary. See the transition-timing-functions.html file in the chapter5 code download folder.

NOTE: The steps timing function doesn't yet appear to work in Opera, but it should get there soon.

I've styled the bars nicely and added a nifty little bit of JavaScript that resizes the height of the bars and their container to perfectly fill the screen when the page loads and when the screen is resized, making for an ideal adaptive example. (There's also a small media query to change the font size when the height gets small; Chapter 8 covers Media Queries in more detail.)

How did I do this? The markup is again very simple (I've removed some of the <div>s for brevity; there are seven in all):

```
<div id="wrapper" tabindex="0">
    <div id="timing1"><p>linear</p></div>
    <div id="timing2"><p>ease</p></div>

        ...

</div>
```

Now on to the CSS. I first selected the nested <div>s:

```
div div {
    height: 100px;
    width: 25%;
    background: linear-gradient(top,rgba(0,0,0,0),rgba(0,0,0,0.4)
    → 70%);
    box-shadow: inset 0 -10px 25px rgba(0,0,0,0.4);
    transition-property: width;
    transition-duration: 3s;
}
```

I set a default height on the <div>s for the benefit of browsers that don't support the JavaScript I've used (they probably won't support the transitions anyway, but hey), a default width of 25%, some shadowing to make the bars look good, and most important, I declared a transition of the width property over 3 seconds.

Next, I set the nested <div> widths to 90%, only when their wrapper <div> is hovered over. Note that it is very powerful to use pseudo-classes in descendant/child selector chains like this:

```
#wrapper:hover div, #wrapper:focus div {
    width: 100%;
}
```

Finally, I set each separate nested <div> to have a different background-color and transition-timing-function, for example:

```
#timing1 {
    background-color: blue;
    transition-timing-function: linear;
}

#timing2 {
    background-color: red;
    transition-timing-function: ease;
}
```

> **TIP:** Notice that I've used a negative number for the Y-position of the first control handle in the cubic Bezier example: cubic-bezier(0.25,-0.5,0.75,1). This causes a "bounce effect" where the transition goes below its beginning value and then comes back up again and on to the final value. This technique can be very useful for some effects, such as a toy boat bobbing up and down in the water after being dropped.

And that's pretty much a wrap for this example and for transitions. With a bit of modification, you could use this example to create a real-world, useful bar graph or perhaps a question page where hovering over the question will reveal the answer. You could use some of the other timing functions to make a transition of a duck moving through water, slowing down as it goes, or a ball falling through the air, gaining speed due to gravity. The other task I tend to use transitions for, beyond the examples you've already seen throughout this chapter, is making information boxes appear. You can see a great example of this on the Monty Python King Arthur example blog-site.html page if you hover over the "More details (+)" lines at the bottom of each blog post summary. The opacity and height of the footer increase, revealing expanded blog post information (**Figure 5.21**).

TRANSITION SHORTHAND AND MULTIPLE TRANSITIONS

Before moving on, you need to know about a couple more small but useful techniques. You can use the `transition` shorthand property to take the place of the other shorthand values, which can save you a lot of lines of code, especially when you have to write five different copies to include all the necessary browser prefixes:

```
transition-property: opacity;

transition-duration: 3s;

transition-timing-function: ease-in;

transition-delay: 1s;
```

These four properties can be represented by the following single shorthand property:

```
transition: opacity 3s ease-in 1s;
```

In addition, if you want to specify multiple different transitions on the same ruleset, you can list them all on the same property separated by commas. This works for shorthand and longhand:

```
transition: opacity 3s ease-in 1s, height 4s linear;

transition-property: opacity, height;
```

You must specify at least transition properties and durations for anything to animate; the other values are optional. If you don't specify a delay, the default is 0s, and if you don't specify a transition timing function, the default is ease.

If you specify multiple longhand properties, those different properties are looped through to make sure all transitions are assigned a value for each property. Let's look at another example:

```
transition-property: opacity, height, width, background-color;

transition-duration: 3s;

transition-timing-function: ease-in, ease, linear;
```

In this case, all four of the transition properties will be transitioned over a duration of 3 seconds, because that is the only value specified in the transition-duration property. Then for transition-timing-function, the first property is given ease-in, the second is given ease, and the third is given linear. But there is one more property. To give this a timing function, you cycle back to the start of the transition-timing-function list: the fourth property is therefore given the ease-in timing function.

You can specify that you want all properties that change upon state change to transition by just writing transition-property: all;

NOTE: To be honest, I very rarely have to write such complicated transitions. I usually just write something like transition: 1s all; (the duration often varies).

ANIMATIONS

The next stop on this journey is CSS Animations. As discussed previously, animations differ from transitions in that transitions are triggered by state changes, whereas animations happen independently. I would argue that animations therefore have a wider scope and are more useful than transitions. For example, you could use JavaScript to apply a CSS Animation to an element anytime you want, perhaps by attaching an animation to an ID selector and appending that ID to the element when a specific event occurs. This makes it easier, for example, to allow users to click links to fire animations.

You can also use CSS Animations with no JavaScript to create intro sequences of elements sliding into place or constant ambient background animations. Browser support for CSS Animations is shown in **Table 5.3**.

TABLE 5.3 Browser Support for Animations

BROWSER	ANIMATIONS
Opera	12 with -o-
Firefox	5 with -moz-
Safari	4 with -webkit-
Chrome	4 with -webkit-
Internet Explorer	10 with -ms-
iOS	3.2 with -webkit-
Android	4 with -webkit-
Mobile Chrome	Since Beta with -webkit-
Opera Mobile	No
Opera Mini	No

Note that in IE10 platform preview 6, support for non-prefixed animation properties has been added.

You'll explore various animation uses throughout this section.

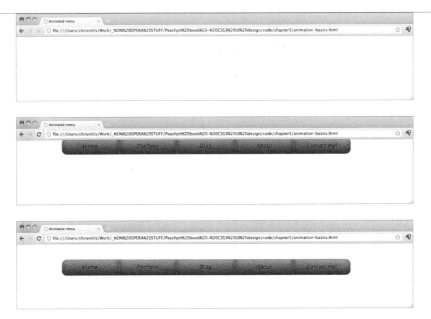

FIGURE 5.22 An animated menu (the animations, unfortunately, look like rubbish on the printed page).

SETTING UP A BASIC ANIMATION

Animation has a few extra features compared to transitions, but it also has many of the same features, such as timing functions, delays, and so on. Therefore, if you've already mastered transitions, a segue into animations should be fairly easy.

Let's start by looking at a simple example: Load the animation-basics.html in the chapter5 code download folder to see a little navigation menu that slides into the browser window when the page first loads—in an Apple website kind of way (**Figure 5.22**). When you mouse over/focus one of the menu buttons, it doesn't just smoothly transition once; it glows smoothly for the whole time it is focused. You couldn't do either of these tasks with transitions (well, not without the aid of JavaScript).

To set up a CSS Animation, you must first specify a set of keyframes for that animation. The animated menu code contains the following two keyframe blocks:

```
@keyframes menu-move {
    from { transform: translateY(-200px); }
    to { transform: translateY(0); }
}
```

```
@keyframes button-glow {
    0%   { color: #000;background-color: #E69EE0; }
    50%  { color: #666;background-color: #FFEEEE; }
    100% { color: #000;background-color: #E69EE0; }
}
```

TIP: All animation blocks and properties require vendor prefixes at the time of this writing; I've removed them here for brevity. In the code example you'll see that this is quite a lot of code, especially because I had to add vendor-prefixed versions of all the animation blocks as well as the animation properties appearing in rulesets, which you'll see later. You write a vendor-prefixed at-rule in basically the same way as a vendor prefixed property—for example, `@-o-keyframes { }`. Note that there's a hyphen between the @ and the prefix, *and* the prefix and `keyframes`.

So the keyframes block is actually a specialized at-rule block. You start it by writing `@keyframes`, add an identifying name of your choosing for the animation, and then add a pair of curly braces. Inside the curly braces, you specify as many keyframes as you want to dictate what happens throughout the course of the animation in terms of what property changes you want to occur. The browser works out smooth animations between the different keyframes.

The two ways of specifying where the keyframes sit along the course of the animation are shown in the preceding code snippet. If you want to specify a keyframe only at the start and end of the animation (0% and 100% along), you can use the keywords `from` and `to`, as shown in the first block. Or you could use 0% and 100% instead.

As you can see, in the second block I've specified three different keyframes, denoting `background-color` changing to a different color and then back again. Because the first and last keyframes are the same, you could rewrite this code block like so:

```
@keyframes button-glow {
    0%, 100%   { color: #000;background-color: #E69EE0; }
    50% { color: #666;background-color: #FFEEEE; }
}
```

But I wouldn't recommend this rewrite, especially not for complicated animations: It is much easier to visualize the animation progression when the keyframes are written out in the order in which they occur.

You can have as many keyframes as you want and as many properties specified inside each keyframe as you want, meaning that complex animations are possible. You can start your keyframes at a value greater than 0%—for example, 50%, 60%, 100%. But nothing will happen for the portion of the keyframes where nothing is specified.

APPLYING AN ANIMATION TO AN ELEMENT

So you've learned how to declare an animation block, but how on earth do you actually apply that animation to something on your page? That's simple; you apply the element to any ruleset you like using the `animation-name` property with the animation's identifying name as the property value:

```
ul {

    ...

    animation-name: menu-move;

}
```

This is very useful because it means you only have to define an animation once, and then you can apply it to as many different rulesets as you want. You could have a whole bank of animation classes set up, and then add them where you need them.

SETTING ANIMATION DURATION

Your animation won't do anything yet: In a similar manner to transitions, you have
to tell it how long to last using animation-duration:

```
ul {

    ...

    animation-name: menu-move;

    animation-duration: 2s;

}
```

This property can take a value with any CSS time units, although you'll most
likely use seconds.

SPECIFYING THE NUMBER OF TIMES TO RUN THE ANIMATION

The menu-move animation will actually work as required already. It will slide into
view once, and only once, because by default animations will play only once. If
you want them to play more than once, you need to specify how many times using
animation-iteration-count. This property accepts a positive number value or
the keyword infinite if you want your animation to go to infinity and beyond (I
tried typing that with a straight face and failed).

The menu-move animation is required only once, so you needn't explicitly set
it. For the button-glow animation, on the other hand, once is not enough. You
want the animation to carry on until your site visitors stop hovering/focusing the
buttons. Therefore, you should use infinite:

```
a:hover, a:focus {

    ...

    animation-name: button-glow;

    animation-duration: 1.5s;

    animation-iteration-count: infinite;

}
```

NOTE: Setting decimal values for animation-iteration-count (e.g. 0.5)
will make the animation play only part of the way through.

ALTERING THE ANIMATION RATE

Again, similar to transitions, you can set different timing functions on animations to make the rate the animation occurs at vary from start to end. Only the property name is different: `animation-timing-function`. The timing functions are all the same. Here again is a list of the different timing functions:

- **linear.** The animation happens at the same rate from beginning to end.
- **ease.** The default value; the animation starts quickly and then gradually slows down.
- **ease-out.** The animation starts quickly, stays quick for longer than ease, and then slows down more abruptly at the end.
- **ease-in.** The animation starts off slowly and then speeds up toward the end.
- **ease-in-out.** The animation starts off by accelerating, is quite fast for most of the duration, and decelerates toward the end.
- **steps().** Instead of giving a smooth transition throughout, this value causes the transition to jump between a set number of steps placed equally along the transition. For example, `steps(10)` would make the transition jump along in ten steps. You can also set an optional second parameter with a value of `start` or `end`—for example, `steps(10, start)` or `steps(10, end)`. This specifies whether the change in property value should happen at the start or end of each step. You won't find much use for this optional parameter, but it is worth a mention.
- **cubic-bezier().** You can use `cubic-bezier()` to specify your own custom cubic Bézier curve to use for the animation. This function takes four arguments: the X and Y coordinates of the beginning control handle, and the X and Y coordinates of the end control handle. For example, `cubic-bezier(0.25, 0.1, 0.25, 1.0)` is equivalent to the ease preset value. For more on cubic Bézier curves, see the "Cubic Bézier Curves" sidebar earlier in the chapter.

In this example, the glowing effect for the buttons was a bit too jerky using the default ease timing function, so I changed it to linear for a smoother feel:

```css
a:hover, a:focus {

    ...

    animation-name: button-glow;

    animation-duration: 1.5s;

    animation-iteration-count: infinite;

    animation-timing-function: linear;

}
```

ADDING A DELAY

Yup, you guessed it; it is also possible to add a delay before an animation starts by adding an animation-delay value. This property is a lot more useful with animation than it is with transitions. For instance, you could have an animated sequence occur on page load or after a button is activated with multiple animations occurring at different times. This type of result is not practical to achieve with transitions.

TIP: You can also give animation-delay a negative value to make the animation start partway through the specified animation-duration.

ANIMATION-DIRECTION: BACK AND FORTH, SIR?

By default, animations occur from the start and go to the end on each iteration. However, it is possible to change this behavior so that the animation will instead take an alternative direction: The first iteration will go forward from 0% to 100%, the second iteration will travel smoothly back from 100% to 0%, the third iteration will go forward, the fourth will go back, and so on. This can be done by including the following line on the element to be animated:

```css
animation-direction: alternate;
```

For example, because I wanted the button glow to run seamlessly, I specified the button-glow animation like this:

```
@-keyframes button-glow {
    0%   { color: #000;background-color: #E69EE0; }
    50%  { color: #666;background-color: #FFEEEE; }
    100% { color: #000;background-color: #E69EE0; }
}
```

If I specified animation-direction: alternate; on the a:hover,a:focus { } ruleset, I could rewrite my keyframes as this:

```
@-keyframes button-glow {
    0%   { color: #000;background-color: #E69EE0; }
    100% { color: #666;background-color: #FFEEEE; }
}
```

I can now halve the animation-duration value, because each iteration would now be half the button glow pulse. This is a more efficient way to write this example and any others where you want the animation to do something and then return to its original state. But not all animations will be like this.

I've included this updated version for you in the chapter5 download folder as animation-basics2.html.

ANIMATION-FILL-MODE

The animation-fill-mode property allows you to specify how the animated element is displayed after an animation ends or during an animation-delay that occurs before the animation starts (i.e., no effect on negative animation delays). The possible values of animation-fill-mode are as follows:

- **none.** This is the default value. When an animation ends, the element it is applied to will go back to using its intrinsic styling. In addition, no styling from the animation keyframes will be applied to the element during an animation delay.

- **forwards.** This value makes an element with an animation applied to it retain the styles defined by the properties in the final keyframe, after the animation ends. The final keyframe will usually be 100% or to. This value is rather useful if you want the animations to finish in their final, not beginning, states—for example, when putting the building blocks of a layout into place upon page load.

- **backwards.** This property value causes styles defined in the first keyframe (usually 0% or from) to be applied to the element the animation is applied to during an animation-delay rather than the default element styles.

- **both.** This value applies the combined effects of forwards and backwards to an element undergoing an animation.

I won't provide isolated examples for you to see now; instead, I'll present some examples later in the chapter that use these values.

SHORTHAND AND MULTIPLE ANIMATIONS

You need to write a lot of code for CSS Animations due to having to write keyframe blocks as well as include multiple properties to control how the animations are applied to elements. Fortunately, you can use a shorthand animation property to significantly reduce the amount of code needed.

The following properties:

```
animation-name: whoosh;
animation-duration: 10s;
animation-timing-function: ease-in;
animation-delay: 3s;
animation-iteration-count: 25;
animation-direction: alternate;
animation-fill-mode: backwards;
```

can be whittled down to this one line:

```
animation: whoosh 10s ease-in 3s 25 alternate backwards;
```

The spec is not very precise in defining the exact order the property values should be included in the shorthand, but it's best to stick with the preceding order to avoid potential browser bugs. Various sources indicate that this order fulfills the idiosyncrasies different browsers currently have.

You need to explicitly include `animation-name` and `animation-duration` for the animation to do anything. If you don't explicitly specify the other values, their default values will come into play, which are:

```
animation-timing-function: ease;

animation-delay: 0s;

animation-iteration-count: 1;

animation-direction: normal;

animation-fill-mode: none;
```

You can also apply multiple animations in a single ruleset by including them in the same property separated by commas. This works for both longhand and shorthand values, for example:

```
animation: whoosh 10s, zap 5s;

animation-name: whoosh, zap;

animation-duration: 10s, 5s;
```

If you're using longhand properties with different numbers of values, you need to specify all the animation names to be applied. If any subsequent properties have fewer values than the number of animations specified, the values will be alternated to fill the gaps. For example, look at the following properties:

```
animation-name: whoosh, zap, bang;

animation-duration: 10s, 5s;

animation-delay: 2s;
```

The whoosh animation will have a duration of 10 seconds, and the zap animation will have a delay of 5 seconds. The bang animation will have a delay of 10 seconds, because the duration values have run out, so they cycle around to the beginning again. All of the animations will have a delay of 2 seconds.

ENHANCING A BANNER AD
WITH ANIMATIONS

In Chapter 4, I introduced you to the Dead Hamster banner ad—a fair stab at creating a banner advertisement with open standards as opposed to Flash, which looks cool and draws people in. Now you'll enhance the banner using CSS Animations, Transitions, and Transforms.

To refresh your memory on the state in which you left the last version, open the example in the poster code download folder. You can also use this file as a starting point from which to add animations. Here you'll look at some new code additions to add exciting swooshy bits to the banner!

> **NOTE:** The finished code example from this section can be found in the poster-animations-transforms-transitions code download folder.

Look at the first frame (`<div id="frame1">` in the HTML). This would look deliciously cool (and not at all like a middle manager's PowerPoint presentation) if you had the different items of text whooshing into the ad, no?

To do this, you first need to set up the animations you need. For the four different pieces of text, try these on for size:

```
@keyframes horizontal-left-150 {
    from {transform: translateX(150px);}
    to {transform: translateX(0px);}
}

@keyframes horizontal-right-400 {
    from {transform: translateX(-400px);}
    to {transform: translateX(0px);}
}

@keyframes horizontal-right-500 {
    from {transform: translateX(-500px);}
    to {transform: translateX(0px);}
}
```

```
@keyframes horizontal-left-600 {
    from {transform: translateX(600px);}
    to {transform: translateX(0px);}
}
```

NOTE: You might think that having presentational animation names goes against the semantic best practices we hold dear, but think about it. Animations are entirely presentational, and you can apply them to multiple elements, so the semantics will change. Presentational is best in this case!

To apply these animations to the different pieces of text, you'll use rules like this:

```
#ad h2 {
    animation: horizontal-left-150 1s 1 1s backwards;
}

#ad #band-name {
    animation: horizontal-right-400 2s 1 2.5s backwards;
}

#ad #album-name {
    animation: horizontal-right-500 2s 1 3.5s backwards;
}

#ad #frame1 ul {
    animation: horizontal-left-600 2s 1 4.5s backwards;
}
```

I used shorthand here, so let's run through each value to make sure all is clear and you know what's going on. In each case:

1. **Start with animation-name.** Each animation is applied to its appropriate ruleset by name.

2. **Add animation-duration.** Each animation must have a duration set on it to work.

3. **Add animation-iteration-count.** Each animation occurs only once, so you don't need to add this in, but I included it to make the code completely obvious.

4. **Add animation-delay.** An animation delay is set for each rule so the pieces of text whoosh in at different times, not all together.

5. **Add animation-fill-mode.** This is set to backwards for all animations, which means that the animated elements take on the styling defined in their from keyframes during the animation delay in each case, and then the animation starts. If you didn't include this, the animation would sit in its default position in each case before being animated from the from position and ending up back in the to position, which is the same as the default. This would look terrible. Try removing the backwards keywords and refreshing the example if you want to see the difference.

> **TIP:** When creating animated effects where you are animating elements from outside their container onto it, you'll usually want to set overflow: hidden; on the containing element, so the moving elements slide into view when they move into it.

For a bit of fun, I also decided to try animating the flaming text shadow by varying the text shadow values across different keyframes. They ended up looking like this:

```
@keyframes flamey-flamey {

    0% {text-shadow: 0 0 4px white, 0 -5px 4px #FFFF33,
    → 2px -10px 6px #FFDD33, -2px -15px 11px #FF8800,
    → 2px -25px 18px #FF2200;}

    19% {text-shadow: 0 0 4px white, 0 -5px 4px #FFFF33,
    → 2px -10px 6px #FFDD33, -2px -15px 11px #FF8800,
    → 2px -25px 18px #FF2200;}

    20% {text-shadow: 0 0 4px white, 0 -4px 3px #FFFF44,
    → 3px -9px 7px #FFDF33, -3px -14px 12px #FF9900,
    → 3px -24px 19px #FF3300;}

    39% {text-shadow: 0 0 4px white, 0 -4px 3px #FFFF44,
    → 3px -9px 7px #FFDF33, -3px -14px 12px #FF9900,
    → 3px -24px 19px #FF3300;}

    40% {text-shadow: 0 0 4px white, 0 -5px 4px #FFFF33,
    → 3px -8px 8px #FFFD44, -3px -12px 11px #FF8800,
    → 2px -25px 20px #FF2200;}

    59% {text-shadow: 0 0 4px white, 0 -5px 4px #FFFF33,
    → 3px -8px 8px #FFFD44, -3px -12px 11px #FF8800,
    → 2px -25px 20px #FF2200;}

    60% {text-shadow: 0 0 5px white, 0 -6px 5px #FFFF55,
    → 2px -7px 7px #FFDD33, -5px -13px 15px #FF7700,
    → 4px -24px 19px #FF4411;}

    79% {text-shadow: 0 0 5px white, 0 -6px 5px #FFFF55,
    → 2px -7px 7px #FFDD33, -5px -13px 15px #FF7700,
    → 4px -24px 19px #FF4411;}

    80% {text-shadow: 0 0 4px white, 0 -5px 4px #FFFF33,
    → 5px -8px 6px #FFEE33, -4px -12px 13px #FF8822,
    → 2px -26px 18px #FF2200;}

    100% {text-shadow: 0 0 4px white, 0 -5px 4px #FFFF33,
    → 5px -8px 6px #FFEE33, -4px -12px 13px #FF8822,
    → 2px -26px 18px #FF2200;}

}
```

In this case I didn't want a smooth transition between each frame: I wanted five clear frames that would repeat; hence, I used duplicate values to make the text shadow stay the same across each different portion of the animation, for example 0–19%.

You can then apply this animation using the following code:

```
#ad #hell {
    animation: flamey-flamey 0.2s infinite;
}
```

This time you're not setting a delay or an `animation-fill-mode`, and the flames will keep flaming infinitely.

The last change in the example was the way #frame2 appears on hover and focus. This time I used a simple transform and transition:

```
#ad #frame2 p {
        ...
transform: scale(0);
transition: 1s all;
}
#ad:hover #frame2 p, #ad:focus #frame2 p {
    transform: scale(1);
}
```

PROVIDING **ALTERNATIVES** WITH **MODERNIZR**

Using the Modernizr feature detection library, let's look at an intelligent way to provide alternative styling for browsers that don't support cutting-edge CSS3 features.

The tour of CSS Animations, Transitions, and Transforms you've just read about was deliberately kept simple, because there is lots of information to take in. But hopefully you've started to form some killer ideas about the cool effects you can achieve using these features. For more involved examples, I recommend doing a Google search. My favorite examples are still CSS3-man (www.optimum7.com/css3-man) and Pure CSS3 AT-AT (anthonycalzadilla.com/css3-ATAT/index.html), both by Anthony Calzadilla.

The trouble is that many of the demos you'll see don't give too much consideration to working in nonsupporting browsers. Perhaps it doesn't matter in the case of throwaway demos, and many examples will degrade gracefully. For instance, look at the preceding animation-basics.html example, which works perfectly well when the animations are not supported; you just don't get to see the fun animations. But what about interfaces in which you rely on animations for viewable content?

A good way to deal with such eventualities is to use feature detection; that is, you can use JavaScript to detect whether the browser accessing the content supports the CSS features you are using, and then serve different styles depending on the result.

The easiest way to do this for noncode ninjas is to use a feature detection library; the best available is Modernizr (www.modernizr.com), created by Faruk Ates, Paul Irish, Alex Sexton, and others. This uses JavaScript to feature detect pretty much every CSS3 and HTML5 feature, and then lets you selectively apply scripting and styles to suit. As of version 2, you can even build and download your own custom version that just includes the tests you want, reducing bandwidth (see www.modernizr.com/download). While you are experimenting at this point, you should just stick to using the full, uncompressed version of Modernizr (click the DEVELOPMENT download button on www.modernizr.com).

Let's run through adding some CSS support detection magic to an example! To keep it simple and easy to follow, you'll revisit the business card 3D flip example. Open the two-faced-cheek-modernizr.html file in the chapter5 code download folder for the finished example, or open the two-faced-cheek.html file for a starting point.

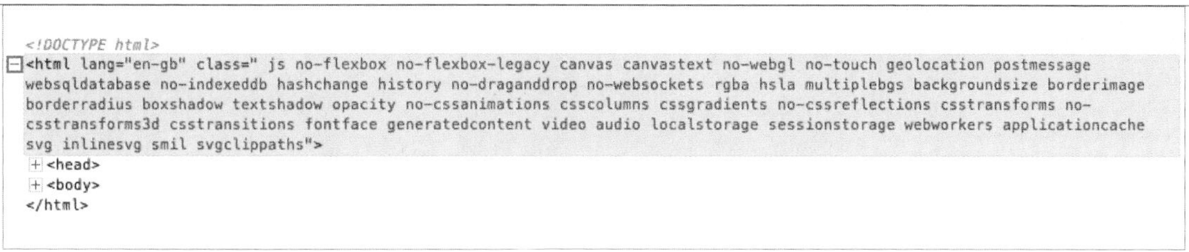

```
<!DOCTYPE html>
<html lang="en-gb" class=" js no-flexbox no-flexbox-legacy canvas canvastext no-webgl no-touch geolocation postmessage
websqldatabase no-indexeddb hashchange history no-draganddrop no-websockets rgba hsla multiplebgs backgroundsize borderimage
borderradius boxshadow textshadow opacity no-cssanimations csscolumns cssgradients no-cssreflections csstransforms no-
csstransforms3d csstransitions fontface generatedcontent video audio localstorage sessionstorage webworkers applicationcache
svg inlinesvg smil svgclippaths">
  <head>
  <body>
</html>
```

ADDING MODERNIZR TO YOUR PAGE

FIGURE 5.23 Modernizr adds classes to your <html> element to indicate which features your browser supports.

To apply Modernizr to your page, you first need to perform two steps:

1. Add a `<script>` element inside the `<head>` of your page to include the Modernizr script, for example:

   ```
   <script src="modernizr-2.5.3.js"></script>
   ```

2. Add a class of `no-js` to your `<html>` tag:

   ```
   <html lang="en-gb" class="no-js">
   ```

Now when you run your page and then look at the code as it is rendered (for example, in a debugging tool like Opera Dragonfly), you'll see that Modernizr has replaced your `no-js` class with a huge string of classes that look something like those shown in **Figure 5.23**.

This string allows you to specify different styles on a page based on whether different features are supported, using descendant selectors. If JavaScript isn't supported or turned off, you'll just be left with the default `no-js` class, and you can provide some kind of safe minimal styles that will probably work everywhere in the absence of more granular support information:

```
.no-js p {
    color: black;
}
```

When JavaScript is supported and Modernizr is able to give you that granular support information, you can start applying fallback styles based on very specific support criteria. Let's look at what the card 3D flip example required for wider-ranging browser support.

FIGURE 5.24 A decent set of alternative styles for browsers that don't support 3D transforms but do support 2D transforms.

PROVIDING ALTERNATIVE STYLES

By default, the card flip example relies on a 3D transform for sighted viewers to be able to see both sides of the card. But this is no good for browsers that don't support 3D transforms, like Opera (at the time of this writing). Nonsupporting browsers will get a class of `no-csstransforms3d` appended to their `<head>` classes, so you can provide alternative styling like so:

```
.no-csstransforms3d #wrapper:hover #front, .no-csstransforms3d
→ #wrapper:focus #front {
    transform: rotate(-30deg) translate(-50%,-100%);
    transition: 0.8s all ease-in;
}
```

The descendant selector applies a 2D transform to the front face of the card only when it is a descendant of `.no-csstransforms3d`. 3D rotation supporting browsers will ignore this styling. In Opera this styling gives you access to the back of the card, as shown in **Figure 5.24**.

But what about browsers that don't support 2D transforms? Older browsers like IE8 or Camino won't support rem units, gradients, transforms, or text shadow, so what about them?

Modernizr won't help with rem units. The best way to deal with them is to provide a pixel-size fallback next to the rem unit version of your property, as discussed in Chapter 1:

```
margin-top: 5px;
margin-top: 0.5rem;
```

Older browsers will just read the first one, whereas newer browsers that support rem units will read both, but the latter line will override the former one.

For other CSS features, you'll need to include at least the following CSS:

```
.no-csstransforms #wrapper:hover #front,.no-csstransforms
    #wrapper:focus #front {
    margin-left: -350px;
}

.no-cssgradients #front, .no-cssgradients #back {
    background: #FF3500;
}

.no-cssgradients #front p, .no-cssgradients #back p {
    /* ideally should be .no-textshadow, but modernizr doesn't seem
        to provide this */
    color: #000000;
}
```

FIGURE 5.25 Simple but basic: I moved the front by changing the margin.

The first rule applies an updated :hover/:focus rule to the flip card so that, if the browser doesn't support 2D transforms, hovering or focusing the card will just move the front over by 350 pixels to reveal the back. The second rule provides a simple, solid background color to replace the posh gradient background in nonsupporting browsers. The third rule just colors the text black, so that it is still readable without the shadows.

This code produces the simple but usable result shown in **Figure 5.25**.

TIP: The fallback code still won't work in IE6–7 due to a horrible bug involving hover effects not working on positioned elements with nontransparent background colors. See http://stackoverflow.com/questions/4378497/ie-bug-absolutely-positioned-element-with-a-non-transparent-background-color for the solution. Go figure!

ANIMATIONS AND JAVASCRIPT

As mentioned earlier, one of the ways I foresee CSS Animations being useful is to trigger animations via JavaScript. To demonstrate this, I created a form example. Web designers hate coding forms and are always looking for better ways to make them more usable, space efficient, and consistent across browsers. So what better way to demonstrate a decent, real-world use of animations than to code an attractive, usable form example?

To see the finished code, check out animated-form.html and animated-form.css in the chapter5 folder. There is nothing remarkable about the HTML for this example. The bulk of it is a very simple, four-input form with a Submit button. But notice that I'm using the same setup as I did in the HTML card flip example (see two-faced-cheek.html). The front face has the form elements in it, whereas the back face has a "Thank you for your feedback!" message in it:

```html
<form id="feedback-form" action="#" class="">
    <div id="front">
        <h1>Give us your feedback!</h1>
        <div>
            <label for="name" tabindex="0">Name<span class=
              "extended-info"> - Enter your first and last name
              so we can identify you more easily.</span></label>
            <input type="text" name="name" id="name">
            <!-- Other form elements follow -->
        </div>
    </div>
    <div id="back">
        <h2>Thank you for your feedback!</h2>
    </div>
</form>
```

TIP: Modernizr is also applied to the form page to provide some fallbacks later on.

Yes I've used the same card flip behavior as before, but instead of animating it via a transition and triggering it on hover/focus via pseudo-classes, I've put the animation in a CSS animation, like this:

```
@keyframes form-rotate {
    from {
        transform: rotateX(0deg);
    }
    to {
        transform: rotateX(180deg);
    }
}

.form-rotate {
    animation: form-rotate 1s forwards;
}
```

The animation keyframes rotate whatever the animation is applied to around the X axis by 180 degrees, and the animation is applied to any element that is given a class of form-rotate. This will be the <input type="submit">.

The other noteworthy part of this example is the <h1>, and the fact that the form slides into the screen and out again when the <h1> is clicked (in browsers that support animations). To move the <h1> to where it is initially, I used a transform:

```
h1 {
    position: absolute;
    transform: rotate(90deg) translate(9.5rem,-23rem);
}
```

To make the whole form slide in and slide out, two animations have been set up:

```
@keyframes form-out {
    from {
        transform: translateX(0rem);
    }
    to {
        transform: translateX(38rem);
    }
}

.form-out {
    animation: form-out 1s forwards;
}

@keyframes form-in {
    from {
        transform: translateX(38rem);
    }
    to {
        transform: translateX(0rem);
    }
}

.form-in {
    animation: form-in 1s forwards;
}
```

But I haven't applied the three classes shown earlier to anything yet, so what gives? I'll do this via some simple JavaScript when the Submit button and <h1> are clicked. The JavaScript looks like this:

```
var submit = document.getElementById("submit");
var form = document.querySelector("form");
var back = document.getElementById("back");
var h1 = document.querySelector("h1");
```

TIP: querySelector and addEventListener are not supported by IE versions earlier than version 9. Therefore, for IE 6–8 support, you'll need to consider using different code.

Here, references to elements are stored on the page in the following variables:

- **submit.** The <input id="submit">
- **form.** The <form> element
- **back.** The back face of the form; the <div> with the #back attribute
- **h1.** The <h1> element

Next, I set up two event listeners:

```
submit.addEventListener("click", rotateForm, false);
h1.addEventListener("click", formOut, false);
```

- **First line.** Adds an event listener to the submit variable reference, which executes the rotateForm function when the Submit button is clicked.
- **Second line.** Adds an event listener to the h1 variable reference, which executes the formOut function when the <h1> element is clicked.

Here is the first function:

```
function formOut() {
    if(form.className==="" || form.className==="form-in") {
        if(Modernizr.cssanimations) {
            form.setAttribute("class","form-out");
        } else {
            form.setAttribute("class","form-fallback");
            form.style.left = "0rem";
        }
        h1.innerHTML = "Hide feedback form!";
    } else {
        if(Modernizr.cssanimations) {
            form.setAttribute("class","form-in");
        } else {
            form.setAttribute("class","");
            form.style.left = "-38rem";
        }
        h1.innerHTML = "Give us your feedback!";
    }
}
```

I've used an if ... else statement to see whether the form is offscreen and I want to move it on or whether it is onscreen and I want to move it off.

form.className==="" || form.className==="form-in" basically specifies "if the form's class is empty OR it is set to form-in, then it will be offscreen; therefore, run the first Modernizr test." modernizr.cssanimations tests whether CSS Animations are supported by the current browser. If they are, then set the form's class value to form-out to trigger the animation that brings it onscreen.

If the Modernizr test returns `false`, the animation won't work; instead you set the `left` property of the form to `0rem` to make the form appear on the screen in one go, and set the form `class` to `form-fallback` so that the second part of the function will run when the user tries to hide the form again (if you don't do this, the second part of the function will never run because the form `class` will always be blank). It's not as nice-looking, but at least it works.

The last part of this section of the code (the `h1.innerHTML` part) changes the text inside the `<h1>` element to a message telling users they can hide it again if they want to.

If the outer `if` test returns false, then the form must be onscreen, and the code inside the `else` block is executed, which runs another `modernizr.cssanimations` test. If this returns `true`, the code changes the `class` value to `form-in` to animate it offscreen again. If it returns `false`, the `left` property is returned to its original value—to move it offscreen again in a less glamorous manner—and the form `class` is set to blank again to return it to its original state.

The last part of the `else` block changes the `<h1>` text back to what it was originally.

Now on to the second function, `rotateForm()`:

```
function rotateForm() {
    if(Modernizr.cssanimations && Modernizr.csstransforms3d) {
        form.setAttribute("class","form-rotate");
        form.style.left = "0rem";
    } else {
        back.style.zIndex = "5";
    }
}
```

Here, if `Modernizr.cssanimations` AND `Modernizr.csstransforms3d` are true, I've used `setAttribute` to set the `<form>`'s class attribute to `form-rotate`. This applies the rotate animation to the form, making it rotate to reveal the "Thank You" message. But setting the `<form>`'s class to `form-rotate` will override the class of `form-out` set earlier, which would cause the form to move offscreen again;

  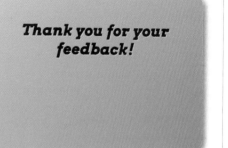

therefore, I've forced the form to remain onscreen by setting the left property to 0 with form.style.left = "0rem".

FIGURE 5.26 The three different states we are animating.

If the Modernizr test isn't true, the browser doesn't support CSS Animations and/or 3D transforms; therefore, I want different styling to occur when the Submit button is clicked. To allow nonsupporting browsers to see the "Thank You" message, I used back.style.zIndex = "5"; to set the z-index of the #back <div> to 5, making it appear above everything else in the stacking order when the Submit button is clicked. **Figure 5.26** shows the three states I'm animating in between.

I've also used some simple transitions to make the help messages appear when the form labels are hovered over/focused on:

```
.extended-info {

    ...

    opacity: 0;

    transition: 1.5s all;

}

div label:hover .extended-info,div label:focus .extended-info {

    opacity: 1;

}
```

Finally, some Modernizr fallbacks are added to allow older browsers to make some use of the form:

```css
.no-cssgradients #front,.no-cssgradients #back {
    background-color: #009999;
}

.no-cssanimations form {
    left: 0;
}

.no-csstransforms h1 {
    position: static;
}

.no-csstransforms .extended-info {
    display: none;
}
```

I'm certainly not expecting you to know JavaScript just to use CSS. If you don't understand this code, pass it to your friendly JavaScript developer and collaborate on it. He or she can probably do a much better job of this than I have. In any case, it's worth exploring such techniques because it's cool to be able to handle the animation with CSS rather than having to write it all in JavaScript. Even if you use jQuery or a similar library, it is still a lot of weight to add to the page just for a couple of simple animations.

WRAPPING **UP**

You should now be clued into how to use CSS Transitions, Transforms, and Animations to achieve some very cool, fresh effects on your web creations. Also, you now know how to use feature detection mechanisms like Modernizr to provide more carefully thought-out alternative experiences to nonsupporting browsers rather than just "IE or not IE" as discussed earlier in the book, for example, with CSS3PIE in Chapter 4.

6

USING **CSS** TO **IMPLEMENT ICONS**

Icons are an essential part of creating web interfaces as familiar signposts, badges of honor, or notifications. They can draw attention to important parts of the page quickly, use less space than words, and can transcend languages. CSS3 offers some useful new tricks to the icon arena; hence, this chapter on icons. After the comparatively heavy learning curve presented by CSS Animations in Chapter 5, you can relax a bit here.

In this chapter you'll learn some slick ways to implement icons on a web page employing cutting-edge CSS and HTML features, such as multiple background images, web fonts, and data- attributes.

ICONS ROCK!

FIGURE 6.1 Aren't you glad that conventions such as these exist the world over! Image courtesy of http://thenounproject.com/noun/unisex/#icon-N050.

You'll find icons everywhere, helping you find your way and get additional information about people, objects, services, and so on. Often, they are invisible and are used almost subconsciously due to the familiarity everyone has with recognized conventions, such as on/off switches, play and pause buttons, airports and train stations, and toilets (**Figure 6.1**)! If you think carefully about icons, you'll find that you use them more often than you realize.

Since the dawn of man, icons have been used for communication. For example, cave dwellers painted on their caves to record details of meetings and food. And the more recent examples of Egyptian hieroglyphics and Chinese symbols most definitely fall under the moniker of icons.

NOTE: I became interested in icons after serving as editor on fellow English gent Jon Hicks's marvelous book, *The Icon Design Handbook (Five Simple Steps, 2012).* In fact, this chapter is influenced heavily by Jon's wonderful work. I highly recommend that everyone purchase his book because it is a real joy to read and provides more in-depth information than I've assembled in this short account.

USING **ICONS** ON **WEBSITES**

Similarly to the real world, icons can fill many roles on websites or in applications. Most commonly, they act as signposts, giving users hints on how to get where they want to go and do what they want to do. Icons can impart these hints quicker and more intuitively than textual descriptions, often due to the fact that they follow established conventions, which can break through the language barrier: Mail, home, and shopping basket icons are classic examples (**Figure 6.2**).

If you need to create an icon to represent something where no convention already exists, you need to choose an image that is as recognizable as possible, easy to depict in different sizes, and attractive enough to draw in the user. Web icons are typically monochrome with transparent backgrounds so they can be overlaid nicely on top of different backgrounds.

Icons are loosely grouped into three different types:

- **Pictograms.** These icons convey a location or idea through resemblance to a physical object, for example, a vinyl record to represent "music" or a car to represent "car insurance" (**Figure 6.3**).

- **Ideograms.** More general than a pictogram, these icons represent ideas or actions, such as "search" or "write a comment" (**Figure 6.4**). Generally, (but not always) they will be intuitive to a certain degree because of users' familiarity with the real-world objects.

- **Arbitrary.** These icons are more abstract creations that generally don't directly relate to real-life objects or concepts. Because they are not real-world objects, they must be learned from scratch and so are not immediately intuitive. **Figure 6.5** provides a good example: This icon set was created for the W3C as part of its effort to brand HTML5 and other cutting-edge technologies to raise interest and awareness (see www.w3.org/html/logo).

I won't go into a great amount of detail on how to choose and draw icons in this chapter, but for those of you interested in finding ideas and inspiration, a Google images search always brings up many, and you can find a huge number of great free icons at thenounproject.com. The images in this section have been taken from the awesome dingbat sets Modern Pictograms and Heydings Common Icons, available on Font Squirrel.

FIGURE 6.2 Familiar web icons: mail, home, shopping basket.

FIGURE 6.3 Pictogram examples.

FIGURE 6.4 Ideogram examples.

FIGURE 6.5 Arbitrary icons from the W3C's HTML5 branding (released under creative commons CC-BY).

FIGURE 6.6 Icons in a menu.

FIGURE 6.7 Intuitive functionality icons: play and zoom in.

FIGURE 6.8 User status icons (taken from Skype).

Icons are a great addition when used in the right contexts, and you should give this some careful thought when considering them. If they solve a problem along the lines of allowing users to find what they want or where they want to go faster and more intuitively, and consume less space, you have a good case for using an icon. But if you are just using icons everywhere with wild abandon, their effectiveness is greatly diminished, and you end up with a horrible Christmas tree-type effect!

Places to consider using icons include:

- **Navigation.** Icons can make great signposts to help direct users to where they want to go. For example, you'll learn how to build the example shown in **Figure 6.6** in the next section "The Basics of Icon Implementation."

- **Functionality.** Intuitive icons allow users to find functionality easily, for example, playing a video or zooming in (**Figure 6.7**).

- **Status.** You need only to look at programs like Skype and messenger applications for good status icon usage, for example, "I'm here," "I'm away," "I'm asleep." See **Figure 6.8** for some examples.

- **Comparison.** Using icons to compare product features is a good way to give users at-a-glance summaries (**Figure 6.9**).

- **User feedback.** Form icons are the classic example for user feedback (**Figure 6.10**): "The format is incorrect," "Missing information," and so on.

- **Emotion.** People use emoticons more and more in communications these days—in text messages, email, chat applications, IRC, and so forth (**Figure 6.11**).

FIGURE 6.9 Icons to compare product features, taken from yolo.co.uk.

FIGURE 6.10 The signup form on mint.com makes good use of icons for form feedback.

FIGURE 6.11 Emoticons are used to convey emotion in a textual form.

THE **BASICS** OF **ICON** IMPLEMENTATION

To implement icons on a web page, arguably the best method is to use CSS background images. Using the <img> tag is workable, but not the best way, because icons are not really content; rather, they support content, plus <img> elements affect content layout on the page and are more fiddly to place where you want.

Let's look at a quick example. You'll find the full code for this in the file basic-icons.html in the chapter6 code download folder. You first need to attach the images to the elements you want them to appear on:

```
ul li:nth-of-type(1) a {
    background-image: url(icons/home.png);
}

ul li:nth-of-type(2) a {
    background-image: url(icons/file.png);
}

ul li:nth-of-type(3) a {
    background-image: url(icons/circle_info.png);
}

ul li:nth-of-type(4) a {
    background-image: url(icons/pencil.png);
}
```

FIGURE 6.12 A simple icon implementation (icons are taken from www.freeiconsweb.com/Free-Downloads.asp?id=1729 and are published under creative commons unported).

A bit more styling is needed to finish this off:

```
li {

    ...

    background-image: linear-gradient(top,rgba(0,0,0,0),
    ⤳ rgba(0,0,0,0.4) 70%);
}

ul a {
    background-repeat: no-repeat;
    background-position: 35% 45%;
    padding-left: 5%;
    background-color: #D660CC;
    behavior: url(PIE.htc);
}
```

In the first rule you're setting a gradient on the actual list item to make the styling on the links more flexible. Then in the second rule you're setting the image to not repeat, because you only want to show it once, and setting a more appropriate position for the icons, because you don't want them to display in the default top-left corner position. You're also setting a bit of left padding to make space for the icon so it doesn't clash with the text and setting a solid background color as a fallback for browsers that don't support the CSS3 styling features also at work here. Some CSS3PIE magic is also included here to provide support for IE6–8 for extra styling peace of mind. Also, note that I've attached Selectivizr to the page to make IE6–8 support the CSS3 selectors I've used in this example, such as nth-of-type. **Figure 6.12** shows the result.

GENERATED CONTENT FOR ICONS

You could also implement your icons using generated content, like so (see basic-icons-generated-content.html in the chapter6 code download folder):

```
ul li:nth-of-type(1) a:before {
    content: url(icons/home.png);
}

/* Other three icons included in the same way as the first one, but
⇢ ommitted here for brevity */

ul a:before {
    position: relative;
    right: 4%;
    top: 5px;
}

ul a {
    padding-left: 1%;
    background-image: linear-gradient(top,rgba(0,0,0,0),
    ⇢ rgba(0,0,0,0.4) 70%);
    background-color: #D660CC;
    behavior: url(PIE.htc);
}
```

This method is also a viable option, although generated content is not supported as widely across browsers (it won't work in IE6–7). You'll explore using generated content more in the "Web Fonts as Icons" section.

CSS SPRITES

The preceding examples work well, but what about implementing multiple icons? Having to pull in a separate image file for each icon introduces a whole lot of HTTP requests: To make your code more efficient, you can use CSS sprites. The idea is that you combine all of your images into a single file, and then show the different icons by varying the background-position property. Your code will look like this (see basic-icons-css-sprites.html):

```
ul li:nth-of-type(1) a {
    background-image: url(icons/sprite-set.png);
    background-position: 35% 10px;
}

ul li:nth-of-type(2) a {
    background-image: url(icons/sprite-set.png);
    background-position: 35% -40px;
}

ul li:nth-of-type(3) a {
    background-image: url(icons/sprite-set.png);
    background-position: 35% -90px;
}

ul li:nth-of-type(4) a {
    background-image: url(icons/sprite-set.png);
    background-position: 35% -140px;
}
```

In each rule the background-position has the same horizontal value but increasing vertical values; each increase pushes the image farther and farther upwards, so that you only have to load a single file but can display different icons

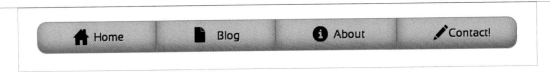

FIGURE 6.13 CSS sprites in action.

as you are displaying a different part of the image in each case. The result is shown in **Figure 6.13**.

MAKING YOUR ICONS MORE BULLETPROOF

In the examples you've seen so far, you have a solid implementation that works well. The only trouble at this point is that if you are using percentages for your container widths; the icon can start to look misplaced or become too big for the containers when the screen gets narrower. To remedy this, you can adopt a few different approaches, either separately or in combination:

- Use `min-width` to limit the shrinking of the containers to an acceptable amount.

- Use **Media Queries** to serve up some different styling at smaller screen widths, for example, a smaller version of the image used for the icon. You'll learn more about media queries in Chapter 8.

- Use `background-size` to constrain the icon to a particular size, proportional to the container.

The solution I considered for my icon set (see basic-icons-background-size. html) incorporates a combination of `min-width` and `background-size`. Let's go through it now: You'll first set a `min-width` on the list:

```
ul {

    ...

    min-width: 750px;

}
```

FIGURE 6.14 Using background-size to scale the icons proportionately to the size of the menu buttons.

Then you'll give the anchors a background-size:

```
ul a {

    ...

    background-size: 10% 50%;

}
```

The effect is shown in **Figure 6.14**.

So, min-width ensures that the menu doesn't get too small and break at narrower browser widths. background-size not only forces all images to adopt the same size, but also fixes that size to be a percentage of the button size, so they will adjust as the buttons become smaller. This may or may not be the behavior you want; it is useful to know it is available to you.

MULTIPLE BACKGROUND IMAGES FOR MODIFIED ICONS

Sometimes you'll use a base icon and then add extra icons to it to modify the icon's meaning somewhat. For example, you could add a plus sign to a document icon to create a "New document" icon or add a down arrow to an application icon to mean "Download update." You could do this by creating each of these separate icons statically, but that would be boring when you have CSS3 at your disposal! Instead, let's include the base icon and the modifiers using multiple background images, and then size and place them programmatically.

FIGURE 6.15 Multiple background images used to make additive icons.

The code to achieve this is very similar to what you used earlier, but it just requires the use of additional multiple background images to include the modifiers. You can see an example of this code in the file modified-icons.html in the chapter6 code download folder. The code looks something like this (**Figure 6.15** shows the result):

```
ul li:nth-of-type(1) a {
    background-image: url(icons/plus.png), url(icons/file.png);
}

/* Other three icons included in a very similar way to the first
→ one, but ommitted here for brevity */

ul a {
    background-repeat: no-repeat;
    background-position: 72px 10px, 50px 10px;
    background-size: 13px 13px, 20px 25px;

        ...
}
```

As you can see, you now have a set of two background images for each icon: one for the modifier and one for the base icon. Two background-positions and three background-sizes also go along with those images.

WEB FONTS AS ICONS

Another option available to you is using web fonts as icons. Using a single character for the icons and applying a web font to them can give you the look you want. This is a good technique in many ways. The text character will be infinitely scalable when zooming in, and there are a wide variety of Dingbats-style fonts to use to create suitable icons. The downsides are that browsers must support @font-face for them to work, font files can be big, and actually adding the character(s) into your HTML will pollute your content and possibly cause accessibility issues for those using screen readers.

Let's review these problems one by one. I've assembled an example for you to dissect in the file web-font-icons.html in the chapter6 folder. To start, you'll find your fonts using any of the resources detailed in Chapter 3. I found my fonts at www.fontsquirrel.com/fonts/list/style/Dingbat.

Next, you'll create the different font formats you need using the Font Squirrel @Font-Face Generator (www.fontsquirrel.com/fontface/generator).

Then you'll import the fonts in your CSS in the usual way using the bulletproof font syntax:

```
@font-face {
    font-family: 'Heydings';
    src: url('fonts/heydings_icons.eot');
    src: url('fonts/heydings_icons.eot?#iefix')
      → format('embedded-opentype'),
        url('fonts/heydings_icons.woff') format('woff'),
        url('fonts/heydings_icons.ttf') format('truetype'),
        url('fonts/heydings_icons.svg#SansationRegular')
          → format('svg');
    font-weight: normal;
    font-style: normal;
}
```

Rather than using images or hardcoding your text characters into your HTML, you'll create them on the fly using generated content:

```
ul li:nth-of-type(1) a:before {
    content: "H";
}
ul li:nth-of-type(2) a:before {
    content: "D";
}
ul li:nth-of-type(3) a:before {
    content: "i";
}
ul li:nth-of-type(4) a:before {
    content: "w";
}
```

This avoids the problem of polluting your markup with surplus characters. However, it can be a bit fiddly trying to work out which text character corresponds to which icon you want to use. You could install the font on your system and then open a word processor and just type out characters until you find them, or open the font in an app like Character Map or Font Book and pick them out of there.

It seems that they are mapped to intuitive characters in this case—"H" for home, "i" for the information symbol, and so on—so hopefully other icon font authors will follow suit and start to adhere to some kind of ad hoc conventions.

FIGURE 6.16 Icons made with web fonts.

All that remains to do now is apply the font to your generated content and position it appropriately:

```
ul a:before {
    font-family: Heydings;
    position: relative;
    right: 4%;
    top: 6px;
}
```

Because you are using fonts, the icons are very easy to size, color, and even add drop shadow effects to. This is awesome!

```
ul a:before {
    font-family: Heydings;
    position: relative;
    right: 4%;
    top: 4px;
    font-size: 1.6em;
    color: #333;
    text-shadow: 1px 1px 1px rgba(255,255,255,0.4);
}
```

Figure 6.16 shows the effect achieved.

TIP: To mitigate the issue of large font file sizes adding significantly to page load, you could reduce the font file using FontForge to include only the characters you need.

HTML data- ATTRIBUTES FOR MORE EFFICIENT ICON CSS

When using the web font icon solution, you'll need to include a separate ruleset for each icon. A way to get around this and lessen the amount of code is to use the new HTML5 data- attribute to store your text characters, like this:

```
<li><a href="#" data-icon="H">Home</a></li>
```

You can put anything you like after the data- part, and store whatever data you like in these custom attributes. Then you'll have your text characters stored in your data-icon attributes; you can put them all on the page using only a single CSS ruleset and eliminate the other four that were present before:

```
ul a:before {
    content: attr(data-icon);

        ...

}
```

You can see my implementation in web-font-icons-data-attributes.html.

PURE CSS ICONS: PECULIAR?

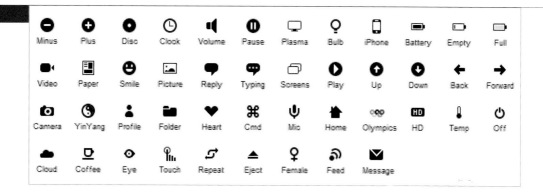

As another alternative for implementing icons, I'll mention the idea of creating icons from pure CSS. Lucian Marin pioneered this technique and created an icon set called Peculiar (http://lucianmarin.com/peculiar). The shapes for these icons were created using pure HTML and CSS. **Figure 6.17** shows the icon set.

FIGURE 6.17 The Peculiar icon set created by Lucian Marin.

As an example, the markup for the Home icon looks like this:

```
<div class="icon icon-home">
    <div class="icon-home-triangle"/>
    <div class="icon-home-rectangle"/>
    <div class="icon-home-line"/>
    <span class="name">
</div>
```

And the CSS applied to this looks like so:

```
.icon-home-triangle {
    border: 8px solid #000;
    border-left-color: transparent;
    border-right-color: transparent;
    border-top-color: transparent;
    height: 0;
```

```
        width: 0;

        position: absolute;

        bottom: 7px;

        left: 0;

    }

    .icon-home-rectangle {

        background-color: #000;

        width: 10px;

        height: 8px;

        border-bottom-left-radius: 1px;

        border-bottom-right-radius: 1px;

        position: absolute;

        bottom: 1px;

        left: 3px;

    }

    .icon-home-line {

        background-color: #000;

        width: 2px;

        height: 5px;

        border-radius: 1px;

        position: absolute;

        top: 2px;

        left: 3px;

    }
```

You can find an example implementation of these icons in the file peculiar-icons. html in the chapter6 folder. To implement the icons here, you need to download the Peculiar icon CSS and HTML from the URL provided earlier, and then copy all the HTML and CSS to your own files. For example, this where I put the Home icon:

```
<li>
<a href="#">Home
    <div class="icon icon-home">
        <div class="icon-home-triangle"></div>
        <div class="icon-home-rectangle"></div>
        <div class="icon-home-line"></div>
    </div>
</a>
</li>
```

You need to make sure the icon HTML is placed inside the container you want it to appear in (in this case the anchor) and that the container will display as a block-level element. In the case of your menu this works fine, because the anchors are already set to display: inline-block; to make the sizing work. Once all the Peculiar CSS is in place, you need to modify it a bit. For starters, the general icon class needs some work:

```
.icon {
    position: absolute;
    top: 16px;
    left: 48px;
    width:16px;
    height:16px;
    transform: scale(1.5);
}
```

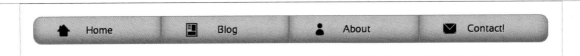

FIGURE 6.18 The menu example using Peculiar icons.

Here I've set the position to absolute so that I can move the icons into position and moved them using top and left. I've also used a transform to set the desired size of the icons. This was needed because the icon shapes are dependent on the 16 x 16 width and height. If you mess with those dimensions, the icons become distorted.

The only step left to do is to set the icons' parent containers—the anchors—to be positioned, so that the position I set on the icons earlier will happen relative to them, not the <body> or another positioned ancestor:

```
ul a {
    position: relative;

    ...

}
```

Figure 6.18 shows the result.

Now, this technique may seem pretty damn complicated for producing a set of simple icons, but it does have its advantages. Creating icons in pure CSS completely does away with those extra HTTP requests needed for downloading images or web fonts, and the file sizes are kept very small.

They are also infinitely scalable and manipulable (you can grab each icon and change its size, shape, color, and so on to suit the situation), and are great for web developers who don't like to use Photoshop very much. Creating such icons does require using border-radius a lot, which doesn't work in IE 6–8, but support can be added via the use of your old friend CSS3PIE, which you first met in Chapter 4. The transform also won't work in old versions of IE, but the overall result looks OK, albeit with smaller icons.

I urge you to learn from these icons and try your hand at creating your own! And please send Lucian Marin flowers and cake, because it is truly a cool idea.

WRAPPING UP

And so wraps up the exploration of CSS icons. I hope you've found it useful, and you'll go forward and use icons effectively and responsibly! The examples all work acceptably in IE 6–8, to a greater or lesser degree. Which one works best for you really depends on your particular situation and the browser support needs of your project.

7

CSS3 **LAYOUT CHOPS**

Now comes the time to turn to the subject of using CSS to create layouts. Traditionally, users of CSS have been poorly served in this area, because the tools available to produce layouts have been limited. However, CSS3 provides a number of modules aimed at bridging that gap.

In CSS2, all you really have for designing web page layouts in a serious way are floats and positioning. In many situations you must still rely on JavaScript to fix CSS layout limitations.

CSS3 gives your layout abilities a real booster shot in the arm by offering many modules designed to fulfill specific needs. In this chapter you'll explore those modules and learn how you can successfully use them now. Let's get this carnival of content contortion started with a brief look at these new features.

Although CSS3 has a number of layout-oriented modules, I'll mainly focus on discussing the following modules because of reasonable current support, future importance, and limited page count:

- **CSS Multi-column layout (www.w3.org/TR/css3-multicol).** Multi-col allows you to split a body of content into a number of different columns with column rules, column breaks, and more.

- **CSS Flexible box layout (www.w3.org/TR/css3-flexbox).** This module defines new values for the `display` property to allow for more powerful layout techniques that control the ordering and spacing of the children of a container, which were previously very difficult to achieve without JavaScript. Vertically spacing multiple elements equally inside a parent container is a good case in point. This module has recently had an overhaul, and most browsers don't support the new syntax at the time of this writing. However, implementation of this module should come quickly, because browser vendors are very interested in it.

- **CSS Grids (www.w3.org/TR/css3-grid).** Grid systems are very popular for creating neat, consistent, balanced web layouts, but traditionally you've had to build your own or use a third-party grid system of some kind. The CSS Grids module provides a standardized, native way to create grids. Again, current browser support is patchy, but more should follow soon.

I'll also cover the following modules briefly at the end of the chapter. These do not have solid browser support as of yet, but they are damn cool and will be important in the future:

- **Regions (http://dev.w3.org/csswg/css3-regions).** This module is intended to allow you to define a series of content regions in a document and an order in which content is placed into those regions as it fills them up.

- **CSS3 Exclusions and Shapes Module Level 3 (http://dev.w3.org/csswg/css3-exclusions).** Shapes allow you to define geometric shapes for content to flow around or inside, whereas exclusions allow you to flow content around those shapes. This module should allow for complicated magazine-style layouts.

- **GCPM (www.w3.org/TR/css3-gcpm).** The idea behind Generated Content for Paged Media is that you can make a container break into pages, which can then be flicked between in a natural, book-like fashion.

Table 7.1 summarizes the support for these features.

TABLE 7.1 Browser Support Matrix for CSS3 Layout Features

BROWSER	MULTI-COL	FLEXBOX	GRIDS	REGIONS	EXCLUSIONS	GCPM
Opera	Since 11.1	No	No	No	No	Since 12****
Firefox	2.0 with -moz-*	2.0 with -moz-**	No	No	No	No
Safari	3.2 with -webkit-*	3.1 with -webkit-**	No	6.0 with -webkit-***	No	No
Chrome	4.0 with -webkit-*	17 with -webkit-	No	16 with -webkit-***	No	No
Internet Explorer	10	10 with -ms-**	10 with -ms-	10 with -ms-	No	No
iOS	3.2 with -webkit-*	5.0 with -webkit-	No	No	No	No
Android	2.1 with -webkit-*	2.1 with -webkit-**	No	No	No	No
Mobile Chrome	Beta with -webkit-*	Beta with -webkit-	No	No	No	No
Opera Mobile	Since 11.1	No	No	No	No	Since 12****
Opera Mini	No	No	No	No	No	No

* Indicates limited multi-col support without support for break-before/after/inside.

** Indicates support for the old version of the Flexbox spec, which is deprecated (see the "Using Flexbox" section for more details).

*** Safari and Chrome at the time of this writing support regions with a different mechanism than that of IE10. See the "Regions" section for more details.

**** At the time of this writing, GCPM was only supported to a limited extent in a special Opera Labs build. See the "GCPM" section for more details.

MULTI-COL LAYOUTS

The CSS Multi-column layout spec provides you with a small, focused set of tools for breaking a body of content into multiple columns. This isn't just limited to text: You can create multi-col layouts with it if you like, and do smart tasks like have images or other elements span more than one column. But it isn't great for full multi-col layouts. For example, you can't specify different widths for individual columns.

So without further ado, let's look at a simple example. You can find my finished example in the file simple-multi-col1.html in the chapter7 code download folder. In the file, note that the multi-col-related properties have been specified with prefixes for Firefox, and the WebKit browsers but not for IE and Opera, which supports them without prefixes. Also note that most of the properties are applied to the parent container of the actual content you want to split into columns, in this case the <section> element that contains the main dummy content.

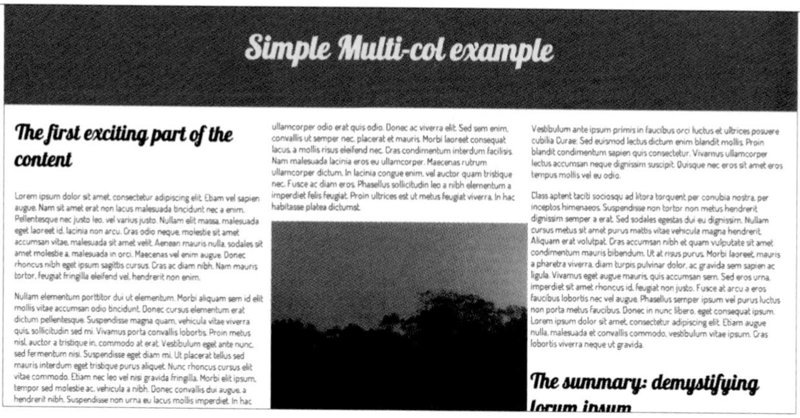

FIGURE 7.1 Multiple columns were never this easy before!

SETTING THE NUMBER OF COLUMNS

To start, you use the `column-count` property to specify the number of columns you want:

```
section {
    column-count: 3;
}
```

Specifying a number of columns equally divides your content into that number of columns across the horizontal space available. This produces the effect shown in **Figure 7.1**.

You can immediately see why this is useful: It is so flexible and easy. Prior to the introduction of this property, you had to break the content into multiple child containers and then float those; if content or layout requirements changed, you had to modify your markup.

> **NOTE:** In my code you'll see that to give the columns some space around the edges and line up at the top, I had to apply some padding to the whole `<section>` and remove the top padding from the first main content `<h2>`. You need to think carefully about this kind of styling when trying to get multi-col layouts to look right. You'll learn more about this in a more complicated example later in this chapter.

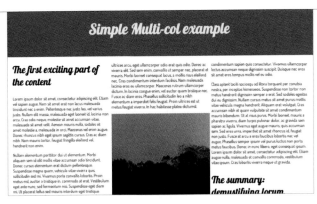

FIGURE 7.2 Varying numbers of columns as the container width is increased.

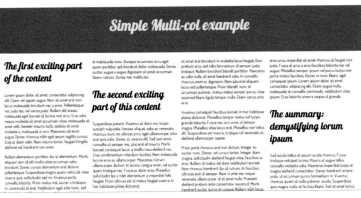

COLUMN WIDTH, NOT COUNT?

Another option available to you for indicating the number of columns you want is to specify a `column-width` property with a unit distance, like so:

```
section {
    column-width: 25rem;
}
```

The effect this has is to make the columns adopt a best-fit approach. If three lots of the specified distance can fit into the available container width or thereabouts, you'll produce three columns. If the width becomes narrower or wider, you may end up with two or four, and so on. The actual column width does vary, because the browser tries to fit the columns as neatly as possible. **Figure 7.2** shows a comparison of different container widths.

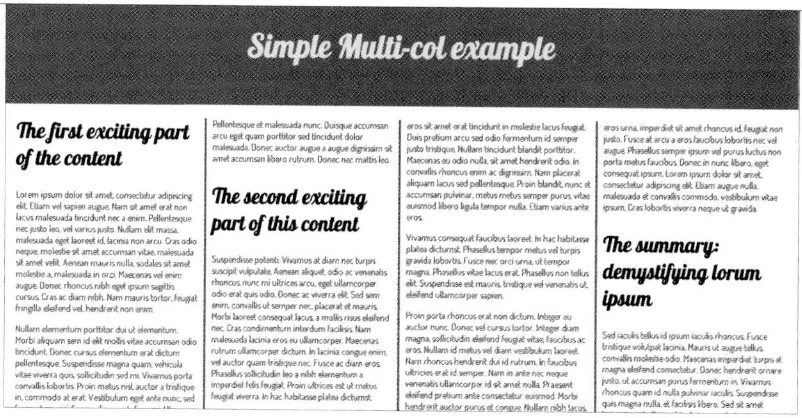

FIGURE 7.3 A much neater effect. You've created dividing rules and column gaps to improve legibility.

SPECIFYING COLUMN GUTTERS

Next, you'll add a couple of properties to specify how to divide vertical rules and space between the columns:

```
section {
    column-width: 25rem;
    column-rule: 3px solid #8B2101;
    column-gap: 2rem;
}
```

This produces the result shown in **Figure 7.3**.

Note that the value given to the column-gap property is divided equally on either side of the column-rule. So in the preceding example, in between each column you'll get a gap of 1 rem, followed by the 3-pixel rule, and then another gap of 1 rem.

Note that the column-rule property is shorthand and works in the same way with the same values as the standard border property. You can even specify the different components in longhand if you like:

```
column-rule-width: 3px;
column-rule-style: solid;
column-rule-color: #8B2101;
```

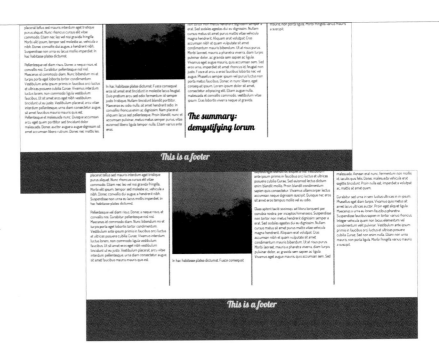

FIGURE 7.4 Demonstrating the difference between auto column fill (left) and column-balanced column fill (right).

SPECIFYING HOW THE COLUMNS ARE FILLED WITH CONTENT

Another property you can specify, `column-fill`, can take two different properties, auto and balance. auto is the default, which just makes the columns fill up left to right and down to a certain length. This can cause an uneven result, as shown on the left in **Figure 7.4**. The better option is often balance, which fills in the content as equally as possible across the columns, leaving less unsightly gaps, as shown on the right in Figure 7.4.

```
section {
    column-width: 20rem;
    column rule: 3px solid #8B2101;
    column-gap: 2rem;
    height: 85rem;
    column-fill: balance;
}
```

The problem with `column-fill` is that it only has an effect when you set a fixed height on the container that you are applying multi-col effects to, as you did in this example. From my experience, you'll almost never want to do this because you can rarely control the exact amount of content you'll want to show across multiple pages using the same template. So `column-fill` is of limited use in my opinion. I've left the code in the example for you to look at but commented it out.

SPAN CONTENT ACROSS MULTIPLE COLUMNS

Usually, you won't want all your content to just sit in one column. The example could definitely do with some sorting out of those top-level headings, and the image is cut off. What can you do, aside from going down to the pub (or better still, logging on to Twitter) and complaining about the web not being print? You can remedy these problems somewhat with the `column-span` property. Look at the file simple-multi-col2.html. It is the same as the previous example, except that it has an image added into the main content body. Let's make the main headings and the image span all the columns, like so:

```
section h2 {
    column-span: all;
}

section h2 + p, section img + p {
    margin-top: 0;
}

section img {
    column-span: all;
    margin: 1rem auto;
}
```

The second exciting part of this content

Suspendisse potenti. Vivamus at diam nec turpis suscipit vulputate. Aenean aliquet, odio ac venenatis rhoncus, nunc mi ultrices arcu, eget ullamcorper odio erat quis odio. Donec ac viverra elit. Sed sem

enim, convallis ut semper nec, placerat et mauris. Morbi laoreet consequat lacus, a mollis risus eleifend nec. Cras condimentum interdum facilisis. Nam malesuada lacinia eros eu ullamcorper. Maecenas

rutrum ullamcorper dictum. In lacinia congue enim, vel auctor quam tristique nec. Fusce ac diam eros. Phasellus sollicitudin leo a nibh elementum a imperdiet felis feugiat. Proin ultrices est ut metus

feugiat viverra. In hac habitasse platea dictumst.

In hac habitasse platea dictumst. Fusce consequat eros sit amet erat tincidunt in molestie lacus feugiat. Duis pretium arcu sed odio fermentum id semper justo tristique. Nullam tincidunt blandit porttitor. Maecenas eu odio nulla, sit amet hendrerit odio. In convallis rhoncus enim ac dignissim. Nam placerat

magna. Phasellus vitae lacus erat. Phasellus non tellus elit. Suspendisse est mauris, tristique vel venenatis ut, eleifend ullamcorper sapien.

Proin porta rhoncus erat non dictum. Integer eu auctor nunc. Donec vel cursus tortor. Integer diam

ante ipsum primis in faucibus orci luctus et ultrices posuere cubilia Curae; Sed euismod lectus dictum enim blandit mollis. Proin blandit condimentum sapien quis consectetur. Vivamus ullamcorper lectus accumsan neque dignissim suscipit. Quisque nec eros sit amet eros tempus mollis vel eu odio.

condimentum mauris bibendum. Ut at risus purus. Morbi laoreet, mauris a pharetra viverra, diam turpis pulvinar dolor, ac gravida sem sapien ac ligula. Vivamus eget augue mauris, quis accumsan sem. Sed eros urna, imperdiet sit amet rhoncus id, feugiat non justo. Fusce at arcu a eros faucibus lobortis nec vel

FIGURE 7.5 Causing selected elements of the layout to span multiple columns.

Note that I've also given the image some top and bottom margins, and removed the top margin from the paragraphs directly after a heading or image to make the paragraphs line up nicely across the columns. **Figure 7.5** shows the result.

column-span seems a bit limited in its effects: The only available values are 1 and all, which seems surprising. I would expect it to break items across a set number of columns higher than 1. In addition, it doesn't seem to work in Firefox at the time of this writing, which limits its cross-browser appeal. In Firefox the headings don't look too bad in one column, but the image looks rather broken. At the time of this writing, work is being done on implementing column-span in Firefox, but no ETA has been announced.

CONTROLLING WHERE THE COLUMNS BREAK

A number of properties defined in multi-col are intended to allow you to set where columns will break. To illustrate this, let's look at the file our-friends-multi-col. html. It is the same as the previous version of this example you saw, but I've added some <h3> elements into the mix and an unordered list to experiment with. As is, the situation isn't great; you'll tend to get unsightly column breaks in places, such as just after the <h3>s.

To remedy this problem, you need to tell the browser where to break your columns! The available break properties and their values are as follows:

- **break-before.** Controls breaking before the element(s) being selected. Possible values are auto, always, avoid, column, and avoid-column.

- **break-after.** Controls breaking after the element(s) being selected. Possible values are auto, always, avoid, column, and avoid-column.

- **break-inside.** Controls breaking inside the element(s) being selected. Possible values are auto, avoid, and avoid-column.

> **NOTE:** There are other break property values besides those listed, but they only apply to paged media: avoid-page, left, page, and right.

To stop the columns from breaking after headings, you could use the following ruleset:

```
h3 {
    break-after: avoid-column;
}
```

It is also best to always break columns before the <h3>s so they appear at the top of the columns. This can be done like so:

```
h3 {
    break-before: column;
}
```

A REAL MULTI-COLUMN LAYOUT

Let's finish off this section with a slightly more complicated example—a more traditional multi-col layout with different elements in each column rather than just a single body of text split into columns. Check out the file our-friends-multi-col.html, the first version of my parody Disney movie. It contains more complicated content: six character bios. Each bio consists of a heading, image, and paragraph:

```
<article>
    <h2>...</h2>
    <img src=" " alt=" ">
    <p>...</p>
</article>
```

The only multi-col property this uses is column-width, which allows the number of columns to change at different widths without modifying the content.

```
section {
    ...
    column-width: 36rem;
}
```

To get the columns to sit well, I set a fixed height on the articles:

```
article {
    ...
    height: 45rem;
    ...
}
```

You are now in possession of a useful little responsive multi-column layout (**Figure 7.6**). This layout is actually very quick to implement and is flexible, compared to using floats.

FIGURE 7.6 Try altering the width of the screen, and you'll see the number of columns adjust from three to two to one—very cool!

MULTI-COL PROBLEMS

Apart from some of the support issues documented earlier, the CSS Multi-column layout module has other problems associated with it. First, it obviously won't work in older browsers like IE6–9. To remedy this, you could use Modernizr to detect support for multi-col (see Chapter 5 for more information on Modernizr) and provide alternative styling for nonsupporting browsers, perhaps using some kind of slightly more limited floated layouts. Modernizr refers to multi-col as `csscolumns`. This is what you are testing for.

Second, multi-col has a fairly limited scope in terms of how it can be used: It was created to be used in specific circumstances where you want to put content into multiple columns and the content isn't too complicated. You can't create full magazine-style layouts or full multiple-column sites with multi-col, because you can't specify widths of individual columns, column breaking seems unreliable, and the spec in general is limited in scope. For such tasks, you need a combination of different layout tools.

USING **FLEXBOX**

Flexbox (www.w3.org/TR/css3-flexbox) is designed to facilitate some complicated layout techniques involving the spacing and ordering of child containers of a box. It is actually a new type of box model. To lay out some elements using Flexbox, you must set their parent container to use the new box model by using a new value of the display property:

```
section {
    display: flex;
}
```

Or if you want your container to be inline, you'd use this:

```
section {
    display: inline-flex;
}
```

Now let's get cooking with some examples.

FLEXBOX SYNTAX **CHANGES**

At the time of this writing, only Chrome Canary supported the new Flexbox syntax shown throughout this section. And it may well be different again by the time you read it; the spec has undergone a lot of changes in the time I've been writing this. In fact, I had to rewrite my Flexbox examples four times during the course of writing this book—such is the folly of trying to work with nascent specs! In any case, the chapter should still nicely demonstrate the concepts of Flexbox.

Other modern browsers currently support Flexbox but with an older version of the syntax from 2009. You can see how the new and old versions of the syntax map at http://wiki.csswg.org/spec/flexbox-2009-2011-spec-propertymapping.

To solve the problem of different browsers supporting different versions of Flexbox, if you are considering using Flexbox in a project, for now I'd recommend that you feed browsers the newest syntax by default, and then feed alternative styles to those that don't support the new syntax using Modernizr.

FIGURE 7.7 Our default, simple layout block is looking OK so far.

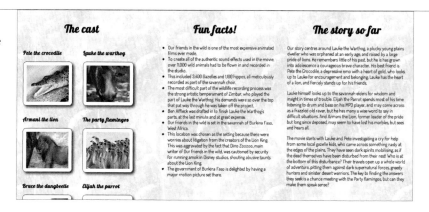

CONTROLLING FLEXBOX CHILD FLOW DIRECTION

Let's begin by briefly looking at an example of laying out some content using Flexbox. (See the file our-friends-flexbox.html in the chapter7 code download folder.) Three `<articles>` with varying content are contained in a `<section>`, and the `<section>` has been set to be laid out as a flexbox with this code:

```
section {
    display: flex;
    flex-flow: row;
}

article {
    width: 30%;
    padding: 1rem 2rem;
}
```

This causes the children to be laid out in a horizontal row (**Figure 7.7**).

If you wanted to lay out your child elements vertically instead in a column, you could do this:

```
section {
    display: flexbox;
    flex-flow: column;
}
```

FIGURE 7.8 Using row wrap to make child elements wrap neatly across different rows down the container is very useful in some circumstances.

And the great thing is that you can also reverse the direction the child elements are displayed in, either horizontally or vertically, by using row-reverse and column-reverse. Try these options to see what happens!

WRAPPING ELEMENTS ONTO NEW LINES

If there are enough child elements to overflow the parent element, you can make them wrap onto multiple lines by adding an extra keyword to the flex-flow property, as shown in the example file our-friends-flexbox-wrap.html:

```
section {
    display: flexbox;
    flex-flow: row wrap;
}
```

This is similar to the previous example but contains six `<article>`s of equal width, not three. This produces the result shown in **Figure 7.8**. Note how, when you reduce the width of the browser window, the layout will go from three to two to one column—a cool responsive effect.

Note: flex-flow is actually a shorthand property for setting the flex-direction and flex-wrap properties on one line. Their possible values are as follows:

- **flex-wrap**. nowrap, wrap, wrap-reverse

- **flex-direction**. row, row-reverse, column, column-reverse

MAIN AXIS, CROSS AXIS

Before you start doing much work with Flexbox, you should understand the concept of *main axis, cross axis*. The main axis is always the axis along which the flexbox children are arranged, and the cross axis crosses that. Depending on the direction your content is arranged, these axes will be swapped:

- If you are using flex-flow: row; or flex-flow: row-reverse;, the main axis will be horizontal, and the cross axis will be vertical. This is illustrated at the top in **Figure 7.9**.

- If you are using flex-flow: column; or flex-flow: column-reverse; , the main axis will be vertical, and the cross axis will be horizontal. This is illustrated at the bottom in Figure 7.9.

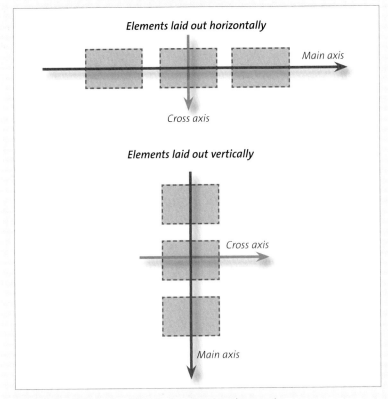

FIGURE 7.9 An illustration of Flexbox's main axis and cross axis.

CUSTOMIZING DISPLAY ORDER OF CHILD ELEMENTS

Another rather killer feature of Flexbox is that it gives you the ability to change the ordering of your child elements. This is done using the order property. For example, going back to the our-friends-flexbox.html example, if you want to grab the first <article> ("Fun facts!") and display it last, you could do this:

```
article:nth-of-type(2) {
    order: 1;
}
```

This initially looks illogical. Surely this code should cause it to appear first, not last. With flex-order, you put your child elements inside *ordinal groups*: The elements from each ordinal group appear from lowest ordinal group number to highest ordinal group number, starting from 0. If multiple elements appear in the same ordinal group, they will then be ordered inside the group according to their position in the original source order.

FIGURE 7.10 Varying the display order of the child elements using order.

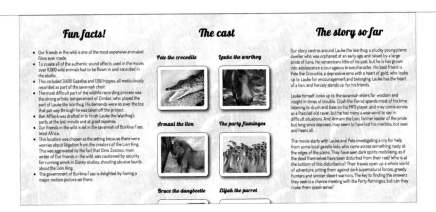

In the preceding code you are putting the first `<article>` into ordinal group 1. But the default ordinal group is 0; therefore, all the other elements will appear before it in their natural source order. If you want to make the fourth `<article>` appear first inside the flexbox, you could use the following:

```
article {

    ...

    order: 2;

}

article:nth-of-type(2) {

    order: 1;

}
```

See **Figure 7.10** for the result.

ALIGNING FLEXBOX CHILDREN

Flexbox also rocks big time when you want to align your flexbox children at the start, middle, or end of a column of content, for example. You can use the justify-content property to align your children along the main axis in whichever direction you've set that to be. The possible values are flex-start, flex-end, center, space-between, and space-around.

I've used this to lay out the <header> content of my example. I wanted the content all centered, horizontally and vertically. This kind of layout is usually quite difficult to do, especially vertically (because you can't rely on the old margin: auto trick for centering), and you usually end up messing around with positioning and inaccurate measurements.

To start with, you should set your <header> to be laid out like a flexbox in a vertical column:

```
header {
    display: flex;
    flex-flow: column;
}
```

By default this will lay out your elements in a column aligned to the left horizontally and sort of near the top vertically. Let's first align them in a better position vertically:

```
header {
    display: flexbox;
    flex-flow: column;
    justify-content: center;
}
```

FIGURE 7.11 Flexbox makes centering and equally spacing elements inside their container very easy.

Flexbox also makes another property available—align-items, which aligns the children along the cross axis, whichever direction that is at the time. You can use this to center the child elements horizontally, like so:

```
header {
    display: flex;
    justify-content: center;
    flex-pack: justify;
    align-items: center;
}
```

Figure 7.11 shows the result of this addition.

NOTES: Possible values for align-items are flex-start, flex-end, center, baseline, and stretch.

There is also a property, align-self, which takes the same values as align-items. align-self, when applied to individual children of a flexbox, can be used to override behavior set on all children by align-items.

THE FLEXIBILITY OF FLEXBOX

The last Flexbox feature you'll look at is the ability to make child elements and their surrounding whitespace flexible. The property you need to do this is flex, as shown here:

```
section {
    display: flexbox;
    flex-flow: row;
}
article {
    flex: 1 1 200px;
}
```

So what do the three arguments inside the function do?

The third value is the preferred size of the child elements. If specified, the size value will be applied to all the children before the other arguments come into effect. So if you set this as 200 pixels, each child element will have a width of 200 pixels (or height, if flex-flow is set to column rather than row).

The first value is the positive flex, a proportion that dictates what share of remaining space available in the parent the children will have. So, for example, if the parent element of the three <article>s was 750 pixels and each one had a positive flex value of 1, as in the preceding code, the extra 150 pixels would be split equally between the children; each one would end up as 250 pixels wide.

If one of the children had a positive flex of 2, it would receive twice as much of the remaining space as the other two, so would end up as (150/4 x 2) + 200 = 275 pixels. The other two would be 150/4 + 200 = 237.5 pixels. The positive flex is the only mandatory argument.

The second value is the negative flex and is also a proportion, except that it works in the opposite direction to the positive flex value. This dictates what happens when the children of the flexbox overflow their parent. In the preceding example, if the parent element was 750 pixels wide and the children had a preferred size of 300 pixels for a total width of 900 pixels, they would overflow the parent by 150 pixels. A negative flex value of 1 given to all of them would cause each one to be reduced by 50 pixels to stop them overflowing their parent; each would end up as 250 pixels wide.

If one of the children had a negative flex of 2, it would be reduced in width by twice as much as the other two, so would end up as 300 - (150/4 x 2) = 225 pixels. The other two would be 300 - 150/4 = 262.5 pixels. So in the case of negative flex, a lower number means less of a reduction and therefore a wider element!

Note: If no explicit negative flex value is set, the default value comes into play, which is 1.

This is complex, so let's go over the workflow here. If you specify all three arguments, the workflow looks like this:

1. The preferred size is applied to all the flexbox children.

2. The remaining space is divided between the flexbox children according to the positive flex value set.

3. If the combined width (or height) of the children causes them to overflow the parent container, the negative flex values, if set, will shrink them down until they fit in. The ratio of these will dictate how much each child is shrunk by.

Note that flex is actually a shorthand property. You can see the three values it holds individually using flex-grow, flex-shrink, and flex-basis.

Time for an example! Look at the our-friends-flexbox-flexible.html file in the chapter7 code download folder. This is the same as our-friends-flexbox.html but with some experimental flex values applied to the <article>s. Be prepared to follow along and change them if you want to experience the different effects.

Let's start by setting the following values on the child <articles>:

```
#cast {
    flex: 1;
}

#facts {
    flex: 1;
}

#plot {
    flex: 1;
}
```

FIGURE 7.12 In the current layout, The Cast and Facts containers have been given an equal proportion of the flexible space. I've included a subtle background on the child elements in this example so you can more easily see what is going on.

FIGURE 7.13 The Cast is now taking up twice as much space as the Facts.

This code produces the result shown in **Figure 7.12**. The three <articles> have been given flex: 1, which gives them a positive flex ratio of 1 : 1 : 1, so they will always take up an equal part of whatever space is available.

Now let's see what happens when you give the #cast container a flex value of 2:

```
#cast {
    flex: 2;
}
```

Figure 7.13 shows the effect. The ratio is now 2 : 1 : 1, so the Cast is now given twice as much of the flexible space as the others.

Let's briefly explore the other two arguments and their effects. Try setting these values on your properties:

```css
#cast {
    flex: 1 400px;
}

#facts {
    flex: 1 250px;
}

#plot {
    flex: 1 250px;
}
```

In this case, you are setting widths of 400, 250, and 250 pixels on the flexible containers; the remaining width is then divided equally between them, because the positive flex is set to 1 for all of them.

Now try these values:

```css
#cast {
    flex: 1 400px;
}

#facts {
    flex: 1 400px;
}

#plot {
    flex: 1 500px;
}
```

Here, the combined widths would cause the containers to overflow their parent, which would look horrible. Fortunately, a default negative flex value of 1 is set on all of the children, which causes them all to shrink by an equal amount of the overflow, meaning that all is well. If you wanted one of the children to be reduced by a larger amount than the others, you could set an explicit negative flex value on it, for example:

```
#plot {
    flex: 1 3 500px;
}
```

Now the flexible boxes are shrunk in size until they no longer overflow their container. Because the negative flex ratio #cast to #facts is 1 : 3, #cast will have ¼ of the total width reduction applied to it, and #facts will have ¾ of the total width reduction applied to it.

This would cause the Plot to be shrunk by ⅗ths of the overflow amount, and the other two to be shrunk by only ⅕th—the shrinking ratio is 1 : 1 : 3.

CROSS-BROWSER FLEXBOX WITH MODERNIZR

As you've seen, Flexbox is very useful for solving some specific types of layout problems. The main problem with it right now is the lack of browser support. The new syntax you've seen so far in this section is only supported in Chrome Canary at the time of this writing.

To make it work across a wider range of browsers at the moment, you'll need to feed other browsers the now deprecated 2009 Flexbox syntax that was implemented by Firefox, WebKit browsers, and IE.

> **NOTE:** The site http://wiki.csswg.org/spec/flexbox-2009-2011-spec-property-mapping provides a fairly useful table showing the mapping between the old and new syntaxes, although this is now somewhat out of date. Peter Gasston, tech reviewer for this book, has written a useful guide to the old syntax at www.netmagazine.com/tutorials/css3-flexible-box-model-explained.

You can put your cross-browser flexbox into action using your old friend Modernizr. Modernizr detects support for the new Flexbox syntax (flexbox/no-flexbox) and the old version (flexbox-legacy/no-flexbox-legacy).

Look at the code download file our-friends-flexbox-modernizr.html. This is the same as the previous example you looked at except that Modernizr is included on the page, and a whole raft of legacy Flexbox properties are applied to browsers that only support the old syntax using Modernizr's descendant selector system. I won't list all of the fallback code here, but you can find it under the "Modernizr fallback rules" flag in the our-friends-flexbox-modernizr.html file.

These properties work fairly well and are fairly self-explanatory, although I found that box-flex (the old syntax of flex) seemed to work slightly oddly and unreliably. Hopefully, browsers will support the new syntax soon so that this kind of craziness will become a thing of the past!

TIP: To provide browsers that don't even support the old Flexbox syntax with alternative layout rules, use .no-flexbox-legacy xxx { ... }.

EXPLORING **GRIDS**

The CSS Grid Positioning Module Level 3 (www.w3.org/TR/css3-grid) is designed to allow web designers to lay out web pages neatly in a stable grid. You most likely already do this, but usually you create your own grid system or use a third-party framework, such as 960 (http://960.gs) or Blueprint CSS (http://blueprintcss.org). CSS3 grids offer a simple native way of creating your own grid system, which has to be a good thing.

At the time of this writing, CSS3 grids are only supported by IE10 and nightly builds of the WebKit browsers (with -ms- and -webkit- prefixes, respectively), so I won't cover them in depth. However, I'll provide you with a solid example of how to use them, because they are bound to be important in the future.

In this example you'll put together a simple grid layout using these nu-schule-kool-toolz (technical term.)

DEFINING THE GRID STRUCTURE

In a similar fashion to Flexbox, CSS3 grids work by using a custom value of the `display` property, `grid`, to designate a container as an area of the page that will be laid out using CSS3 grids (look at the file simple-grid.html in the chapter7 code download folder to follow along with this first example):

```
body {
    display: grid;
}
```

You then divide this container into columns and rows using the `grid-columns` and `grid-rows` properties, like so:

```
body {
    display: grid;
    grid-columns: 30rem 40rem 30rem;
    grid-rows: 1fr 1fr 1fr 1fr;
}
```

The `grid-columns` property specifies three columns in the grid, and they are 30 rems wide, 40 rems wide, and 30 rems wide, respectively. In this case, the `grid-rows` property is using a new CSS unit called `fr` (fraction), which means *I will be this many parts of the total big.* So in this case you have four rows that are all `1fr` big for a total of `4fr`. Therefore, each row spans 1/4 of the total height of the body.

You could also use percentages, other CSS length units, or `auto` to specify columns, for example:

```
body {
    display: grid;
    grid-columns: 30% 40% 30%;
    grid-rows: 1fr 1fr 1fr 1fr;
}
```

In this alternative version, I've changed `grid-columns` so that the columns are percentages (you can see this alternative example in simple-grid2.html). Percentages work the way you'd expect them to, although you need to be careful about using weird combinations of percentages and absolute unit values: If they end up as less than 100% in one or both dimensions, you'll waste space and produce unexpected results. If they end up as more than 100%, your content may be cut off.

FITTING YOUR CONTENT ONTO THE GRID

Next, you need to start fitting your content onto the grid. This is done by applying some special properties to the child elements of the container that is set to display as a grid. In this simple example, the children look like this:

```
<header>
    <h1>Header</h1>
</header>
<div id="block1">Block 1</div>
<div id="block2">Block 2</div>
<div id="block3">Block 3</div>
<div id="block4">Block 4</div>
<footer>
    <h2>Footer</h2>
</footer>
```

You can fit these elements to the grid you defined earlier using the following properties:

- **grid-column** specifies the column the child element will be placed in, or start in, in the case of children that span multiple columns.

- **grid-column-span** specifies the number of columns that the child element will span (optional).

- **grid-row** specifies the row the child element will be placed in, or start in, in the case of children that span multiple rows.

- **grid-row-span** specifies the number of rows that the child element will span (optional).

FIGURE 7.14 A simple grid layout in action.

So, for example, you could lay out your content like this:

```
header {
    grid-column: 1;
    grid-column-span: 3;
    grid-row: 1;
}

footer {
    grid-column: 1;
    grid-column-span: 3;
    grid-row: 4;
}

#block1 {
    background-color: blue;
    grid-column: 1;
    grid-row: 2;
    grid-row-span: 2;
}

/* And so on - look at the code file for the rest of it */
```

This simple grid layout is shown in **Figure 7.14**.

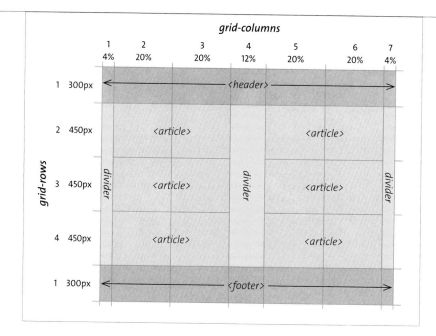

FIGURE 7.15 A schematic of the example grid.

You can use nested grids if you like to create all kinds of complicated layouts, although if you consider doing this, your information architecture might need revisiting! I'm sure this simple example gives you a good idea of how powerful these grids can be, especially considering that you can create liquid grids as well as fixed grids, and you can place elements wherever you like on the grid regardless of source order and structure.

A REAL GRID EXAMPLE

Now let's look at a more complex example. Here you'll go back and re-lay out the "our-friends" in the wild example again using CSS grids. As you follow along, you can look at the file our-friends-css-grids.html in the code download to find the right code if you go wrong at some point.

As grids become more complex, it's best to start drawing them out on paper (or some other medium) and then refer to the sketch as you start placing your content. The grid you'll use looks something like the one shown in **Figure 7.15**.

FIGURE 7.16 Using CSS grids to lay out our lovely animal friends.

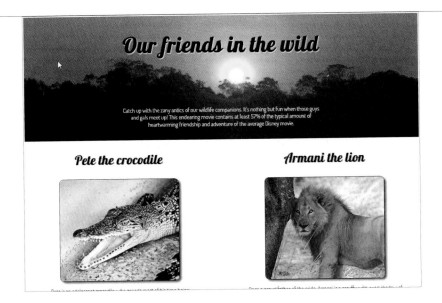

I've provided you with the columns and rows declarations free of charge:

```
grid-columns: 4% 20% 20% 12% 20% 20% 4%;
grid-rows: 300px 450px 450px 450px 300px;
```

Now you need to work out rulesets to place all the content in the places shown on the schematic. Look at the example file if you get stuck! The final example looks the one shown in **Figure 7.16**.

GRID PROBLEMS

IE10 is the only browser with decent support for CSS grids at the time of writing. However, I believe it was worth talking about them, because all the browser vendors have shown an interest in them of late.

You could also argue that they are not quite as flexible as other layout methods you've seen already. One aspect of grids that surprised me is that you can only place immediate children of the grid layout element on the grid. But I think it depends on how you use them. For example, you could use a simple grid to place a header, footer, and three columns easily, and then lay out the content inside them using a different mechanism, such as Flexbox. A combination of these layout methods would prove effective in your layout design.

OTHER **LAYOUT MODULES**
WORTHY OF **MENTION**

A few other CSS3 layout modules are also worth mentioning, although I'll just talk about them briefly, because their browser support and finished status is even more nonexistent than those you've learned about already.

REGIONS

The CSS Regions Module Level 3 spec (http://dev.w3.org/csswg/css3-regions) defines a set of functionality for specifying different elements to flow content into. This was supported in IE10 and Chrome/Safari nightlies at the time of this writing. But at the time, the spec looked to be very much in flux and likely to change—hence my unwillingness to cover it in much detail.

However, for completeness I'll walk you through it. See the file simple-regions-ms.html in the chapter7 code download folder for an example that will work in IE10. Here you have a set of `<div>`s for laying out content into:

```
<section id="layout">

    <div id="region1" class="region"></div>

    <div id="region2"><img src="images/sunset.jpg"
    ➞ alt="sunset image"></div>

    <div id="region3" class="region"></div>

    <div id="region4" class="region"></div>

    <div id="region5" class="region"></div>

</section>
```

The actual content is stored in a separate file—region-content.html—and included at the bottom of the main example page using an iFrame:

```
<iframe id="region-content" src="region-content.html">
```

The region's magic works as follows: You identify the source of the content (in this case, the iFrame) by its ID and give it a keyword of your choosing:

```
#region-content {

    -ms-flow-into: my-regions;

}
```

FIGURE 7.17 Using CSS regions to lay out content into a grid.

FIGURE 7.17 Using CSS regions
to lay out content into a grid.

You then dictate where the content should flow into by applying your keyword to the relevant elements. In this case, I wanted the content to flow into the four `<div>`s that have a class of `region`:

```css
.region {
    padding: 1rem;
    background-color: red;
    border: 1px solid white;
    -ms-flow-from: my-regions;
}
```

This is how it currently works in IE10, and it produces the layout shown in **Figure 7.17**. Note how I've actually created this layout using a CSS grid. Indeed, you can lay out the page in any way you want, and then put the content into elements of your choosing using regions.

Try resizing the browser window and note how the content keeps reflowing inside the regions: The reason is that I've set the width of the grid rows using percentages. The content starts to flow into the first region in the source order and then continues to the second region when the first is filled, and so on.

WebKit-based browsers currently support regions but with a different syntax that isn't limited to using an iFrame to contain the content:

```
#region-content {
    content: -webkit-from-flow("flow_name");
}

.region {
    -webkit-flow: "flow_name";
}
```

An example of this that will work in Chrome Canary only (at the time of this writing) can be seen in simple-regions-webkit.html. Be warned though: To enable CSS regions in this browser, you currently need to type **about:flags** into the Chrome Canary URL bar, enable CSS Regions in the settings, and relaunch.

> **TIP:** In the same manner as multi-col, you can use break properties to specify where content should and shouldn't break when it is nearing the edge of your regions. See http://dev.w3.org/csswg/css3-regions/#region-flow-break for more details.

EXCLUSIONS

The idea behind the CSS Exclusions and Shapes Module Level 3 (http://dev.w3.org/csswg/css3-exclusions) is that you can define a shape or specify an element and then flow content around that shape/element, thereby creating complicated layouts. You might see these types of layouts in a magazine with text flowing around an image of a mountain or a floated image halfway between two columns of text. You can think of exclusions as a way to create more powerful floats. Indeed, CSS3 did have a feature called positioned floats, which was invented by Microsoft, but this seems to have been merged with the Exclusions spec now.

Exclusions aren't supported anywhere at the time of this writing, but I'll at least give you an idea of how they are supposed to work. To make a more interesting float, you could have a simple section with a figure inside it, like this:

```
<section>
    ...
    <figure> ... </figure>
    ...
</section>
```

You should be able to absolutely position the figure inside the section, and then turn it into an exclusion using the wrap-flow property:

```
figure {
    position: absolute;
    color: #fff;
    top: 30%;
    left: 40%;
    wrap-flow: both;
}
```

You can then give it padding and a margin, like so:

```
figure {
    position: absolute;
    color: #fff;
    top: 30%;
    left: 40%;
    wrap-flow: both;
    wrap-padding: 10px;
    wrap-margin: 10px;
}
```

wrap-flow specifies what side of the exclusion element, in this case the figure, you want the text to flow around. You can specify auto, start, end, both, maximum, or clear:

- **auto** is the default: If you set this value, the surrounding text will not wrap around the exclusion; it will just sit underneath the exclusion element as if it doesn't exist.

- **start** means that content will wrap around the start of the exclusion, but the space after the end of it will be left empty of content.

- **end** means that content will wrap around the end of the exclusion, but the space before the start of it will be left empty of content.

- **both** means that the content will wrap around the start and end of the exclusion.

- **maximum** will cause content to wrap around the side of the exclusion that has the largest amount of space next to it.

- **clear** means that content will only wrap around the top and bottom of the exclusion; the space to the left and right (start and end) of it will be left empty.

wrap-margin specifies how much margin you want left between the exclusion element and the rest of the content.

wrap-padding specifies how much padding you want left between the exclusion element and the rest of the content.

If you have multiple exclusions interacting inside the same space, they should wrap around one another in reverse order of how they are placed in the document. See http://dev.w3.org/csswg/css3-exclusions/#exclusions-order for more details.

If you want your content to flow around a more complicated shape, you can define what the shape of the exclusion will be using the shapes part of the Exclusions spec: See http://dev.w3.org/csswg/css3-exclusions/#shapes. You'll be able to create circles, ellipses, and so on to shape your exclusions or even base those shapes on images.

GCPM

Finally, let's look at the CSS Generated Content for Paged Media (GCPM) module (www.w3.org/TR/css3-gcpm). This module is currently supported only by the experimental "Opera Reader" technology, but it is lots of fun to play with. You can set your whole web page (or a small part of it) to be paginated using rulesets defined in a special paged at-rule:

```
@media -o-paged {

    ...

}
```

To set the whole page content, you can do this:

```
@media -o-paged {

    html {

        height: 100%;

        overflow: -o-paged-x;

    }

}
```

When you load this page in a supporting browser, the whole page content will be paginated, and you can flick through the pages by swiping left and right on a touch device, and by using arrow keys on a non touch device.

Opera Reader/GCPM has many more features besides. See Håkon Wium Lie's website at http://people.opera.com/howcome/2011/reader for experimental builds and a more complete treatment.

WRAPPING **UP**

In this chapter you explored some of the new layout features contained among the CSS3 modules, including multi-col, flexbox, exclusions, and generated content for paged media.

A significant number of these features are currently not supported across browsers, and unfortunately, some of them don't degrade gracefully, causing layouts to completely break in those browsers that don't support them. However, browser vendors are working hard on adding support for them. In the meantime, you can provide alternative styling to nonsupporting browsers through tools like Modernizr, and you should be prepared for the revolution when it comes.

8

RESPONSIVE AND ADAPTIVE DESIGN

One of the biggest challenges faced by web developers and designers today is optimizing websites so they look and perform well across a wide range of devices that differ significantly in screen size, processing power, and so on. You no longer just have to think about different browsers on a desktop or laptop. You now have to consider mobile phones (both modern smartphones and older feature phones), tablets, web-enabled TVs, and other devices.

This may sound like a nightmare, and with more web-enabled devices no doubt appearing every year, you might think it'll get worse. How on earth do you provide a good web experience across all these devices?

In this chapter I'll discuss high-level strategies and implementation options available for combatting such problems.

A **BRIEF HISTORY** OF
WEB BROWSERS

When the web was first introduced in the early to mid-90s, it was basically viewable using web browser software installed on personal computers (first desktops, and slightly later, laptops). These computers had monitors with resolutions of 640 x 480 pixels, 800 x 600 pixels, and later on, 1024 x 768 pixels. This didn't really change much until the middle of the 2000s when mobile phones became powerful enough to run real web browsers (OK, before that was a lame standard called WAP, but I won't bother discussing it here; you can look it up if you are interested).

Fast forward a few more years and a huge variety of devices are now capable of browsing the web:

- Modern smart phones do a great job of rendering websites, for example, iPhones, Android-based devices, and BlackBerry and Nokia phones running Opera Mobile, Mobile Chrome, Fennec, and other browsers.

- Several varieties of tablets are available too, mainly iPads and a slew of Android-based devices, again running similar browsers to those described previously but with larger screens.

- TVs are increasingly becoming web-enabled: You can view the web on TVs (from companies like Sony, Samsung, and Ikea) with built-in browsers and on games consoles run through TVs (like the Nintendo Wii and the PlayStation 3).

- Portable game consoles like the Nintendo 3DS and Sony Vita all have web browsers as well.

- Many people in the world still browse the web using feature phones that don't have very good web browsers installed or use a proxy browser, such as Opera Mini to gain access to web content (see the "Opera Mini" sidebar).

OPERA MINI

Opera Mini is a proxy-based browser that doesn't work like a normal web browser. Usually, you install a browser on your device that has full rendering capabilities. When a web page is browsed to, the code, images, and other assets that make up that web page are downloaded to your device and interpreted and assembled into a web page by the browser for you to interact with. But Opera Mini does not have full rendering capabilities; it is merely a thin client that can display a static format similar to PDF called OBML (Opera Binary Markup Language). The web-page code and assets, when requested, are actually downloaded to a server farm to be assembled into the web page and are then compressed into this OBML format.

The OBML page is then sent to the device to be displayed. This system has some big advantages: First, OBML is a static, compressed format. The size of the pages you are viewing can be reduced by up to 90 percent using this system, meaning much smaller downloads, which is great for those on slow networks and those still paying for web access by the kilobyte. Second, because rendering is done on the server, the Mini client is very small and simple; therefore, it can run on low-powered phones—pretty much anything with a JVM (Java Virtual Machine).

Opera Mini does have its disadvantages too. Rendering will not look as nice, because many styling features, such as box shadows and web fonts, are turned off to save on bandwidth and processing power requirements. In addition, OBML just provides a static snapshot of the page you are viewing at the time it was rendered; therefore, animated content (CSS animations, JavaScript-based animations, Flash, or even animated GIFs) won't work, and background script operations, such as Ajax page updates, won't work either. This means that web applications that rely on heavy scripting may not perform very well, depending on whether the developer responsible tested in Opera Mini and used progressive enhancement to still provide a workable experience without JavaScript.

But most websites work well on Opera Mini. The point is not to provide a perfect browsing experience, but to provide a fast, usable browsing experience that works on nearly any device. It is worth installing Opera Mini on a high-powered device, such as an iPhone. If you are stuck on a slow, mobile phone network and desperately need to use the web, Opera Mini can be very useful.

FIGURE 8.1 Graceful degradation of CSS3 bling in Opera 12 desktop (left) and in Opera Mini 6 (right).

Broadly speaking, there are three main strategies for optimizing web content across different devices. Let's look at each one in detail.

DO NOTHING SPECIAL

Do nothing special sounds great, huh? The truth is that as long as you create web content using open standards and best practices, as detailed in this book and other decent learning resources, your content will probably be accessible across most devices. The web is responsive by default. The <body> element will cover 100 percent of the browser window width unless you tell it not to. And if you use floats to arrange repeated content blocks in rows and size containers in percentages rather than absolute measurements, your layout will have some degree of flexibility as browser windows become narrower.

In addition, many HTML5 and CSS3 features will degrade gracefully in nonsupporting browsers. As you can see in my CSS bling example in Opera 12 (**Figure 8.1**, left) and in Opera Mini 6 (Figure 8.1, right), many of the bling effects don't work in Opera Mini, but the content is still readable.

NOTE: The Opera Mini screen shot shown in Figure 8.1 is actually taken from the Opera Mini simulator, which is available at www.opera.com/developer/tools/mini.

FIGURE 8.2 Most mobile phone browsers have zoom functionality, as illustrated here in the Opera Mobile Emulator for desktop (available at www.opera.com/developer/tools/mobile).

Mobile device browsers tend to display a zoomed-out version of web pages and then provide zoom features to enable you to see different parts of the content more closely (**Figure 8.2**).

SERVE DIFFERENT SITES TO DIFFERENT DEVICES

So doing nothing can make your content accessible on most browsers, but often you'll want more control over how your content looks on different devices, and your client will want a more tailored approach. How many times has your client or boss said, "I want an awesome iPad app"? Also, various browsing contexts will often call for different content. Mobile phone users frequently want to just browse to a website quickly to find train times, look up a map, or play a little throwaway game because they are bored. They don't want to see pages of staff bios or a giant movie featuring your company's CEO explaining your company history.

It is therefore a good idea to, for example, serve mobile users a different set of content by default—a mobile version of the site that just contains the most important features a user might want to use on the move. Traditionally, this is done by detecting what user agent string a browser has and redirecting the browser to a mobile version of the website, perhaps at mysite.mobi instead of mysite.com.

Although this might seem like a good idea, it is fraught with problems and you must be careful. First, you'll have to publish and maintain two or more versions of your site (desktop version, mobile version, iPad app, TV app, etc.), which adds more time and cost to the project.

Second, doing browser sniffing is error prone and shortsighted. If you are just detecting the iPad, for example, because you have a specific iPad app, it might not be so bad. But it usually makes more sense to develop sites to work across all devices, not just one. Also, user agent strings are deliberately ambiguous, because back in the early days of the web, developers started using user agent sniffing to arbitrarily target browsers they wanted to support, leaving other browsers locked out, even if they could render those sites perfectly well. To get access to these sites, browsers started aping other vendors' user agent strings, so you'd end up with user agent strings like this:

```
Mozilla/5.0 (Windows; U; Windows NT 5.1; en-US) AppleWebKit/525.13
→ (KHTML, like Gecko) Chrome/0.2.149.27 Safari/525.13
```

And even if your code is serving the right content to the right browsers now, it may not in the future when new browsers come out that have different user agent strings. You'll have to keep updating your code to take these new browsers into account! As an example, when Opera hit version 10, the user agent string was changed to include a version number of 9.81, because so many developers were using browser sniffing code that returned Opera 10+ as Opera 1, thereby blocking browsers from accessing sites that would render them fine. Hilarity ensued. Really.

It is much more effective and less error prone to test whether browsers support the features your sites need, as you've been doing with Modernizr, rather than testing whether the browser is one of the ones you *think* will support your code.

TIP: You should always provide a link to switch between site versions too, in case a mobile user wants to use the desktop version of the site instead. Users hate having their choices taken away!

TERMINOLOGY **CONFUSION!**

You were probably wowed when you first read the delicious buzzword-laden title of this chapter. I included both "responsive design" and "adaptive design" because you'll probably hear these two terms and various other word combinations to describe the techniques this chapter covers in your travels around the interwebs.

In fact, I was confused about when to use which term. So, after doing a bit of research on the subject, the best distinction between "adaptive" and "responsive" that I came up with is as follows:

- **Responsive design** refers to the use of technologies like media queries and flexible units to create flexible web page/app layouts that are optimized to suit different-sized viewports.

- **Adaptive design** is pretty much another term for "progressive enhancement," which of course was defined in Chapter 1, and examples have been shown throughout the book. Adaptive design refers to any design that allows a website to adapt and provide an acceptable experience in browsers of different abilities. You could think of responsive design as a subset of adaptive design.

You'll also hear the term "mobile web" quite a lot, especially from manager types; it's used to describe the web created for mobile devices, or some such thing. I recommend that you stay away from this term as much as possible.

Designer and all-round "good bloke" Stephen Hay summed it up nicely when he said: *"There is no mobile web. There is only the web, which we view in different ways. There is also no desktop web. Or tablet web. Thank you."*

Creating different sites for different devices is not really the right way to think about accessing web content; you should strive to optimize the same content for different devices.

A better way to think about "mobile" is a state of being rather than a device. When users are mobile, they are more likely to be using various devices to browse the web, have less bandwidth available, and be interested in different information and functionality. This leads to a separate set of requirements for people who are stationary and those who are on the move. Therefore, different versions of your site will require different UX work.

OPTIMIZE ONE SITE FOR DIFFERENT BROWSERS/DEVICES

The third method for optimizing web content across devices generally involves using responsive/adaptive design techniques to create a single set of content that will automatically change depending on features of the browser accessing it, such as screen width and height, resolution, and more.

Usually these techniques involve:

- **Feature detection** to see if a feature will work in a browser and serving fallback content if it doesn't (e.g., using Modernizr).

- **Using flexible layout techniques**, such as CSS multi-col and percentages for container widths, so that layouts will breathe and still look good on smaller screens and browser windows.

- **Serving smaller images**, videos, and other media to smaller screen devices that don't need the bigger versions and could really benefit from being saved some bandwidth.

- **Using smart layout optimization** technologies, such as CSS media queries and viewport, to change how content is displayed depending on screen width, resolution, orientation, and other features of the browsing device.

Support for the nu-school features discussed in this chapter is summarized in **Table 8.1**.

TABLE 8.1 Browser Support for Responsive Design Features

BROWSER	MEDIA QUERIES	\<SOURCE> MEDIA ATTRIBUTE	VIEWPORT META TAG	@VIEWPORT CSS
Opera	Since 9.5	?*	n/a**	n/a**
Firefox	Since 3.5	?*	n/a**	n/a**
Safari	Since 4	?*	n/a**	n/a**
Chrome	Since 4	?*	n/a**	n/a**
Internet Explorer	Since 9	?*	n/a**	n/a**
iOS	Since 3.2	?*	Since 3.2	No
Android	Since 2.1	?*	Since 2.1	No
Mobile Chrome	Since beta	?*	Since beta	No
Opera Mobile	Since 10	?*	Since 10.0	Since 11.0
Opera Mini	Since 5	?*	Since 6.0	No

* It was difficult to find any concrete, detailed support data for the \<source> media attribute. But from my tests, it seems to work well across all the latest desktop and mobile browsers.

** The Viewport meta tag and @viewport aren't relevant to nonmobile browsers.

Optimizing one site for different browsers/devices is the strategy mainly covered in this chapter. It is arguably the best and most future-proof way of optimizing your content for different browsers/devices. In reality, most modern sites will use a combination of this strategy and the preceding strategy—serving different sites to different devices—to provide a decent experience to various devices. Let's move on and look at some groovalicious, modern web-design techniques.

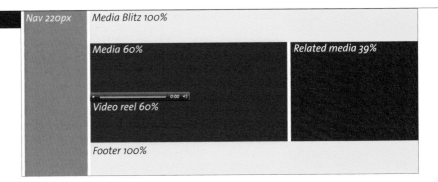

FIGURE 8.3 A raw flexible layout.

So far in this book, I've deliberately not considered responsive design very much because I wanted to dedicate this chapter to it! However, you've already seen some of the elements of responsive design without even knowing it, mainly the flexible techniques I'll talk about in this section.

CONTAINERS THAT BREATHE

The first important optimizing technique is sizing containers in percentages to allow your containers to breathe a little so the layout will still look OK and fit in slightly different screen sizes. This is demonstrated by the main example I'll use in this chapter, which is a responsive media site called Media Blitz. You can find the finished version in the media_blitz folder in the code download files. So hop on over to the chapter8 folder and open the file media-blitz-1-base-layout.html file to start with. This file literally just includes the raw container layout information (**Figure 8.3**).

This layout was pretty easy to put together. The code should be self-explanatory if you know your basic CSS. Don't worry about the height of the content right now. Instead, focus on the fact that however you resize your browser window, the different blocks keep to the indicated proportions because the containers are all sized using percentages.

NOTE: In the future when browser support is better, you'll be able to create flexible layouts in a much easier way, with less markup, using some of the advanced layout techniques in Chapter 7. For now, I've just stuck to good ol' floats.

FIGURE 8.4 The flexible layout with the content filled in. Love that retro feel!

FIGURE 8.5 Media elements overflowing their containers = ugly!

Now open the file media-blitz-2-with-content.html, which looks like **Figure 8.4**. This file is the same as the previous version but with some content filled in for you to work with.

RESPONSIVE MEDIA LAYOUTS

The layout I've created so far looks perfectly reasonable. As you increase and decrease the width slightly, it breathes. The sizes of the different containers change, and their relative proportions change, meaning that you can still see all of the layout.

Text will reflow flawlessly in these situations, but you can soon run into problems with images and video. If an image or video overflows its bounds, the result will get ugly, as shown in **Figure 8.5**.

FIGURE 8.6 Using max-width: 100% to make media flexible.

A good way to get the media elements to also breathe inside their containers is to set max-width: 100%; on those elements. So even when the images and videos are larger than their containers, they will be constrained inside. And as the containers shrink or grow, the media elements will shrink and grow with them (**Figure 8.6**).

To give you some examples, I've used this trick on the main playing video, the related reels, and the other "videos" in the reel:

```css
video {
    max-width: 100%;
}

#related article {
        ...
    width: 35%;
    margin: 2rem 2%;
    padding: 2rem 3%;
}

#related img {
    display: block;
    margin: 0 auto;
    max-width: 100%;
}

#video-reel article {
    width: 33%;
    display: inline-block;
    opacity: 0.7;
}

#video-reel img {
    max-width: 100%;
}
```

FIGURE 8.7 Setting an upper bound on the layout width using max-width.

Another good way to use max-width when creating responsive layouts is to set an upper bound on your layout width. When your layout starts to look ghastly in very wide viewports (and let's face it, big "cinema-screen" monitors are increasingly common these days), you can control the result using something like this:

```
body {
    max-width: 1300px;
    margin: 0 auto;
}
```

When the upper bound is reached, the layout will no longer grow but instead be centered inside whatever space is available, as shown in **Figure 8.7**.

TIP: max-width is not supported in IE7 and earlier; therefore, I've set width: 100% as a fallback in the iefixes.css file included in one of my conditional comments (along with pixel fallbacks for all the units set in rems, which aren't supported in IE8 and earlier). But you must be careful with this: width is way less flexible than max-width. If the container is smaller than the image, the image will maintain its set width and overflow the container.

MEDIA QUERIES

The Media Blitz example is looking good now, but it is still not great. When you resize the screen less than 1024px in width, the <h1> wraps onto two lines, and the media elements start to look tiny and insignificant. This is unacceptable given that they are supposed to be the main content of the site!

Wouldn't it be great if you had a mechanism to dynamically alter the layout of your site based on features such as width and height?

Well, here's the good news: The Media Queries spec (www.w3.org/TR/css3-mediaqueries) allows you to do just that! In a nutshell, it extends the functionality of CSS3 media types, which allow you to apply styles to markup based on whether it is onscreen, being printed, and so on:

```
@media print {
    /* print styles go here */
}

<link rel="stylesheet" media="print" href="print.css">
```

Media queries go even further, allowing you to apply styles based on media types plus the result of tests on the condition of media features, such as browser viewport width, screen orientation, resolution, and more. Here is a simple example:

```
@media screen and (max-width: 800px) {
    /* put your styles here */
}
```

This code block specifies the following: *For the screen media type only, if the width of the browser window is 800 pixels or less, apply the styles within the block. If these conditions aren't true, completely ignore the rules within the block.* You can immediately see how powerful this feature is. It means that you can start applying different styles to your site depending on features like screen width, so you can provide one layout for a wide viewport, one for a narrow viewport, and as many more as you like!

If you want to apply your custom styles to any media type, you can use the keyword all, or just omit the media type. The following are equivalent:

```
@media all and (max-width: 800px)
@media (max-width: 800px)
```

You can use the not keyword to indicate that you want to apply your styles in any case other than the one evaluated as true by the media query. For example:

```
@media not screen and (max-width: 800px) {
    /* put your styles here */
}
```

You can chain further conditions onto the ends of your media queries to enforce stricter conditions, for example:

```
@media screen and (max-width: 800px) and (orientation: landscape) {
    /* put your styles here */
}
```

If you want to apply the same set of conditional styles when multiple conditions are true, you can put the different sets of conditions on the same line, separated by commas, like so:

```
@media screen and (max-width: 800px), print and (max-width: 29.7cm)
{
    /* put your styles here */
}
```

The most common media features you'll want to test are as follows:

- **min/max-width and min/max-height.** Apply styles depending on the width or height of your browser window's viewport: the part of the window that the web page is actually displayed in.

- **min/max-device-width and min/max-device-height.** Apply styles depending on the physical width or height of the device rather than the viewport. The importance of this distinction will become apparent later in the chapter.

- **aspect-ratio/device-aspect-ratio.** Apply styles based on aspect ratio or device aspect ratio. The former is defined as the ratio of width over height, and the latter is defined as the ratio of device-width over device-height.

- **orientation.** Apply styles based on whether the target device is in portrait or landscape mode. This feature is useful for targeting different layouts on devices like iPads, Android phones, and other tablets and smartphones that change between portrait and landscape when you change the way you hold them.

- **min/max-resolution.** Apply styles based on minimum and maximum device resolutions. This is useful if you want to, for example, serve larger icons and increase text size on devices with high resolutions, like iPhones with retina displays.

- **min/max-device-pixel-ratio.** A proprietary Apple media feature that is similar to min- and max-resolution but seems better supported currently.

You can find a full list of media features at www.w3.org/TR/css3-mediaqueries/#media1.

APPLYING SOME MEDIA QUERIES TO THE EXAMPLE

Let's return to the Media Blitz example and improve it at different screen widths using media queries. You can see the final result of these additions in media-blitz-3-with-media-queries.html and media-blitz3.css. At the bottom of this new CSS file, you'll find a series of @media blocks that kick in when the screen width decreases below certain thresholds. I won't cover every ruleset inside these blocks in excruciating detail, because each is pretty obvious, but let's just look at the whole of the first one to help you get the idea:

```
@media all and (max-width: 1024px) {
    nav {
        float: none;
        width: 100%;
        margin-left: 0;
    }
}
```

```css
#main-panel {
    margin-left: 0px;
}

nav ul {
    width: 100%;
}

nav li {
    display: inline-block;
}

nav li a {
    display: block;
    margin-right: 3rem;
}

nav hr {
    width: 90%;
}

body {
    display: table;
    width: 100%;
}

nav {
    display: table-caption;
    table-layout: fixed;
    caption-side: bottom;
}
    }
```

FIGURE 8.8 The result of the first media query kicking in. The navigation menu moves from the side of the site down to the bottom, and the rest of the content expands to span the entire width of the browser.

You force these rules to kick in when the browser window is less than 1024 pixels in width. When they kick in, you remove the float from the ‹nav›, change its width to 100%, and get rid of the left margin from both the ‹nav› and the #main-panel so that the location of the navigation menus changes from the side of the layout to the top of it. You then set the list items to display: inline-block so they sit alongside one another rather than on top of one another, do a couple of other minor adjustments there, and then use some CSS tables magic to relocate the navigation to the bottom of the site instead of the top. **Figure 8.8** shows the result.

WHICH **MEDIA QUERIES** SHOULD YOU **USE?**

It is often a challenge to work out exactly which media queries to use. You need to determine how many different layouts your site needs and at what width you should change layouts. Also, consider whether you need any other types of media query. The solution depends on what target audience/devices you are designing for. If you are creating an app that is designed only for iPad and iPod, you'll probably get away with having a layout for the iPad screen size and one for the iPhone size, which breathes a bit for portrait/landscape orientation:

```
@media screen and (max-width: 480px) { ... }
@media screen and (max-width: 1024px) { ... }
```

You might go further and optimize the layout for portrait/landscape:

```
@media screen and (orientation: landscape) { ... }
@media screen and (orientation: portrait) { ... }
```

If you need to target more devices, you might well expand your list of queries to suit other screen sizes. Targeting devices like this is referred to as setting *device breakpoints*.

My personal preference is to use *content breakpoints* instead: I usually ignore target devices completely and just add in media queries to fix the layout when it breaks. This methodology is more flexible and therefore better overall for supporting a wide range of devices. But it is often a bit more complicated than just creating a couple of well-thought-out layouts for specific screen sizes. The choice is yours.

Width- and orientation-based media queries are certainly the most common media queries you'll use, although with so many high-resolution devices now available on the market, you might also want to provide different images or layout features depending on resolution: see the "High-fidelity Devices" section later in the chapter.

FIGURE 8.9 The third, narrower layout is potentially good for a tablet in portrait mode or a small-resolution desktop monitor.

The next media query simply reduces the font size and spacing of the navigation menus to make them fit better at slightly smaller widths:

```
@media all and (max-width: 870px) {
    nav {
        font-size: 3rem;
    }
    nav li a {
        margin-right: 1rem;
    }
}
```

The third media query performs a number of tasks but basically narrows down the Related Reels sidebar to a single column and alters the layout of the Video Reel section.

```
@media all and (max-width: 800px) {

    ...

}
```

Figure 8.9 shows the result.

FIGURE 8.10 The fourth and fifth layouts work well for portrait and landscape mobile phones.

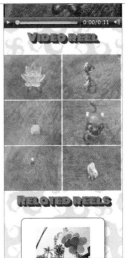

The fourth media query puts all the major containers in a single column but puts the Related Reels into two columns again:

```
@media all and (max-width: 600px) {

    ...

}
```

The final media query kicks in at 350 pixels or less, which reduces the Related Reels to a single column again and makes the <h1> smaller:

```
@media all and (max-width: 350px) {

    ...

}
```

Figure 8.10 shows the final two layouts in action.

CSS TABLES MAGIC

In media-blitz-3-with-media-queries.html, when the first media query kicks in, the navigation menu moves to the bottom of the screen. This is the result of the following two rulesets:

```
body {
    display: table;
    table-layout: fixed;
    width: 100%;
}
nav {
    display: table-caption;
    caption-side: bottom;
}
```

The table-related properties are part of CSS2. They were created to allow web developers to lay out groups of elements with a tabular structure without abusing table markup. An obvious application of CSS tables is to lay out forms in an easier fashion (see the file form_csstables.html in the chapter8 code download folder). This is basically achieved using markup like this:

```
<ul>
    <li><label><input></li>
    ...
</ul>
```

and CSS like this:

```
li {
    display:table-row;
}
label {
        display:table-cell;
}
```

The technique I've used in my media query example is the only known way to move the position of a child element from side to top to bottom reliably without changing the source order. It is a useful technique to keep in mind, although bear in mind that these properties don't work in IE7 and earlier.

MOBILE FIRST

Let's now turn the media query example on its head by looking at the Mobile First technique invented by Luke Wroblewski. This technique reverses what you did in the preceding section. You create the mobile layout first as the default layout, and then apply wider layouts as the browser width increases.

The Media Blitz example is recreated using Mobile First in the file media-blitz-4-mobile-first.html. I won't show all of the code here, but be sure to dig through the file so you can appreciate the differences between media-blitz-3 and media-blitz-4. The former starts with the wide-screen layout and layers on styles suitable for narrower screens. The latter starts with the narrow-screen layout and layers on styles suitable for wider screens. As a brief example, the <h1> is initially set to its smallest size:

```
h1 {
    font-family: 'Monoton', cursive;
}
```

and then is increased in size by subsequent media queries:

```
@media all and (min-width: 350px) {
    h1 {
        font-size: 6rem;
    }
}
```

This reverse method has many advantages: One of which is that it is often easier to start by designing a simple, narrow (mobile) layout and then add on complexity to work up to a richer wide-screen (desktop) layout than it is to design a complex, all-singing wide-screen layout and then try to factor that down to an effective (uncluttered) narrow layout.

MEDIA QUERY POLYFILLS

One problem with Mobile First is that browsers that don't support media queries will get a mobile layout rather than a desktop layout. To fix this, you could include a JavaScript polyfill in your page. The two worth checking out are css3-mediaqueries.js (http://code.google.com/p/css3-mediaqueries-js) and respond.js (https://github.com/scottjehl/Respond). Both work in the same sort of way. You just include the JavaScript in your page after the CSS declarations. All my responsive examples from number 4 (media-blitz-4-mobile-first.html) on include the following:

```
<script src="respond.min.js"></script>
```

In terms of which one to use, css3-mediaqueries.js is larger in size but more robust, whereas respond.js works only on width/height media queries.

FLASH: RESPONSIVE SHORTCOMINGS

Although the media query polyfills work well, one glaring problem is that the video fallback that comes into play when the Media Blitz example is loaded in IE6–8 is, well, Flash. When Flash is loaded into a browser, the browser allocates some space for it and then hands control of that space over to the Flash Player; the resulting content doesn't play nicely with web standards.

The Flash movie therefore can't be reduced in size or otherwise manipulated using CSS (width, max-width, etc.), so the Flash video will stay the same size regardless of how the size of the rest of the page around it changes. In a responsive design, when the screen width gets too narrow, the layout will start to look horrible as the Flash movie stomps all over it.

Therefore, I've set my Flash Player fallback to a bit smaller than the HTML5 <video> equivalent and set the <body> element to a fixed width of 1024px inside one of my IE conditional comments so that the design is now fixed, eliminating the problem. It's not perfect, but think of it this way: Users of IE won't be using a narrow-screen device anyway, and at least they get a layout they can use.

Another advantage of Mobile First is that you can easily serve smaller background images to smaller devices, and then swap them out for bigger images using rules in wider media queries. For example, in simple-responsive-header-image1.html, a background image spans the whole `<header>`, which runs across 100 percent of the screen width. I've included it like this:

```
header {

    ...

    background: url(images/sunset.jpg) center;

}
```

Setting it to display in the center ensures that the nice sun in the center of the image will always display in the center of the header. But there's more you can do here.

Take a look at simple-responsive-header-image2.html. The original 1024px wide image is 41 KB, which doesn't make much difference to a user with a fast connection but could slow down response time somewhat for a mobile user on a slow mobile network. To mitigate this, I've included a 480px version in the default CSS:

```
header {

    ...

    background: url(images/sunset-480.jpg) center;

}
```

Therefore, narrow-screen browsers get a much smaller image. The full-size image is then served up in a media query like so:

```
@media all and (min-width: 481px) {

    header {

        background: url(images/sunset.jpg) center;

    }

}
```

Devices that have a browser window width of 480px or less will only load the small image, and devices with a browser window width of over 480px will load the larger image.

Of course, the preceding technique doesn't work for images put on the page using <img>. Often, you'll want to serve smaller content images to smaller devices too. This is a much harder problem to solve. Fortunately, intelligent people have been thinking about this problem. For a robust solution that relies on some server-side magic, check out Matt Wilcox's excellent Adaptive Images technique. All you'll need is at http://24ways.org/2011/adaptive-images-for-responsive-designs.

RESPONSIVE VIDEO

For video, the solution to making it responsive is a bit different. HTML5 <video> has a rather nifty responsive mechanism included—a media attribute on the <source> element in which you can insert a media query test. If the test is passed, that video source is the one loaded into the <video> element, unless of course another <source> element later on in the source order overrides it.

In media-blitz-5-responsive-video.html, you can see this in action:

```
<video controls>

    <source src="videos/320/crystal320.mp4" type="video/mp4"
    ⇢ media="all and (max-width: 480px)">

    <source src="videos/320/crystal320.webm" type="video/webm"
    ⇢ media="all and (max-width: 480px)">

    <source src="videos/720/crystal720.mp4" type="video/mp4"
    ⇢ media="all and (min-width: 481px)">

    <source src="videos/720/crystal720.webm" type="video/webm"
    ⇢ media="all and (min-width: 481px)">

    ...

</video>
```

When the screen width is 480px or less, the 320 video is loaded; when the screen width is more than 480px, the 720 video is loaded.

NOTE: I cheated slightly in media-blitz5.css. I set the <video> element to width: 100%, not, max-width: 100%, so that the video will always span the full width of the screen, even when the 320 video is displayed across the full-screen width at 321–480px. This is not a great idea, especially when the width gets much bigger, because the video will start to look very grainy. You need to be especially mindful of this on very high-resolution devices like the iPhone 4.

FIGURE 8.11 This isn't what was expected! Why aren't the narrow-screen media queries being applied on mobile browsers?

There is more to optimizing content for mobile devices using media queries than you might first think. If you view one of the media query examples you've seen so far in this chapter on a mobile phone, you'll see the surprising result shown in **Figure 8.11**.

> **NOTE:** You might also get slightly odd positioning or other behavior of the video depending on the mobile device viewing the content, because some mobile browsers will play the video inside the browser, whereas others hand off the video playing to the device's native player.

The problem here is that mobile browsers lie. When a mobile browser renders the average site, it doesn't render it at the actual browser width and display it as is. Instead, it renders the site at a higher assumed width—Opera Mobile, for example, uses 850px (and sometimes goes wider, depending on how wide the page being rendered is)—and shrinks the result to fit on the mobile screen.

You can understand why browser creators would do this. Historically, most sites are not created with responsive techniques in mind; therefore, they would look crappy if rendered at widths of 480px, 320px, or less. But in this responsive world, you should override this behavior so that your media queries behave like you want them to.

You could do this by changing your width/height media queries to always test for the equivalent device-width/device-height as well. For example:

```
@media all and (max-width: 800px), @media all and
→ (max-device-width: 800px) {

    ...

}
```

But having to do this for every @media block means a lot of extra typing and hassle, so let's look at a better solution: viewport.

<META NAME="VIEWPORT">

A better, less messy way to make media queries behave themselves is to use the viewport meta tag. Invented by Apple to make web apps display more reliably on iDevices, it was adopted by other browser manufacturers because it is a jolly good idea.

To get your media queries to behave (**Figure 8.12**), you can add the following line into your HTML <head> (see media-blitz-6-with-viewport.html in the code download folder):

```
<meta name="viewport" content="width=device-width">
```

This makes the browser render the site at its true width, triggering media queries as appropriate.

The viewport meta tag is not just limited to forcing browsers to tell the truth about the site's width or height. You can also do the following:

- **Set a specific width or height to render at.** This is done using a number for the width or height value. For example,

  ```
  <meta name="viewport" content="width=320">
  ```

- **Set an initial zoom factor for your content.** This is done using initial-scale and a zoom factor:

  ```
  <meta name="viewport" content="initial-scale=1.5">
  ```

  Such values work just like CSS scale transforms: 1.5 means "zoom in by 50%," 0.75 means "zoom out to 75% of initial size," and so on.

- **Set the target pixel density.** As you'll see later in the "High-fidelity Devices" section, devices with high resolutions will often have multiple physical device pixels for each pixel on your page (sometimes called CSS pixels). To alter how many or just set a CSS pixel to equal 1 device pixel, you can use `target-densitydpi=device-dpi`. For example:

`target-densitydpi=device-dpi` or

`target-densitydpi=160`.

```
<meta name="viewport" content="target-densitydpi=device-dpi">
```

- **Set a maximum and/or minimum allowed zoom factor for your content.** If you want to limit how far your users can zoom in or out, you can use `maximum-scale` and `minimum-scale`, like so:

```
<meta name="viewport" content="maximum-scale=2, minimum-scale=0.5">
```

- **Turn off the ability to zoom.** This is done using `user-scalable=no`:

```
<meta name="viewport" content="user-scalable=no">.
```

TIP: Zooming is a very important accessibility feature for many users. You should really think carefully before you limit it or turn it off completely. A viable use case would be a game UI where you want it to remain full screen and don't want it to be zoomed (in which case, you might want to provide an in-game zoom mechanism). Or, you might want to just limit zooming to acceptable levels that don't make your app look too terrible at either end of the spectrum but still retain acceptable levels of zooming for low-vision users.

@VIEWPORT

You might be thinking that this viewport thing smells like presentation rather than content so should probably be handled using some kind of CSS construct rather than an HTML meta tag. Some clever folks at Opera agree and have produced the @viewport rule spec (http://dev.w3.org/csswg/css-device-adapt/#the-viewport-rule), which defines the same functionality as Viewport meta tag but as a CSS construct. The different options available in Viewport meta tag all have their equivalents in @viewport, except target-densitydpi (hopefully, this will be added later):

```
@-o-viewport {
    width: device-width;
    width: 320px;
    zoom: 1.5;
    max-zoom: 2;
    min-zoom: 0.5;
    user-zoom: fixed;
}
```

Note that @viewport currently works only in Opera Mobile 11 and later, but in my opinion it is a better implementation than Viewport meta tag, and should catch on in the future.

HIGH-FIDELITY DEVICES

As if the techniques you've looked at so far weren't complicated enough, many devices from Apple, HTC, LG, Nokia, and more are now coming out with high-resolution screens. For that reason, text and images are in danger of becoming illegibly small.

To compensate for this potential problem, mobile browsers on high-resolution devices *lie to you twice.* Not only do they render sites at a broader width than the physical device width, but they also apply a default zoom to the content. So a CSS pixel can actually equal multiple device pixels (yes, folks, bizarrely enough, pixels in CSS are actually a relative unit). For example, in Opera Mobile running on an HTC Desire S, the zoom factor is 1.5, and in the default browser on iOS 4, the zoom factor is 2.

How do you deal with this extra level of complexity? Generally, it's not that much of an ordeal, because most of the features on your web page will still look crisp when scaled. It's mainly just images and video you need to worry about. If you are concerned about your images not looking as crisp as they could, you could reference a slightly larger image than required in your <img> element and then constrain the size, so when it is scaled up in high-resolution browsers, it stays crisp:

```
<img src="images/tribal-sun-640px.jpg" width="480">
```

Or in the case of CSS background images, you could check for a certain pixel ratio via a media query and use additional rules inside the media query to "fix" the issue in browsers that pass the test.

For example, you could use background-size to cancel out the effects of the device zoom in the case of a background slice:

```
#wrap {
    background: url(images/wood.jpg);
}

@media screen and (min-device-pixel-ratio: 3/2) {
    #wrap {
        background-size: 255px;
        /* Original image is 1.5 times this size - 383px */
    }
}
```

Or when dealing with icons, you could serve a larger background image to devices with a higher pixel density, for example:

```
ul li:nth-of-type(1) a {
    background-image: url(icons/home-32.png);
    border-radius: 20px 0 0 0;
    background-position: 25px 50%;
}

@media screen and (-o-min-device-pixel-ratio: 3/2) {
    ul li:nth-of-type(1) a {
        background-image: url(icons/home-48.png);
    }
}
```

You can see working examples of these techniques in the file high-resolution-example.html. Note that at the moment min-device-pixel-ratio is supported differently across browsers: Opera Mobile uses ratio values, for example, 3/2, whereas WebKit-based mobile browsers support it with decimals, such as 1.5. In the example file you'll see multiple versions of the media query with different vendor prefixes used to serve the different browsers values they recognize.

If you want to stop mobile browsers from applying their default zoom, you could use the target-densitydpi viewport feature to tell the browser, *I really do want to make 1 pixel equal 1 pixel; tell the whole truth, damn you!* like this:

```
<meta name="viewport" content="width=device-width,
 target-densitydpi=device-dpi">
```

A RESPONSIVE **HEAVY METAL BANNER AD**!

As promised earlier in the book, I'll round off this chapter by returning to the heavy metal banner ad and making it responsive. I'll make it pair down to the smaller "large rectangle" ad size of 336 x 280 in devices with screens narrower than 800px and change it to a narrow banner that spans 100 percent of the screen width in very narrow devices (less than 480px in width). I'll also use the media attribute in my video <source>s to stop the video being served to narrow-screen devices and include a background image instead in such cases. See the poster-responsive folder in the root of the code download for the finished new version.

FIRST ALTERNATIVE: 800PX OR LESS

The middle-sized ad is achieved via the following media query:

```
@media all and (max-width: 800px) {

   ...

}
```

A fair amount of work was required here to adjust all the styles and get the ad looking good at this narrower size. I won't discuss all the CSS changes in the media query, because there is nothing new here. To see all the new styles, search for the preceding media query in the code and check them out.

Note that I didn't tweak the animations: When I tested the narrow size in animation-supporting browsers, all the animations seemed to still look fine.

SECOND ALTERNATIVE: 480PX OR LESS

For all of the new styling in this section to work correctly, I used viewport to make mobile browsers render at the real device width:

```
<meta name="viewport" content="width=device-width">
```

Here is how I set up the alternative styling for narrow-screen browsers. Note that I've completely hidden the <video> to save on processing in small-screen devices:

```
@media all and (max-width: 480px) {
   video {
      display: none;
   }
```

```css
#ad {
    width: 100%;
    height: 90px;
    background-image: url(bg-alternative.jpg);
    font-size: 13px;
}

#ad, #ad div {
    width: 100%;
    height: 90px;
}

#ad #band-name {
    top: -10px;
    left: 20px;
}

#ad #album-name {
    top: 50px;
    right: 40px;
}

#ad #frame1 ul, #ad #frame2 p {
    visibility: hidden;
}

#ad h2, #ad #band-name, #ad #album-name, #ad #frame1 ul {
    animation: none;
}

}
```

FIGURE 8.13 Et voilà, responsive advertising!

Here I implemented some simple styling to alter the ad's dimensions. I also hid the video player and some of the text, and turned off all the animations (except the awesome flames), because I felt the ad would be too cluttered at a smaller size. Smaller, less-powerful devices also appreciate less load on their processors.

And that's it! **Figure 8.13** shows the three different sizes of the ad.

WRAPPING **UP**

This chapter has given you valuable insights into optimizing your web creations so they'll look better and perform better on different types of devices, from tiny mobile devices to wide-screen monitors. Along the way you looked at media queries, viewport, adaptive image and video techniques, and more. I think you'll agree that this chapter was a lot of fun, so go forth and play!

INDEX

HTML, trouble with 3D CSS, 178
HTML content, creating base of, 10
HTML Lint website, 47
HTML5. *See also* semantic HTML5;
  template
  benefits, 39
  browser support for, 40
  DOCTYPE, 41
  embedded video, 40
  error handling, 40
  features, 39
  outlines, 56
  sectioning, 56
  shiv, 45–46
  validating, 47
HTML5 elements. *See also* elements
  <article>, 51–53
  <aside>, 54–55
  <audio>, 48–50
  <canvas>, 62–63
  <figcaption>, 56–57
  <figure>, 56–57
  <footer>, 54
  <header>, 54
  <hgroup>, 56
  <mark>, 59
  <nav>, 55
  <section>, 51–53
  <time>, 57–58
  <video>, 48–50
HTML5 form elements, 60–62. *See also*
  form improvements
hyphenation, controlling, 92–93

I

IAB (Internet Advertising Bureau), 142
icons
  arbitrary, 221
  background images, 229–230
  background-position property, 227
  background-size property, 228–229
  comparison, 222–223
  CSS sprites, 227–228
  emotion, 222–223
  functionality, 222
  generated content for, 226
  guidelines for use of, 222–223
  ideograms, 221
  implementing, 224–230, 235–238

making bulletproof, 228–229
Media Queries, 228–229
min-width property, 228–229
navigation, 222
Peculiar set, 235–238
pictograms, 221
setting gradient on list item, 225
status, 222
user feedback, 222–223
web fonts as, 231–234
IE conditional comments, 68–69
IE Print Protector script, 46
IE versions
  backgrounds in, 135
  CSS3PIE, 130
  gradient support for, 130–131
images, serving responsively, 308–310
Internet Explorer
  animations, 189
  bling boxes, 109
  CSS3 Color Units, 16
  font formats, 74
  layout features, 243
  rem units, 20–21
  responsive design features, 291
  text features, 87, 94
  transforms, 152
  transitions, 179
iOS
  animations, 189
  bling boxes, 109
  CSS3 Color Units, 16
  font formats, 74
  layout features, 243
  rem units, 20
  responsive design features, 291
  text features, 87, 94
  transforms, 152
  transitions, 179
Irish, Paul, 11, 204
  "Bulletproof @font-face syntax," 77
  Modernizr library, 67

J

JavaScript, triggering animations with,
  208–216
JavaScript libraries
  css3-mediaqueries-js, 65
  CSS3PIE, 66–67

Modernizr, 67
respond.js, 65
Selectivizr, 67
Jehl, Scott, 65

K

kerning text, 101
King Arthur example, adding fonts to,
  75–77
Krug, Steve, 8

L

language CSS3 selector, 24
Lauke, Patrick, 62
Lawson, Bruce
  HTML5 semantics, 53
  HTML5 video player, 50
  IE conditional comments, 69
layout modules. *See also* CSS
  Multi-column layout module;
  Flexbox; grid structure
  CSS Exclusions and Shapes, 242,
    277–279
  CSS Flexible box, 242
  CSS GCPM (Generate Content for
    Paged Media), 280
  CSS Grids, 242
  CSS Multi-column, 242
  CSS Regions Level 3, 275–277
  GCPM, 243
  Regions, 242
layout techniques
  containers, 292–293
  max-width, 295–296
  responsive media layouts,
    293–296
layout width, setting upper bound
  on, 296
letters in elements, selecting, 26
ligatures
  dealing with, 95–96
  discretionary, 98
linear gradients
  color stops, 121–122
  negative unit values, 122
  repeating, 123
  RGBA colors, 122
  syntax, 123